AFRICAN POLITICS

IN PERSPECTIVE

by
DOROTHY DODGE
Macalester College

NEW PERSPECTIVES
IN
POLITICAL SCIENCE

VAN NOSTRAND REINHOLD COMPANY
NEW YORK   CINCINNATI   TORONTO
LONDON   MELBOURNE

320.96
D66a
84808
Sept 1973

Van Nostrand Reinhold Company Regional Offices:
Cincinnati, New York, Chicago, Millbrae, Dallas

Van Nostrand Reinhold Company Foreign offices:
London, Toronto, Melbourne

Published by Van Nostrand Reinhold Company
450 West 33rd Street, New York, N. Y. 10001

Published simultaneously in Canada by
D. Van Nostrand Company (Canada), Ltd.

15 14 13 12 11 10 9 8 7 6 5 4 3 2

To my mother

Preface

MANY CURRENT STUDIES OF NON-WESTERN POLITICAL SYSTEMS
are attempting to devise new methodologies and terminology for
the analysis of emergent societies. The works of Gabriel Almond,
David Apter, Henry Bretton, James Coleman, and Herbert Spiro
are well known examples. The traditional approach has been revised, since Western concepts, such as two party systems, separation of powers, or judicial review, may not be applicable to
non-Western political systems and may introduce value judgments.
The new studies refer to themselves as functional-structural, and
propose to describe governments in relation to their functions, for
example, interest articulation or interest aggregation. It is hoped
that this approach will avoid the imposition of traditional Western
concepts upon non-Western civilization and minimize the tendency
to test emergent political systems in relation to Western values and
standards.

The functional-structural approach would have certain advantages for the present study. However, a number of problems are
encountered. Any survey of Africa south of the Sahara is a
formidable undertaking since it is difficult to become even generally
familiar with political developments in such a large number of
states. Emergent Africa presents the researcher with additional
dilemmas. Events move so swiftly that materials may be out of
date almost before they are made available. In addition, data that
would be of value is not always obtainable. For example, discussion of voting behavior is inhibited by limited or admittedly unreliable election statistics. Census reports that would assist the
study of the population involve similar difficulty as may be illustrated by the inability of the United Nations demographic survey
to compile an accurate population total. The age, educational

background, economic status, occupation, and the religious or ethnic affiliation of the legislative members would be of interest in discussing the legislative role, but many states do not publish such breakdowns. Government economic plans are readily available, but reports on implementation and administration often are lacking. Although a few individual states do publish the desired materials, they are not always available in the United States. These examples illustrate some of the problems for the researcher.

If the student of African politics could spend sufficient time in each of the states, the data that is presently lacking could undoubtedly be compiled. In this regard, appreciation is expressed to Macalester College for making possible a research grant for study in Africa in 1962. Although the period of time was inadequate for the above proposal, the grant was invaluable in the present study. In view of the shortage of data, reliance must often be placed upon the journals, newspaper reports, and research in individual countries done by scholars in the field. An additional bibliography is provided at the end of each chapter to assist the student in becoming more familiar with these materials. It should be noted that West Africa, particularly Nigeria, has received considerable attention; East and Central Africa, especially the Congo and the former Central African Federation, an almost equal amount; and the former French areas very little.

Confronting these problems of data unavailability, the following discussion is centered on the more traditional institutional and constitutional approach, since these materials are published by each of the states south of the Sahara. Although the functional-structural method might be preferable, such a survey must wait until the needed data is compiled for all of Africa south of the Sahara. It is hoped the institutional-constitutional survey may serve as a baseline for such future studies.

DOROTHY DODGE

Contents

ix

AFRICAN POLITICS
IN PERSPECTIVE

CHAPTER 1

Political Culture

WHY STUDY AFRICA?

BEFORE WORLD WAR II, STUDY OF AFRICAN POLITICS AND GOVernment in the United States was limited. This country had no colonies on the African continent, and trade with the area was restricted by European colonial policies. Lack of extensive contact contributed to limited popular interest in internal African affairs. We tended to look to London, Paris, or Brussels for interpretation of African developments and events.

The postwar period brought a marked increase in study and research. The strength and power of the independence movements that swept the African continent causing the unexpected collapse of Colonial Systems drew attention. At the end of World War II, many observers assumed that African independence would not be achieved for at least seventy-five to one hundred years. Contrary to these expectations, the late fifties and early sixties saw a nearly bewildering procession of newly independent states. This movement attained such momentum that current estimates of all Africa's attaining independence by 1970 are considered conservative. With independence, new African leaders have assumed prominence in international politics. Their appearance stimulated interest in their backgrounds, the policies of the parties they represent, and the governmental systems they lead.

This new interest was sharpened by the Congo crisis of 1960, which emphasized the problems of instability, secessionism, and transition from colonial status that face the Congolese and other African peoples. The inability of the Congolese leaders to achieve a workable compromise on constitutional procedures and institutions and the outbreak of violence precipitated United Nations intervention. Debate developed over the wisdom of colonial policies, the preparation for independence, and the solutions to the problems of instability and disorder. Patrice Lumumba's request for Soviet military assistance in regaining power raised the threat of an East-West military confrontation in the heart of Africa if stability were not restored quickly and East-West military intervention curtailed.

These Cold War struggles focused attention on the foreign policies of the African states. The new governments expressed support for the nonaligned or neutralist approach to international politics. Their leaders publicly disapproved any attempt to extend the East-West conflict to Africa, make formal alliances with any major power bloc, or participate directly in the struggle. They assumed an active role in international meetings of the nonaligned states, such as the Belgrade Conference, and were vocal in their criticism of colonialism and neocolonialism, nuclear testing, and the armaments race. These statements caused concern for United States-African relations and cooperation. Communist Chinese and Soviet attempts to draw the African states closer to the Communist bloc deepened United States concern. Both blocs expanded economic aid programs and cultural exchange to counter one another. The Sino-Soviet split further intensified Communist activity. The Chinese have been accused of supporting rebel Congolese groups in the hope of establishing a Chinese-oriented government. Russia announced her decision to aid the rebel forces also.

The admission of thirty-five states to membership has given Africa a new prominence in the United Nations. Its votes represent a balance between East and West. The new states formed an African bloc or caucus to promote a common front on issues coming before the organization and to encourage united voting on resolutions of concern to Africa. For example, it has attempted to remove the Republic of South Africa from membership in United Nations bodies, prevent its representatives from addressing United Nations sessions, and institute an economic boycott of South Africa's products. The African bloc has not achieved all its goals, but its activities have focused more attention on African policies and problems. Although African voting unity has not been consistent, cohesion has been high enough to cause the Soviet and Western blocs to seek its votes and favor. The bloc also has attempted to caucus with the members of the Asian bloc to increase its voting strength and influence. Although other factors could be mentioned, the independence movement and newly acquired international influence have played a primary role in the current interest in African government and politics.

METHODOLOGY

A variety of approaches might be adopted in undertaking a study of African constitutional patterns. The method selected for this series of comparative area studies is to stress institutional patterns held in common by the states of a given geographic area. This approach reduces Africa's great political diversity to manageable, if somewhat arbitrary proportions. It lends itself to an overview of patterns and trends that may be developing. The analysis of common institutional patterns also permits classification and comparison. The approach, however, has definite limitations. Emphasis upon common characteristics omits discussion of significant diversity and difference. It is difficult, if not impossible, to make any general statement that will be uniformly accurate throughout an area. In the case of Africa south of the Sahara, the exceptions may be particularly numerous. The states do not possess common historical development, common colonial experience, common tribal cultures and political traditions, common language, common religious affiliation or experience. Despite these significant diversities, analysis of contemporary African governments and politics reveals a number of similar patterns of political organization and structure. These patterns are not found in all African states and are not necessarily identical. They are held in common by a sufficient number of states, however, to make them significant. This study, therefore, will attempt to describe and analyze these common patterns rather than stress differences and diversity.

The value of the latter approach is recognized, but since space precludes such an attempt, the student of African politics is urged to investigate each African state in detail to learn more about individual and distinctive political institutions and characteristics.

WHAT DO AFRICAN STATES HAVE IN COMMON?

Many of today's common institutional patterns result from the fact that the majority of the African states are at a comparable stage of political and economic development. The African states are emergent political societies in the sense of having gained independence recently and being in transition from the established colonial system. After achieving independence, the African states all face similar difficulties in building effective and stable governments that will promote the goals of economic and social well-being for their peoples, as well as international status and respect.

To reach these goals, the governments must find solutions to a number of problems characteristic of emergent political societies. These problems center around the need to develop governmental systems that balance stability and change and that permit change in accordance with general popular approval. If some degree of stability does not exist, the new state will find itself in chaos. On the other hand, if stability is insisted upon or forced, response to the pressures for change may be restricted and the goals of social and economic well-being will not be achieved.

The creation of an effective governmental system is assisted if certain conditions exist in the state. Among these are common acceptance by its citizens of political institutions and procedures, popular confidence in and respect for the ruling elite, and a sense of nationalism and common destiny. These factors promote national unity and stability.

Decolonization produces some political instability. The transfer of power from the colonial administration forces the emergent society to search for areas of common agreement on new political institutions and procedures through which internal social conflicts may be resolved. Common popular agreement has proven elusive. The new governments might have turned to pre-European procedures and institutions for common political experience. However, tribal political traditions often differ significantly from each other. States composed of only one tribal group would have less difficulty. Since national boundaries encompass several tribal units, common institutions may not exist. The political institutions and processes of the old colonial system also represent common experience. However, they are discredited in the popular mind because of their association with colonialism and Western control. The independent governments seek the development of African, rather than Western, institutions. Popular acceptance of the colonial structure is limited also by lack of experience with or understanding of the colonial institutions. Although colonial policies varied, widespread popular participation in the governing process did not exist in many states until a few years prior to independence. Lacking common traditional institutions, African leaders have turned to Western models. Since adoption of Western models does not solve the problem of popular acceptance and understanding, the emergent states may encounter serious instances of instability in the transition period. These difficulties may become more acute as the government attempts to reconcile widespread internal conflicts of interest.

The transition from colonial status involves the replacement of the old colonial administrators by an African civil service. The governments need to build popular confidence in and respect for this new African official class. Until after World War II, relatively few Africans served in administrative positions. High level directive and discretionary posts were reserved for colonial civil servants until immediately before independence. These policies made the development of an African ruling elite more difficult. African civil servants have only limited experience upon which to base their new responsibilities. Expansion of the civil service has required the hiring of untrained and inexperienced personnel. Building confidence in the new civil service may be more difficult when the level of administrative efficiency does not meet desired standards. The impartiality of the new personnel has also been questioned. Nigeria has reported several protests over the tribal affiliation of civil servants. Fear has been expressed, for example, that a Yoruba would not administer fairly in respect to members of the Ibo tribe, or the Ibo to the Yoruba. The protests insist that each tribal group be given a proportional share of administrative posts. If tribal affiliation becomes the dominant criterion in hiring of civil servants, the best trained may be passed over. Actually, study of administrative practice has turned up a few isolated cases of possible discrimination along tribal affiliation lines, but such incidents aggravate lack of confidence. Tanzania has reported problems in the establishment of its governmental authority in all areas of the state. Members of the Masai tribe tend to look to the former British colonial officials for administration and benefits. Therefore, TANU officials are not recognized and find it difficult to assure compliance with their rulings. These examples of lack of confidence may be limited, but they indicate areas of difficulty.

The building of a sense of unity is a third area of possible instability. The end of colonial rule removed one force holding the African states together. The new governments are searching for other areas of internal political cohesion. Such unity generally rests upon a sense of nationalism and common destiny. This sense may not be well developed in Africa south of the Sahara. For one reason, colonial boundary lines had little relationship to African political organization prior to the arrival of the Europeans. The boundaries inherited by the independent African states were drawn according to the lines of economic penetration or political arrangements of the colonial powers. Frequently, tribal groups were divided between colonies. Since independence, there has been pressure for tribal reunification. The question of reunifying the Ewe tribe has created tension between Ghana and Togo since neither state wishes to lose territory. In some cases, tribal units having few common political, social, or cultural traditions were grouped together. Such diversity has made agreement on destiny and goals difficult for the Nigerians and inhibited the development of a sense of national unity and cohesion. In other cases, smaller tribes were grouped with one or two larger tribes. Since the larger tribes comprise a majority of the population, the smaller ones may become uneasy. KADU, the opposition political party, played on concern of Kikuyu domination in its campaign for a regional form of government in Kenya.

African leaders fear campaigns similar to that of KADU. The revival of tribal loyalties and rivalries could precipitate internal discord and undermine national unity. Governments stress national interest and loyalty to the state in an attempt to overcome possible movements toward regionalism or secession. The danger is always present that too much emphasis may be placed upon internal political unity. In their eagerness to promote stability, the new governments may attempt to force agreement and conformity resulting in the adoption of authoritarian institutions and procedures severely limiting the areas of diversity. The suppression of civil liberties, the elimination of opposition political parties, and the curtailment of minority rights and protections may follow. The emergent governments face the difficult challenge of finding solutions to the quest for unity that promote the degree of cohesion necessary to assure effective political systems and still allow diversity and individualism. Balance between unity and diversity is difficult enough even in established political societies.

African governments also face a consistent demand for change. Their leaders are under pressure to improve the social and economic well-being of their people. In the African mind, independence has been associated with an immediate rise in educational opportunities and social or economic status. The independence movements must assume some responsibility for this association since their platforms tended to equate independence with immediate improvement. The colonial system was blamed for slow development and limited opportunities. The African people anticipate that their governments will be able to achieve noticeable gains in a short time. Consequently, pressure for change is constant and politically critical. The emergent governments are literally under the gun to produce results in the early years of independence or lose power and popular support. However, they face major hurdles in achieving these desired goals in the short run.

The emergent governments recognize that raising the standard of living will require industrialization in order to expand production and employment opportunities. Large-scale industrialization requires tremendous capital investment. Several factors limit the availability of investment capital in the African states. For one thing, the emergent governments have inherited economies that are basically agricultural and rural. The economies are dependent upon one or two crop productions to raise necessary foreign exchange. Governments hope to expand agricultural output to raise income levels. Since agricultural methods often are inefficient, expansion of production requires major educational projects to teach new techniques. Land-reform programs also are essential to expand production. Although the governments have undertaken development programs for agriculture, results will not be immediate. Even if it is achieved in the short run, expansion of agricultural production may not solve the problem of higher income levels. In many cases, the raw material exports produced by the African states are presently in oversupply on the world market. Demand for these products tends to be inelastic. An increase in production may further glut the world market and depress prices. Expanded production, therefore, may result in little, if any, increase in income levels. Diversification of production is proposed as one solution to this problem.

A second factor limiting availability of investment capital is that independence produced a temporary break in the aid and trade ties with the former colonial power. Although there has been a tendency for these ties to re-form gradually, some economic dislocation resulted. Several states avoid such ties as a matter of policy to avoid post-independence economic dominance by the old colonial power since continued dependence is referred to as "Neocolonialism." Until new markets can be formed, breaking of colonial trade ties depresses the economy. Just when an expanding economy is needed, therefore, a temporary recession may occur.

The emergent governments do not have significant internal supplies of private capital for development and industrialization. Average yearly income varies from state to state, but generally it is inadequate for more than a minimal standard of living. It is difficult, therefore, to tax out the large amounts needed to pay for development projects and programs. Stringent taxation policies would find little support among African peoples who are demanding higher living standards. To supplement the lack of internal private capital, governments have attempted to encourage foreign private investment. Their ability to attract foreign capital has been curtailed by the unwillingness of foreign investors to risk funds in the unstable political atmosphere that may follow the granting of independence. For example, in the eighteen months prior to independence, significant amounts of foreign capital left Kenya because of this concern. The possibility of nationalization and reprisal against Western business has deterred post-independence investment in many areas. In addition to capital, industrialization is dependent upon such factors as resource availability and development; adequate transportation, communication, and distribution facilities; and the availability of skilled labor which do not always co-exist. For example, several American companies have abandoned projects for African branches because of lack of skilled labor and distribution facilities.

This discussion of some of the problems facing the governments of Africa in the early stages of independence does not pretend to present a complete picture. However, it does indicate some factors in the African search for a balance between stability and change. The similarity of governmental programs and policies which the newly emergent African states have adopted results from their need to succeed in this search. The following discussion will investigate in more detail African political tradition prior to the arrival of the West, colonial policies and institutions, the rise of the independence movements, contemporary governmental institutions and structures, political party structures, and governmental programs for advancement and progress.

THE LAND AND THE PEOPLE

It is difficult to generalize about Africa since it is an area of great diversity and size. The continent extends 5,000 miles north-south and 4,700 from east-west. Its 11½ million square miles are classified into eight vegetation zones. The rain forests, often called the "evergreen" area, are characterized by a high mean temperature and very heavy rainfall without any marked dry season. Parts of the Congo basin, Spanish Guinea, Gabon, Southern Nigeria and the Cameroons are listed as rain-forest zones. The monsoon region, which includes parts of the Ivory Coast, Liberia, Sierra Leone, Guinea, and Portugese Guinea, also experiences high mean temperatures and heavy rainfall; but monsoon zones have a marked dry season lasting for three months on the average. The savanna or tropical zone has an average rainfall from 30 to 50 inches annually, with a dry season extending from four to seven months during which the days are hot and humidity low. During this period, the land is virtually useless, often cracking as vegetation withers and dies. Parts of Nigeria, Dahomey, the Ivory Coast, and Guinea experience this pattern. A semi-arid zone stretches across the continent characterized by an eight to nine month dry season and an average mean temperature from 60° to 80°F. The desert areas are virtually rainless with temperatures reaching into the 100's during the heat of the day, except for plateau regions. The tropical highlands, including parts of Guinea, Nigeria, the Cameroons, Uganda, Tanzania, and the Congo have an average mean temperature from 64° to 70°F with rainfall varying from area to area. In the temperate highlands, the average mean temperature varies from 50° to 64°F and rainfall is adequate to class this zone of

Ethiopia, Kenya, Tanzania, Rhodesia, and Zambia as humid. Finally, the alpine regions are characterized by mountains exceeding 8,000 feet, such as Mt. Kilimanjaro or Mt. Kenya. Despite the diversity among these zones, African climate is generally described as having a high mean temperature and a rainy season. In the lowlands, the mean temperature averages between 77° to 81°F and varies less than 6° from the coldest to the warmest months. Cloud cover is usual in the period of high sun, which results in summer sometimes being cooler than the winter. In contrast, the mean temperature in the highlands averages about 57° to 61°F. Although temperatures over the continent are high enough to minimize the need for heated shelters and warm clothing, high temperatures and humidity may produce physical discomfort in many areas.

Continental rainfall patterns vary considerably. For example, one million square miles receives over 60 inches annually while another million square miles receives less than 6. All areas except the Congo Basin and the highlands around Lake Victoria and the Guinea coast experience a dry season of longer than three months, resulting in annual periods of abundant food and shortage. In areas where the rainy season follows an extended dry period, such as Senegal, the farmer is physically weakened by hunger, heat, and inactivity just before he enters a period of intensive physical labor. Since these vegetation, temperature, and rainfall zones cut through many states, they may experience several patterns. For example, along the coast, Liberia receives 200 inches of rain a year but only 70 inches in the hinterland.

Physical descriptions of Africa divide the continent into a number of distinct areas. East Africa is referred to as the roof of the continent with the Ethiopian highlands reaching 14,000 feet at their maximum. Central Africa is characterized as a series of plateaus of different levels linked by rivers and deep gorges such as Victoria Falls. The Congo Basin has been likened to a saucer of 1,000 feet elevation at its center, rising to 4,000 feet at its edge and covered by marshes, swamps, and lakes. The Middle Nile Basin is the meeting place of the great waters of the continent. Finally West Africa is the lowest point on the continent and characterized by savanna along its coasts.

The total population of Africa is estimated between 161 to 167 million. An accurate count is difficult because a reliable census does not exist in many states. Although demographic statistics differ, they indicate that racial diversity is part of the African pattern. The Bushmen, numbering under 55,000, are believed to have migrated to South Africa from the North. They are described as short, with a yellowish-brown skin that tends to wrinkle easily. Divided into three distinct tribes, each speaking its own language, the Bushmen live in small communities of from 50 to 100 members governed by a headman. The primary occupation is hunting and the group is described as nomadic. Bushmen are found presently in Bechuanaland, South West Africa, and Southern Angola, but the population is in decline and has mixed with other groups. The Hottentots are similar in appearance to the Bushmen but they are taller. They number under 15,000 and are believed to be a mixture of the Bushmen and the Hamites. The Hottentots are primarily pastoral, keeping cattle and sheep. The pygmies are found in the thickest rain forest areas of the Congo, Gabon, and the Cameroons and are estimated at more than 100,000. Living in small communities, they engage primarily in hunting. The 60 million Negroes are scattered throughout Africa south of the Sahara. "True" Negroes remain only in limited areas along the Guinea coast including parts of Nigeria, the Cameroons, and the Congo. The rest are believed to represent a mixture with other races of Africa. The Hamites are classed as European and are believed to have originated either in Asia or Arabia. The Eastern Hamites were found in ancient or modern Egypt and the Northern Hamites, the Berbers, in Algeria or Morocco. The Hamites presently number around 35 million. The Nilo-Hamites, representing a mixture of the Negroes and Hamites, are found in Eastern and East Central Africa. Although their appearance is similar to the Negroes, their culture and speech is predominantly Hamitic. They tend to be a nomadic pastoral people engaged in cattle keeping. The Nilotes, also a mixture of Hamites and Negroes, are found in the Nile Valley, particularly in Sudan and are also primarily pastoral. They number under 10 million at present. The estimated 55 million Bantus of Central and South Africa also are believed to be a mixture of Hamite and Negro, but are differentiated from the Negroes primarily on the basis of a distinct language. In fact, the Bantu classification centers on the peculiar language rather than physical characteristics or culture. The 2 million Semites or Arabs are found in the Sudan, the Ethiopian highlands, and Zanzibar.

Population density is low, averaging less than 20 persons per square mile for the continent and only nine for Africa south of the Sahara. However, density varies greatly from area to area. The West African or Sudanese zone, comprising 28% of the land mass, contains 40% of the population concentrated into two belts, the grassland or savanna and the rain forests. There is little land without some concentration of population. The Central African zone representing 28% of the land mass has only 20% of the population. Its greatest density is found in the Northern Congo and the highlands of Angola and Rhodesia. Many areas of Central Africa have only scattered population. East Africa comprises 40% of the land mass and holds about 40% of the population. Its greatest density is found in Western Eritrea, Central Ruanda-Urundi, South Central Kenya, and Zanzibar, where the population exceeds 125 per square mile while other parts of East Africa are under 10. The variations in density may be illustrated further by the figures for a few states. Nigeria with a total population of 55½ million has a density of 39 per square mile; Senegal with 3 million, a density of 17, Congo-Leopoldville with 12½ million, a density of 6; and Ghana with 6½ million, a density of 30.

Life expectancy in Africa is estimated to be around 37 years. For example, in the Congo-Leopoldville it is 37; Nigeria, 37; Ghana, 38; and Rhodesia, 48.76. The population of Africa south of the Sahara grew from 53 million in 1930 to 92 million in 1962. The average rate of increase is estimated at 2.3%. This also varies to some extent from state to state. The Nigerian rate is 1.9%; Senegal, 2.6%; and Tanganyika, 2.8%. On the basis of this rate of increase, it is predicted the population will swell to 350 million by the turn of the century. The population of the African states is young, with many states having 40% of the population under 15 years of age. The low life expectancy rate may explain the preponderance of population under 20 years old.

Ninety percent of the African population live in rural areas. Three out of every four persons depend upon agriculture for their livelihood. Land tenure patterns may have been influenced by the plentifulness of land and the relatively limited uses to which it could be put. They also were directly related to the traditional emphasis upon the clan, village, tribe, or kingdom and kinship ties and loyalties. Traditional land patterns follow a communal ownership system in which land belonged to all members of the group. An individual had the right to use a given piece of land as long as he continued to work it. Even if the individual left the group for a period of time, he could claim the same piece of land upon his return. Individual holdings varied in size, but were based upon what an individual required to support himself and his family. Since the traditional system required that the members of the group share the fertile and less fertile land with each other, an individual's holding generally consisted of a series of small patches scattered over the area claimed by the tribe, clan, or village. Every member of the group had a claim to the land in its territory. Land was not considered salable or rentable, but transfer from one member of the group to another was permissible with mutual consent. Tribes that built permanent settlements developed more exact land demarcation systems as did many areas of dense population. This pattern of land holding presents modern governments with real headaches as they try to increase agricultural production by modernization and mechanization. Recent studies of African agricultural potential raise additional problems for the expansion of current production levels. Contrary to the popular belief that Africa is a lush tropical area in which anything will grow, these studies point out that African soil is poor in comparison to many other areas of the world.

Subsistence farming was the general pattern in the traditional society. Hunting was the primary source of food in the rain forests, but some bush-fallow cultivation also developed. In the cooler and drier highlands, more intensive cultivation evolved. Although a number of the tribes of East and South Africa were pastoral, cattle keeping was difficult at best with preservation of meat, milk, and cheese almost impossible. In West Africa, the tsetse fly and ticks limited cattle keeping. Present statistics still indicate an annual cattle loss adequate to feed ten million people. The savannas also provide poor grazing land. The subsistence agriculture pattern was disrupted by the introduction of cash crop production. Colonial policies encouraged its expansion and by the 20's and early 30's, it had become big business. Cash crop areas developed patchily, and subsistence agriculture continued alongside it. Cocoa, cotton, and palm products headed the list of exports but coffee, peanuts, and sisal also played a part in the export totals.

Urbanization is limited. Less than ten percent of the population live in communities of over 5,000. The pattern of towns is very varied, with two-thirds of them concentrated in West Africa and one-fourth in Nigeria. Yoruba towns such as Ibe, Iwo, or Ibadan represent a high percentage of these urban areas. These Yoruba towns were part of the traditional pattern, and their origin may have been as rural settlements since sixty percent of their males still engage in agricultural production. Forty-seven percent of the population of the Western Region is concentrated in these towns in contrast to fourteen percent in Eastern Nigeria.

The scattering of urban settlements may be illustrated by survey-ing urban population percentages in various areas of the continent. Nigeria and Ghana, which have a high population density, also have a high urban percentage of over nine percent. Malawi and Uganda, also with a high population density, have very few urban areas. The percentage for Uganda is 0.7%. Zambia, which has the sparsest population, also has the highest urban population of 18.4%. Angola and French Equatorial Africa with low population densities also have low urban percentages of less than 6%. Co-lonial policies helped stimulate the growth of many large cities, particularly along the coast. Accra had been a small fishing village prior to the arrival of the Europeans. These cities have tended to grow rapidly, many doubling their population in the more recent period. For example, Abidjan, which had a population of under 1,000 in 1900, has grown to over 300,000. In 1950, urban popu-lation was estimated at 7.1% but now represents 10%.

One explanation for the low percentage of urban population until the recent period may be the traditional communal organization of society based upon subsistence agriculture. The Europeans found it difficult to attract Africans to the plantations, mines, or urban areas since they had little need for money and were reluctant to leave their clan. The 1956 survey of African population estimates the total wage-earning force to be under 10%. Of these, 36% were engaged in agriculture, 11% in mining, 13% in manufactur-ing, 12% in construction, 5% in commerce, and 10% in domestic service. These surveys of African population also indicate that the labor force tends to circulate between urban centers and the rural areas rather than to migrate permanently as in Europe. African labor has moved to urban areas or plantations in search of employment and wages in order to pay tax assessments and to expand purchasing power. After gaining the cash desired, however, they tend to return to their tribal communities. Questionnaires sent to "permanent" urban dwellers in a few major cities indicated that a high percentage planned to return to the village after retirement.

Contemporary African governments place great emphasis upon the industrialization of the continent, which may stimulate a rapid growth in urbanization. The ability to industrialize may depend to some extent upon mineral resource deposits. Three primary regions of mineral wealth exist: the Katanga-Zambia copper belt, which is fifty miles wide and stretches for two hundred and fifty miles; the Kimberlite diamond region of East Central Africa including Tanzania, Angola, Katanga; and the Rhodesian chromium, nickel, and iron ore areas. In addition to these three regions, many states have important deposits of minerals. Sierra Leone, Liberia, and Guinea produce 1.4% of the world's total of iron ore. The Congo-Leopoldville, Zambia, and Uganda have three-fifths of the world's total cobalt deposits. Ghana is one of the world's major producers of magnesium. Fourteen percent of the world's total production of tin comes from the Congo and Nigeria. Finally Africa produces 80% of the world's supply of diamonds. Although export of these minerals provides foreign currency, facilities to process these mineral resources have not been developed to any great extent in Africa. Such facilities must be expanded before the goal of industrialization and urbanization is attained.

POLITICAL TRADITIONS IN PRE-EUROPEAN AFRICA

In the discussion of emergent Africa's problems of stability and change, certain questions were raised about the pre-independence period: the possible influence of traditional and colonial institutions and procedures upon present African governmental patterns; colonial policies in Africa and the preparation for independence. A brief investigation of the political institutions and procedures of pre-European Africa and the colonial period may shed some light on the questions raised.

Anthropologists and sociologists have undertaken thousands of detailed studies of pre-European tribal customs and culture. Their research has revealed that over 700 distinctive languages existed in pre-European Africa. No accurate count of individual tribal groups has been made, but the large number of distinctive language groups may give some indication of the multiplicity of tribal units, although tribal and language units may not necessarily be equated. The following discussion will illustrate the diversity of tribal institutions and procedures in the pre-European period, although the tribal units selected as examples will not show every distinctive tribal system or practice.

Some 19th century surveys pictured Africa as a vast, unorganized, anarchistic, and undeveloped continent before the arrival of the West. Such studies reinforced the notion of the "white man's burden" prevalent at the time. Although records of pre-European Africa are not always readily available, recent studies have found evidence of well developed and complex political and social organizations. The African traditional system included a wide variety of political institutions and procedures.

The basic unit of the tribal system was the family. Originally, one family or several families may have moved into an area to cultivate the land or herd livestock. Gradually distinct family groups were created in the area. The size varied to some extent with the type of agricultural production. The Bantus of South Africa, Rhodesia, Kenya, Tanganyika, Uganda, and the Congo often did not maintain permanent settlements. Cattle keeping was an important part of the economy. Cattle were prized as a sign of wealth and were used in payment for brides and legalization of marriage. Many of the Negro tribes of West Africa engaged in grain production and permanent settlement was more common. Cattle keeping was not part of their economic system.

To maintain order, the families evolved a system of authority to settle disputes, promote stability, and redress injuries and grievances. Some groups also developed common procedures to protect their land and themselves against invasion and attack. As these steps were taken, the groupings tended to become differentiated from each other and a distinct tribal unit emerged. In the evolution of the system, certain individuals were given authority in the social organization. The headman of the family generally assumed the responsibility to promote his group's welfare and maintain order. When a number of families came together, one family might be chosen to rule the group. This selection sometimes occurred as a result of conquest or because one family was the first to settle in a given area. The headman of these families became the chief.

In all the tribes, the family was the basic unit of the system. It served as the integrator of society. The family was responsible for production, religious and cultural beliefs, order and authority, marriage arrangements, and maintaining continuity with the past. The family, in other words, was responsible for passing the traditional system to the next generation. The clan was the enlargement of the family system and assumed the same responsibilities as the family for the well being of the larger unit.

Marriages were arranged by the clan with an eye to the strength and wealth of its members. Dowries or bride payment often were required. Polygamy was practiced by some tribes to assure that all female members were protected by the males in the group. Some of these marriage practices have caused administrative problems for contemporary African governments. In the Ivory Coast, for example, new marriage laws have been passed requiring civil marriage ceremonies, licenses, and registration in order that records can be accurate. Polygamous marriages have been outlawed and must be dissolved.

Land was a basis of livelihood. Land tenure and land cultivation were important social, political, and religious factors. The chief, or headman, was the custodian of the land, and land tenure was generally communal. Loss of land was a serious matter, and land was sold only in extreme hardship cases. Technically, the chief had the power to regulate land tenancy and cultivation. In the communal systems, all members owed certain responsibilities to the clan. In event of calamity or disaster, clan members were expected to assist the less fortunate.

Some tribes gradually developed a pyramid, or hierarchy, of centralized authority, with a king at the top of the system. Zulu tribal organization illustrates this type of centralized authority. The tribe was pastoral, scattered in homesteads in Zulu territory. Its homesteads were grouped into hundreds of clans united under a chief. Originally these clans traced descent from the Zulus, but gradually other families became part of the structure because of their allegiance to the Zulu king. At the top of the structure was the king who was empowered to speak for the entire nation and who had judicial, administrative, and legislative authority over his people. He also performed religious ceremonies and "magical" rites for the protection and well-being of the tribe.

In theory, the king's power was absolute, but in practice he operated within defined limits. He was expected to seek the advice of his council, and refusal to follow their recommendations could lead to difficulty. Tribal policies and programs were presented to the council for discussion. The council members debated issues freely but were expected to avoid direct contradiction of the king. He adopted the practice of speaking last to avoid open clashes with the council. The king attempted to control discussion by informing key councilors of his wishes prior to the meeting. If he could persuade them to support his views, the danger of a clash was avoided. A successful and respected king was one who could maintain the confidence of the council and rule with their support and approval.

Below the Zulu king in the pyramid were the regional chiefs. They could check a king's abuse of power since their right of revolution against excessive use of power was recognized. At the base of the pyramid were the local chiefs. The king was forced to rely upon them for tax collection and troop supply in time of emergency. The local chiefs divided their tribes into fighting units and hunting units, and regiments of fighting units were quartered near the king for his use. Although fighting units could be called only by the king and under his personal control, each regiment was attached to a local chief and commanded by princes, chiefs, or brothers of the chief. These officials could check the king's use of troops by refusing to follow the king's orders.

The Bemba tribe of Northern Rhodesia also developed a centralized organization. The chief of the tribe combined executive, ritualistic, and judicial powers. Although his authority was not to be questioned, his powers were checked by the Bakabilo, holders of hereditary offices that descended from a few of the older clans of the tribe. These positions were primarily ritualistic rather than conciliar although the Bakabilo did serve as regents upon the death of the chief. A chief's exercise of power could be limited by their refusal to perform ritualistic functions for him. Since their offices were hereditary, the chief could not remove them. However, difficult members occasionally were exiled by chiefs when limitation attempts went too far. The chief's immediate family also could intervene to attempt a check on his abuse of powers.

Another tribe that developed a large-scale political organization was the Yoruba tribe of Western Nigeria. At the head of the system was a king who ruled over one million people at the peak of the empire's development. The king was selected by the elders on the basis of lineage and ability. The Yoruba king also ruled with a council and was expected to discuss policy with them. He could be removed when he exceeded the limits of his power. The Yoruba method of removal was to present the king with a parrot's egg as a signal for him to commit suicide. Sub-chiefs and headmen similarly were limited in the use of their powers. The Bushongo of the Congo and the Tukolov of Senegal also developed similar centralized structures.

The centralized political system of Northern Nigeria differed from those discussed above. When the Fulani invaded the area in the thirteenth century they brought their imperial structure. The North was divided into thirty-eight emirates with populations ranging from seventy thousand to one million people. The emir was responsible for the proper performance of the Islamic religious rites, the economic development of the emirate, and the maintenance of order and justice. He generally controlled educational programs, land distribution, and religious policies. The emir's position was reinforced by the belief that proper performance of the Islamic religious rites required support of the social and economic system. At the top of the structure was the Sultan of Sokoto. Theoretically, he had final authority over the empire. In practice, the system was loosely controlled, and power tended to center in the emirates, which operated nearly autonomously.

These examples of centralized tribal organization reveal certain similarities of governing procedure. In theory, the chiefs or kings were assumed to hold autocratic powers over their subjects, but in practice their powers were limited. The chiefs were normally required to rule through some type of council. Successful chiefs kept the support of at least a majority of the council on tribal questions. Members of the tribe could approach individual councilors in order to present their views and air grievances. By this procedure the king was informed of tribal wishes and feelings. Some students of African tribal structure have suggested that certain aspects of a constitutional monarchy system were present in this type of tribal structure, since definite limits to the power of the chief were recognized. If the chief exceeded these limits, there was an understanding in many tribes that he could be removed. Many methods existed from popular consent to suicide.

The chief's powers were primarily adjudicative. In this role he interpreted the ancient customs and laws and attempted to determine which party came closer to satisfying the traditional procedures and requirements. The executive function was not emphasized since each individual was expected to abide by the rules and mores of his group without the necessity for formal enforcement procedures. These norms were as old as the tribe itself, and respect for the past and antiquity was strong. The rules that had been adopted by previous generations were handed down from father to son with little questioning. Although some rules and taboos of the tribe lost their meaning over a period of time, their validity was rarely questioned, and they were carried on although the reasons for doing so were no longer clear. Those who broke tribal rules and taboos suffered social disapproval and threat of expulsion from the tribe. Death could be inflicted for a serious violation of the rules. The legislative function tended to be poorly developed in the tribal system. Since law and custom were considered unchangeable, the legislative function of altering the *status quo* was not desired.

Methods for selecting chiefs were well developed but varied from tribe to tribe. Lineage was a key consideration in most cases. Military ability and administrative skill also played a part in the selection process. In some tribes, the chief's position was hereditary. In Zulu land, fathers normally were succeeded by their sons. In the Bemba tribe descent was traced through the female rather than the male line. It was believed that the blood of the mother carried the family line and that the father provided the spirit. Contemporary African governments are attempting to revise the matriarchic system that existed in many tribes. For example, President Felix Houphouet-Boigny of the Ivory Coast recently promulgated legislation requiring that every citizen of the state must have a patronymic (family) name and that the child shall take the name of the father. Families have been urged to come together to pick a patronymic name, which then will be registered with the authorities.

Inheritance laws have been revised to end inheritance through the maternal line. Property of the father under the old system went to his nephew. Confusion over blood lines and family names resulting from the matriarchic system necessitated the new legislation.

Whether the tribe followed the patriarchic or the matriarchic system, blood lines were of great importance. They controlled the rank, position, and rights of the members of the tribe. Political power tended to concentrate in the hands of the original lineage status group. The significance of lineage may be illustrated by the Bemba belief in the influence of the dead over the living. In this tradition the spirit of a dead chief survived as a guardian of the land and the village where he dwelled. His spirit protected his lineage group. His successor had the power to appeal to him at certain sacred spots. Such appeals were believed to promote the fertility of the land and the welfare of the members of society. When a chief died, his successor passed through a special ritual and acquired the name and symbols of succession of the dead man. This practice emphasized the continuity of the line from the beginning. After receiving the name of the deceased, the new chief was believed to possess the magic powers of his predecessor.

Not all tribes provided an automatic hereditary succession. In some coastal areas of the Gold Coast and in Ashanti Province, chiefs were elected by a complex process. The queen mother was responsible for nominating a chief from the members of royal lineage. She was expected to consult at length with the elders over her choice. Criteria for selection included military capacity and leadership potential as well as royal lineage. When the queen mother and the elders reached agreement on a candidate, the queen mother announced the selection to the tribe. The members had the power to vote approval of her choice. After his election, the chief assumed responsibility for protection of the tribe, custodianship over the land and economy, and authority to adjudicate conflicts and injuries. He was obliged to consult a council on important issues. Abuse of power could result in destooling proceedings, which also involved the vote of the tribe. Since periodic destoolings occurred, chiefs were careful to maintain popular approval and confidence.

In other areas of the Gold Coast, tribal selection of chiefs was based upon the practice of gerontocracy, or rule by elders. Chiefs were elected following the process described above, but there was a hierarchy of elections system in which chiefs were elected periodically to higher and higher offices. At the top of the hierarchy was an elected chief whose power involved more absolute power than in the tribes described above. By the time a chief had gone through the pyramid to the higher ranks, he was an old man. Age was not the only criterion, however, since experience also entered into the considerations for selection. Some chiefs in the hierarchy were passed over if there was a question about the wisdom of their policies.

Not all African tribes developed a centralized hierarchy with authority over the members of the tribe. Among the Luguru of Tanganyika the principal political unit was the clan. The Luguru viewed themselves as a cultural group inhabiting a defined territory. Since each clan ruled itself, no central offices were created. The headman, selected by the clan, was responsible for order within his clan and for negotiating questions that might arise with other clans. Since the clan was a smaller unit than those of the centralized systems, more freedom of discussion and choice entered into clan procedures. Lineage heads were chosen for their intelligence and integrity. In some clans, the body of adult women was empowered to make the selection. In other clans, the adult males proposed a candidate to the assembled lineage women for election. These nominees had to be acceptable to the majority in the clan to be selected. Nominees were not approved automatically, and several votes often were necessary before a choice was made. The lineage heads so selected could be removed by popular consent.

The clan dwelling also was the basic political unit of the Tallensi of the northern Gold Coast. The Tallensi numbered about thirty-five thousand and were fixed cultivators, generally producing cereal grains. Being engaged in fixed cultivation, they built permanent and stable settlements. The senior male member of the family had authority and was responsible for its affairs. No centralized administrative, judicial, or military functions were maintained. The Tallensi did not unite for war as did many tribes. Each settlement or clan was expected to handle its own affairs and provide its own defense. The Kikuyu of Kenya and the Zoromu of Tanganyika are also examples of decentralized tribal systems.

Very briefly, these were the general outlines of the African traditional system before the arrival of the West. Contrary to the

19th century thesis that pre-European Africa constituted a vast, anarchistic, and undeveloped wasteland, these tribal systems reveal well-developed procedures for governing and for selection of officials. These procedures and processes were deeply rooted in tradition and in custom, and they were supported and understood by tribal members.

Significant differences in tribal structures and procedures are apparent. Some tribes had centralized institutions and others did not. Procedures for selection of governing officials varied. Some were hereditary and some were elected. Some tribes provided for removal but these procedures differed. Although each tribe developed institutions and procedures for governing, the dissimilarity of practices among them was significant. Now that they have achieved independence, states in which, for example, a centralized tribal structure was grouped together with a decentralized one face a serious problem of lack of common traditional institutions to which they might turn in the contemporary period.

THE COLONIAL PERIOD

The arrival of Western traders, missionaries, settlers, and colonial civil servants brought the African traditional system into contact with new cultures and new political structures and procedures. The impact of Western civilization shook the foundations of the traditional system and played a significant role in the eventual rise of modern African nationalism.

The European powers became interested in Africa for a variety of reasons. As trade with the Orient developed, Africa became significant as an area for obtaining water and food stuffs. Dutch arrival at the Cape of Good Hope in 1652 was a search for needed supplies. The slave trade in the seventeenth century brought increased numbers of traders from Europe to areas of Africa. As this trade expanded, large numbers of the strongest and healthiest young men and women were seized for transportation overseas. West Africa was particularly hard hit by the trade. Clan members were scattered by this process and clan life upset by the loss of their younger members. The actual devastation is difficult to measure. After the slave trade was outlawed, many ex-slaves were returned to the West Coast of Africa and liberated. Ghana received a significant number of them. The ex-slave group tended to be a disruptive influence. They had lived outside of Africa for a long enough period of time to become "detribalized." They no longer recognized traditional authority and did not wish to return to clan life or responsibilities. Exposure to Western life caused them to question, and in some cases reject, tribal customs and mores.

With the ending of slave trade, European interest in trade expansion increased. The industrial revolution promoted European concern over raw material areas and markets. Mercantilist philosophies encouraged the acquiring of colonial areas to supply the mother country. As a result, European governments chartered trading companies to expand trade and development of Africa. These companies were empowered to negotiate economic treaties with local authorities and to settle some areas. In the early years, trading company officials served as the colonial administration. Since they were concerned primarily with economic expansion and profit, the impact of their policies upon the African traditional system received little attention or concern.

European entry into Africa also was stimulated by the power struggle that developed among the states. Colonies and overseas expansion were associated with power and prestige. States attempted to expand their areas of influence in order to attain a major power status. In some cases, territories were taken to check another power's expansionist drives. Tribal authority boundaries and the traditional system largely were ignored in the process. Having gained territory, the powers were often unclear about the policies they wished to follow or their purposes in the area. Since the European powers entered Africa for a variety of reasons, colonial policy often evolved to meet the requirements of control, economic penetration, and a minimum of administrative expenditure. Conscious evaluation of the wisdom or results of a policy was not necessarily part of the process.

BRITISH COLONIAL POLICY

The British indirect rule system is an example of such an evolved policy. The indirect rule system was developed in Nigeria. Britain established control over Nigeria by 1900 and amalgamated the Colony of Lagos and the Northern and Southern Protectorates in 1914. The colonial service was charged with putting down resistance and promoting trade and development. Since the British

Government expected the colonies to be largely self-supporting, little in the way of funds was available for administrative expenditure. The Niger Company originally received a charter from the British Government to develop trade in the Niger River area. Expansion of trade was relatively easy along the coastal area, since it was a level grassland or plain about forty miles wide. Behind this coastal strip lay a dense forest area, which made travel difficult. The Niger Company concentrated on developing trade along the coast. Few British settlers or traders moved into the interior or northern area since the dense forest hindered penetration. When the colonial service took over administration of Nigeria, control and pacification of the North presented a problem. Sending troops to occupy the region was difficult in view of a limited budget. The utilization of British settlers and traders as an administrative and enforcement arm of the civil service was not feasible since their numbers were too small to be effective. Lord Lugard hit upon the scheme of utilizing the native administrative structure already existing. Since the North was divided into Moslem emirates, which had been created when the Fulani conquered the Hausa, he reasoned that the emirate system was tailor-made for indirect rule.

Under the Governor in the colonial administrative structure was a Lieutenant Governor for the Northern Protectorate. He was assisted by a permanent secretariat and departmental officials responsible for medical care, public works, forestry, agriculture, education, police and penal institutions, and politics. The Lieutenant Governor and his staff operated autonomously, and the civil service staff of the region was administered separately from the South.

In the traditional system, the emirs were responsible for collecting taxes on their lands, cattle, and trade. The Sultan of Sokoto at the head of the structure received annual payments from these tax collections. In utilizing the native administration structure, the British retained the right to impose taxes and ultimate control over the land. British district officers were appointed to advise and oversee the emirates. They were responsible for law enforcement, tax collection, and trade expansion in their districts. One general tax, a graduated land tax, was established, and all others were abolished. The Colonial Service supervised its collection. The British ended the traditional practice of the tax collectors living at the emir's court and periodically dispatching agents to make collections. They required the emirs to live permanently in their districts and headmen to establish permanent residence in their villages. In the early period the taxes were divided equally between the colonial government and the emirs. The British recognized the special power and position of the Sarduna of Sokoto and allowed him to keep seventy-five percent of the taxes collected in his district. The colonial office checked the accounts and expenditures of the native funds to regulate possible corruption and misuse. The emirates had a chief minister, the Wayiri; a chief justice, called the Alkali, who was schooled in the Koran; and a chief of police, the Dogari, who were under the direction and control of the emir. The colonial administration utilized them to enforce colonial rules and regulations.

The indirect-rule policy was considered the best administrative procedure to follow since it involved a relatively small number of British troops and colonial officials. The use of native authorities and structures already in existence avoided the creation of a complex colonial administrative structure on local and district levels and kept government expenditures at a minimum. All areas of Nigeria were not pacified in the period when indirect rule was adopted. It was assumed the use of native authorities would assist pacification since they would collect taxes and enforce law and order. The colonial civil service also recognized that its personnel had only limited knowledge of the local areas and conditions. The use of native authorities was a means to overcome some of the difficulties resulting from ignorance of local procedures and practices since it might avoid the introduction of drastic reforms that would dislocate and disrupt the society. The native authority system also was similar to that adopted in India, where the British had administered through the Indian princely states. Since the policy was effective in India, it was hoped that it could be applied with equal success to African institutions.

Although indirect rule solved the problems of administration and pacification for the Colonial Service, it had side effects that were not considered at the time of its adoption. The status and position of the traditional authorities were reinforced by this policy, since British power and prestige supported their traditional power. The Fulani-Hausa empire was based upon a feudal land system, and the British colonial service inadvertently became its protector and perpetuator. Forces of modernization and liberalization found it hard to make headway against an entrenched emirate structure reinforced by the British Colonial Service. The autonomy that developed in the administration of the North encouraged a regional rather than a national outlook. Northern and Southern Nigeria tended to develop along different lines. In the South there was greater contact with British traders, Christian missionaries, and Western education. The growth of commercialization, urbanization, and nationalism followed. In the North, trade was limited, Christian missionaries were discouraged, and educational policy remained the prerogative of the emir. These differences in experience aggravated the problem of creating national unity after Nigeria became independent.

Since indirect rule worked effectively in the North, it also was applied to other regions of Nigeria. Problems were encountered, since the tribal institutions differed from those of the Fulani-Hausa system. For example, Iboland in the Eastern Region was inhabited by a tribal group that had not developed a centralized hierarchy of authority. The basic unit of the tribal system was the clan. In some clans, hereditary chiefs existed, but this was the exception rather than the rule. The British Colonial Office was not presented with an existing centralized tribal structure that could be utilized for administration of taxation, law enforcement, education, and economic expansion. The British officials selected those who appeared to be the persons entitled to exercise authority in the Ibo tribe and made them administrators of colonial policy. However, these "warrant chiefs" were not necessarily recognized by the Ibo as persons of authority. Since the colonial administration certified them, they performed these functions whether or not they held clan positions. No native treasuries were created at first, since they had not existed prior to the introduction of indirect rule. The warrant chiefs became known as instruments of British policy. Riots occurred over taxation policy, and there was anger at the warrant chiefs' collection of taxes and assumption of power. The use of the indirect rule system in an area where a decentralized tribal unit existed created a new tribal class and discredited them almost immediately because of their close association with the colonial system.

The use of indirect rule in Yoruba land of the Western Region had a somewhat different result. The Yoruba had developed a hierarchic organization with a monarch at the top. Unlike the semi-autonomous emirate system of the North, it was centralized. Since the indirect-rule system worked through the local and district native authorities, Yoruba subchiefs, district chiefs, and headmen existed whom the colonial office could certify as native authorities. However, the use of these officials ignored the tribal leaders at the top level of the hierarchy and undercut their authority. Although such procedures suited the requirements of indirect rule, they tended to upset the Yoruba traditional system.

The Nigerian indirect-rule policy served as a model in varying degrees in other British areas. In the Gold Coast, indirect rule was never completely adopted. In the early years, the Gold Coast was administered by the African Company of Merchants. The British Government formally established firm control over the Gold Coast after separating it from Sierra Leone in 1874. The coastal areas were placed under direct Colonial Office administration. The geography of the Gold Coast is similar to that of Nigeria. The Northern areas were difficult to penetrate, and few British traders or settlers had moved into the North. Indirect rule was adopted since the North could be less closely controlled. In the mixed system adopted by the Gold Coast colonial administration, the traditional social life remained unimpaired whenever it was not contrary to British standards of morality and justice. Native chiefs were used as an arm of the adminstration wherever possible. The British reserved the right to impose taxes, legislate policy, appropriate land, confirm the successors to chieftainships, and depose those of whom it did not approve. In the traditional systems, complex and elaborate procedures existed for selecting new chiefs. Lengthy discussions with the tribal elders, queen mother, and commoners occurred before a new chief was named. The assumption of this power by the colonial administration upset the working of the traditional system. Tribal selection was based upon lineage, military ability, and leadership. The Colonial Service emphasized the training and ability of the chief for administrative functions. In tribal practice, the power of a chief was balanced by the requirements for consultation in which every member of the tribe had an opportunity to participate to some degree and by the provisions for destooling in cases of abuse of power. The position of the chief suddenly shifted under the colonial system, and his authority was based on British law rather than resting on the traditional check and balance. The tribal system tended to break down as the chiefs became increasingly identified with the British administration. Although tribal authorities administered the rules, no one was fooled concerning the British officials who supervised behind the scenes. British rules of procedure did not tend to be accepted by tribal members as the traditional system broke down, since they were not completely understood and there was resentment over British interference and authority.

In order for the traditional authorities to perform administrative functions effectively for the Colonial Service, training in administrative procedures was necessary. British mission schools were opened, and tribal chiefs were instructed to send their sons to school. It was hoped that this would assist in creating a native authority personnel capable of enforcing British rules and administering native funds. Some chiefs sent slave-sons to school out of anger over British interference. As these slave-sons became educated, they gradually moved into administrative positions or European firm offices. The creation of an ex-slave class as a new elite further upset traditional procedures and structures. Training of the chief's sons for administrative responsibility also ignored tribal selection processes. In tribes where descent followed the matriarchic system, authority passed to the wrong person. Tribal procedures that followed election or gerontocracy also were disrupted.

Mission schools in Ghana, as well as in other areas, brought Christianity to Africa. The chief's position was based in part upon traditional religious practice. The sanctity of the chief and his special "magical" powers stemmed from these religious beliefs. The introduction of Christianity weakened this base of power. The "white man's burden" philosophy influenced some missions and caused them to look down upon African culture and traditions. Some African religious practices conflicted with Christianity. Animism and polytheism were contrary to Christian teachings. The practice of polygamy also caused difficulty. In accepting Christianity, the African was expected to abandon many of these traditional beliefs and practices. This necessitated in many cases a rejection of tribal authority and responsibility. The African Christian gradually formed an opposition to the tribal authorities. A breach was created between him and his tribal members that was difficult to heal due to lack of mutual understanding. Africans often point to mission activity as a significant force in the development of African nationalism. Having broken with the traditional system, the African Christian began to search for status in the colonial system. He became not only an opponent of the authority of the traditional system but of the colonial system as well.

Islam had not had the same disruptive influence on the traditional system since it tended to proselytize only the formal aspects of the belief system. A mixture of the traditional and Islamic beliefs developed. In some cases, the imitation of dress, the practice of fasting, or the observance of prayers were all that was necessary to claim membership. Baptism was not required, and polygamy was not necessarily prohibited. Polytheism was the primary area of irreconcilable conflict. Since it was more easily adapted to traditional religious practice, Islam grew rapidly in some areas of the African continent. Adoption of Islam also was encouraged by Arab prestige gained as a result of their earlier military power and ability. In the slave-trade period, some Africans accepted the faith because enslavement of those who professed the religion was not permitted. In areas where Islam had penetrated significantly, as Northern Nigeria, British colonial policy limited or prohibited Christian missionary activity in the belief it might prove too disruptive. This policy strengthened the influence of Islam and its leaders. In Northern Nigeria this led the British to acquiesce in the perpetuation of a feudalistic system. Religious policy as well as indirect rule reinforced their position.

Tanganyikan Governor Sir Donald Cameron, who had served on the colonial staff in Nigeria, attempted to adapt the Nigerian indirect-rule policy to Tanganyika. Tanganyika had been a German Colony prior to World War I. The Germans had established a direct rule structure that resembled a military occupation. Little attention had been paid to traditional authority lines, and there had been a tendency for tribal authority to weaken under German control. After the war, Tanganyika was placed under the League Mandate System with Britain as the mandate power. In attempting to liberalize the German administrative policies, the British Colonial Staff turned to indirect rule. Re-establishment of tribal authority was considered essential to the promotion of greater self rule. The Colonial Service was sent throughout Tanganyika to study tribal structures and patterns. As a result of this study, the indirect-rule system was modified in order to re-establish the proper tribal authorities in power.

The mandate status of Tanganyika encouraged significant divergences from the Nigerian indirect rule pattern. For example, native authorities were not forced to administer policies with which they did not agree. Colonial district officers were responsible for gaining compliance with British policies by means of persuasion. In the 1930's, colonial officers encouraged conferences of the chiefs. In 1932, fifty-two chiefs met to discuss common policies and programs for the state. After 1932 these conferences became annual. The colonial staff also encouraged the growth of African organizations to promote joint development. Many tribal planter associations were formed. Co-operative distribution and marketing became a significant function of these associations. The colonial staff also paid particular attention to the expansion of educational opportunities in Tanganyika. Village school facilities were increased. African languages were used in the schools, and the curriculum was designed to avoid a radical break with traditional culture and patterns. English and Western history and philosophy entered into the curriculum at the higher levels, but the Colonial Service attempted to avoid a frowning upon traditional civilization and culture.

In the other British areas of East and Central Africa, the colonial office also adopted some forms of indirect rule. However, colonial policies were influenced by the white populations that settled in such countries as Kenya and the Rhodesias. In these territories, land policy became a critical issue between white settler and African. Colonial policy reserved all land for ultimate disposal by the crown. Land policies created native reserves and alienated large tracts for exclusive white settlement and development. Native populations were told to take their herds to new areas in order to create "white reserves." The white highlands policy of Kenya restricted 16,000 square miles for settler development. Alienation of land was a serious problem for the African tribes since land was the basis of the traditional system and was the source of all income and livelihood. Taxation policy in the white settler areas often was designed to force the African laborer to work in the white plantations, mines, or industries. Shortage of labor and the reluctance of the African to leave the village precipitated such legislation. The movement of Africans away from the villages, the breakup of families and the absence from the village of able-bodied males for significant periods of time further weakened the traditional structure. Since indirect rule was adopted for administration of the native reserves, but not for the white settler areas, inequalities began to develop between the white settler and the African in political participation, educational facilities, and economic standards and opportunities. White settler interests tended to dominate policy making.

Each colony had its own local department of education. General principles for their guidance were established by the colonial office. In 1925, the colonial office recommended that curriculum be adapted to the aptitudes, occupations and traditions of Africa. Advisory boards composed of members of the medical, agricultural, and public works departments assisted the Education Departments in implementing these policies. Elementary education was to be in the vernacular. In areas where a mission school network existed, the boards of education worked through these schools. Uganda and Nyasaland are examples. In Northern Nigeria and Tanganyika's Lake Province, native administration schools were used. Government schools were established in most urban areas. Elementary curriculum placed great importance on religious and moral training. Some vocational training was given in handicraft and agriculture. Secondary education was provided for able students. Higher educational facilities were opened in the 1930's. Makerere College in Uganda, Yaba College in Nigeria, Achimoto in the Gold Coast, and Fourah Bay in Sierra Leone provided higher education facilities. Overseas training was expanded also.

After World War II, British colonial policy was revised to encourage greater African participation in the government. The Civil Service permitted increased numbers of Africans to enter. Before the war, only twenty-three Nigerians held positions in the Civil

Service. By 1948 their numbers were expanded to 182. By 1956, 600 of the 3,679 members of the service were Nigerian. To train additional Africans for career service, scholarships were made available for overseas study and college facilities were expanded in the African states.

Popular participation in the political process was fostered by the establishment of locally elected councils to handle local policy questions. These councils gradually replaced the tribal authorities' administrative and legislative functions. Traditional authorities were opposed to these revisions because they represented a loss of position and prestige. As British post-war policy moved progressively toward the eventual independence of the African states, the colonial administrators faced the problem of reconciling the traditional-authority, indirect-rule system with a modern parliamentary model.

New constitutions were written to allow greater African political participation in central governmental policies. The governor, prior to the war, was assisted by a legislative council. This council generally was composed of a majority of official members appointed by the governor. Africans gradually were admitted to membership, but their numbers were limited. After the war the legislative councils were reformed to permit direct election of a majority of their members. The 1946 Gold Coast constitution provided for an African majority in the elected legislative council. Following the 1946 constitution, a series of governmental decrees moved progressively toward African control of the government. The 1951 reform abolished the legislative council and replaced it with an elected legislative assembly. Gold Coast citizens who were twenty-five years of age, British subjects, and able to read English were able to stand for election after the deposit of a fifty-pound fee. In the Northern areas, an electoral college system using the territorial councils allowed the chiefs greater influence over the selection of representatives. After 1954, the legislative assembly was composed of majority and opposition party benches. Indirect election was abolished and territorial councils no longer elected representatives. This ended the last vestige of the indirect-rule system and the chiefs' control over selection of representatives. The new independence party movements became dominant, and the chiefs tended to lose their place in the political structure. In 1951 a cabinet was created to advise the governor; it gradually became the principal instrument of policy. The governor appointed the prime minister on majority party recommendation and removed cabinet ministers only at the request of a two-thirds vote of the assembly. Kwame Nkrumah became prime minister after the adoption of the 1954 constitution and introduced a motion asking for independence.

Similar liberalization occurred in other British colonies. Centralization of control over local institutions brought the liberalization process into conflict with the indirect-rule system. As the central government assumed control over local institutions and policies, indirect rule was ended. In order to preserve the influence of the traditional authorities, several constitutions provided for some degree of regionalism or federalism.

For example, the 1946 Richards constitution in Nigeria created regional assemblies with electoral college systems in which the influence of the traditional authorities was perpetuated. Regionalism also permitted the continuance of local differences in educational policy, economic organization, and political procedures. It was opposed by the more nationalistic elements of the society who desired a centralized, uniform, and national system. Regionalism was viewed as a danger to national unity and stability. These fears may have been well founded. When Nigeria began negotiations on a constitution in the pre-independence period it was impossible to reach a compromise on a unitary system. Regionalism was continued in the post-independence constitution. British indirect rule was one factor in the adoption of this system.

Liberalization of the constitutions and expansion of African participation in government also was undertaken in the British white settler areas. Reforms moved more slowly because of white settler fears over African domination. Africanization of the civil service came gradually, but top positions were European dominated until a few years before independence. Reform of parliament was based upon a guaranteed number of seats arrangement. For example, the Kenyan parliamentary seats were divided among the European, African, and Asian communities. African majorities did not come until less than ten years before independence. One explanation for the delay in reform is that it was not expected that independence would come as quickly in the white settler areas. Southern Rhodesia still maintains strict controls over African participation in government, and African majorities have not been achieved in parliament or the civil service.

The development of parliamentary systems of government and centralized administrations undercut the indirect-rule system and removed the native authorities from the positions that the British had deliberately fostered in an earlier period. African nationalists criticized the indirect-rule policy for perpetuating ancient and autocratic institutions and for attempting a divide-and-rule technique. Traditional authorities, resenting the loss of their positions and power, opposed the nationalist movements and in some cases attempted revolts against the new governments. Later chapters will discuss these problems in more detail.

FRENCH COLONIAL POLICY

French colonial policy did not follow one uniform pattern. Policy vacillated from one period to another depending on French views and the problems of administration. However, underlying the colonial policy was a belief in the unity of the overseas areas with the mother country. Overseas territories were expected to perform certain patriotic duties for France. Among these were supplying troops, contributing financially to the support of the colony, and furnishing raw materials for French industry. Senegal was conquered by France between 1854 and 1865. Since Napoleon III was in power in this period, colonial policy for Senegal developed along the authoritarian lines then prevailing in France. Colonial structures for other areas of Africa were modeled after the Senegalese pattern and the authoritarian lines tended to be perpetuated. The French created a centralized colonial structure. In 1895, a Governor General with headquarters at Dakar was appointed for all French Africa and made responsible for co-ordinating French policy in all colonies. The Governor General was assisted by a *Conseil du Gouvernement* composed of sixteen official members, a deputy from Senegal, four elected members representing Dahomey, the Ivory Coast, Sudan, and Guinea, the president and one non-citizen member of the Colonial Council of Senegal, and two unofficial members of the *Conseil d'Administration*. This council met annually to discuss policy questions. Regional groupings were formed to promote control and administration. French West Africa was composed of the eight colonies of

Senegal, Sudan, Guinea, Ivory Coast, Dahomey, Mauritania, Niger, and Upper Volta. The Federation of Equatorial Africa was formed from the three colonies of Gabon, Middle Congo, and Ubangi-Shari. Togo was administered separately and had financial autonomy. Chad was controlled by military government until the 1920's. Since the Cameroons were placed under the League Mandate system, they also were administered separately.

Each colony had its own Lieutenant Governor who was responsible for policy within his jurisdiction. In practice, the Governor General controlled policy decisions for each territory. The Lieutenant Governors and their colonial staffs served primarily as local administrators of French policy. The Lieutenant Governor was assisted by a *Conseil d'Administration*. The composition of the council varied somewhat from colony to colony. Generally, it was composed of three official members, two French citizens elected by chambers of agriculture and commerce, and three French subjects who were elected by subject groups holding administrative posts and by certain chiefs. The Council was consulted on budgetary, taxation, and commercial questions.

French policy has sometimes been described as direct rule by French administrators supported by French soldiers. In the period of pacification, military organization occasionally was adopted. For example, Guinea was divided into seventeen *cercles* each headed by a commandant. The commandant was responsible for the maintenance of law and order in his *cercle*. To emphasize his authority, he was empowered to imprison Africans without trial or charge for a two-week period. Direct rule often involved a deliberate attempt to break tribal authority in order to establish firm French control. However, in many cases the French colonial administration was forced to utilize the services of the subordinate chiefs. French administrators, as well as the British, were plagued by lack of personnel and funds and the difficulty of pacification. They concluded that directives were more likely to be carried out if they came through the chiefs. After pacification, the native authority system generally was abandoned. In the Ivory Coast, rebellions in 1900 and 1916 caused a temporary revival of tribal chief power but the system was dropped after the revolts were quelled.

In selecting chiefs as administrative aids, the French made little effort to pick the recognized leaders of the tribes. Instead, emphasis was placed upon ability, literacy, and loyalty to the French. The village headman was generally the only African given authority in the colonial administrative system, and his powers were limited to the enforcement of district and local policy. The French structure did not permit independent initiative by the traditional authorities as did the British. Since chiefs were viewed as colonial lackeys, they gradually lost their influence and prestige. Direct rule also encouraged uniformity of development and centralization of authority. Regionalism and sectionalism were discouraged. After independence the French territories had less difficulty than the British in establishing unitary systems. There was little problem of removing the traditional authorities from power, since French policy had already stripped them of authority and influence.

Exceptions to the direct rule pattern were the four special communes created in Senegal in 1872. Their inhabitants were accorded special status and rights. The *originaires* were considered citizens and had the right to elect their own municipal governments. In 1872, local self-government was instituted in the communes of St. Louis and Garée. Adult males were given the suffrage and elected members to the local council. A mayor was selected by the council from among its members. After 1910, a majority of council members were African.

French educational policy followed the concept of the union of France with her overseas territories. The colonies were to be assimilated into the French system and civilization. Perhaps as a result of "white man's burden" philosophy, French civilization was viewed as far advanced to the African. It was expected that all intelligent Africans would willingly adopt French culture after proper exposure to it. The assimilated African was able, in theory, to enter any profession on an equal basis with the European. Assimilated Africans could become naturalized citizens with full legal rights. Citizenship requirements varied from period to period. They included loyalty to France, ten years service in the French empire, the ability to read and write French, a good character, means of support, and no criminal record. Few Africans achieved this status. There was a complicated application procedure that discouraged many who were eligible. Others did not apply because citizenship status did not necessarily guarantee equal rights. By 1922, only two thousand naturalizations had been granted.

The great majority of Africans were not eligible for citizenship. Since educational facilities were not available equally to all, there was limited opportunity to master spoken or written French. In 1900, only 2,500 pupils were enrolled in school. French educational policies placed greater emphasis upon training gifted Africans who could become members of an assimilated African intellectual elite. Those of average ability were instructed only in subjects of use in village life. In the early years of the colonial administration, the majority of students received one year of education. The curriculum consisted of spoken French, mental arithmetic, and hygiene. Instruction in new agricultural techniques was provided to increase production and raise quality. Promising students received two or three years' additional schooling. If they showed outstanding ability, they were sent to a regional school and then to the *École Primaire* for craft or professional training. In 1903, twenty-three Senegalese bush schools were opened to expand village facilities. In 1910, the first secondary school was created at St. Louis. Emphasis upon the assimilation of the population of the overseas areas gradually brought about the emergence of a highly trained intellectual elite, which moved into higher economic and social status. Administrative positions were opened to them, and eventually they were allowed to stand for elective offices. After 1914, African membership in the French parliament was expanded.

By the 1920's, the French colonial service recognized that the assimilationist policy could not be applied effectively to every member of the overseas territories. Contrary to the notion of the superiority of French culture, many Africans were not attracted to French civilization. Colonial policy was altered to place even greater emphasis on the training of the elite. It was assumed that an assimilated intelligentsia would fill the top leadership positions. The decision to emphasize the education of the most gifted student left the vast majority of Africans without adequate educational facilities and opportunities. Progress for them was limited and difficult. French Equatorial Africa's educational facilities were particularly limited.

The French policy of assimilation represented an attack upon the traditional authorities and culture. Little attention was given to the disruption of the tribal systems caused by this emphasis.

Many present-day African leaders criticize French policy for having educated the intellectual elite away from Africa and creating a professional class that was more French than African. Although a few members of the elite may have accepted the view that African culture was inferior, many did not lose their African identification. The educated elite spearheaded the drive for greater autonomy and freedom. Frustrated in their attempts for autonomy within the French Union, they gradually turned to demands for complete independence.

French post-World War II policy was deliberated at a conference of local administrators held at Brazzaville in January, 1944. This conference re-emphasized the idea of unity between France and the overseas areas. Although independence for the colonies was not visualized as a desirable goal, greater local autonomy was proposed. The colonial areas participated in a constituent assembly in 1946 that drew up a new constitution for France and its overseas territories. In November 1946, under the new provisions, all residents of overseas areas were declared French citizens, and the franchise was broadened. Territorial assemblies were created in each colony and councils for the Federation of French West Africa and of French Equatorial Africa were established. The territorial assemblies were to be elected by universal suffrage, but an electoral-college system was followed in practice. The broadening of the suffrage and the election of delegates to the constitutional and territorial assemblies encouraged the development of political parties. The postwar period also saw the abolition of forced labor and the power of two weeks imprisonment without trial. France expanded economic assistance after the war. Investment funds were created to promote sorely needed economic development and closer economic integration with France. In educational policy, provisions were made for teaching French and African languages and some revision of the assimilationist approach. Facilities for the less gifted were expanded. In order to strengthen the idea of the French Union, the term "colony" was dropped, and overseas territories were permitted to elect representatives to the French National Assembly. Since they elected only a handful to the 600 member French parliament, they formed an insignificant percentage of the total membership. To gain majority support for their programs, these delegates allied themselves with French parties and formed an African united front. Only the French Communist Party took any real interest in the African delegates in the early period, and African deputies came into close contact with the French Marxists. France has been criticized for introducing Marxism into her African territories by this policy. However, this may not be significant since other Africans came into contact with Marxism through educational and labor union experiences. A more significant criticism of this policy may be that the political elite of the French areas were sent overseas for extended periods of time to serve as deputies or cabinet members. Residence in France made it difficult for them to stay in close contact with political movements and developments in their territories, and some deputies lost contact with their constituents. It also deterred the building of highly organized territorial parties.

A second significant postwar revision of colonial policy came with the passage of the so-called *loi-cadre* in 1956. The government received the power to modify the status of the overseas territories by decree. The size of the territorial assemblies was increased, and suffrage was extended. The electoral college system, which had been adapted to assure some control over the selection of representatives, was abolished. Executive councils were created in each territory, and African ministers were given more powers. These actions relaxed French controls and responded to the demands of growing nationalism in the territories. Despite these actions, pressures continued for greater territorial freedom and autonomy.

The 1958 Constitution of the Fifth French Republic recognized the necessity of meeting these demands for increased political autonomy. The French Union was modified and a "Community" was proposed between France and the overseas territories. The Community envisioned each territory as a self-governing state. Foreign policy, defense, fiscal programs, raw-material development, education, and communications would be commonly administered by the Community. The Community organization was to consist of a president, an executive council, a senate, and a court of arbitration. Each territory was to be represented in the common organs and participate in the common decisions and programs. However, French representation on the council was equal to that of the African territories. President de Gaulle proposed that every territory should have the opportunity to accept this new proposal by means of a referendum. Rejection would constitute severance by the territory of its ties with France. States voting *yes* on the referendum would have the option for independence if they should desire it in the future. The Community organization continued the concept of the unity of France and the overseas territories. However, complete internal autonomy and community action on questions such as foreign affairs replaced the older notion of French dominance and control.

Guinea returned an overwhelming *no* vote on the referendum and chose to break her ties with France. Complete independence was granted, and French colonial administrators left Guinea in a very short period of time taking with them everything movable, even the light bulbs from the government buildings. French aid and trade ties were broken, and Guinea faced the difficult problem of assuming separate existence. Ghana extended credit to assist Guinea over the immediate post-independence economic dislocation. Although the other territories voted *yes* on the referendum question, in a relatively short period of time they also sued for independence, and the notion of the French union with her overseas areas was dead. Many of the leaders of the overseas territories criticized France for adopting the internal self-government policy since it created separate and sovereign independent states, which tended to "Balkanize" the former French areas rather than encouraging them to adopt a united federal structure. Attempts have been made to re-establish some form of unity among the states by such agreements as the Brazzaville treaty. However, the dream some African leaders have of political union among the former French areas has not yet been achieved.

BELGIAN COLONIAL POLICY

Perhaps Belgian colonial policy has been more thoroughly analyzed and studied—certainly it has been more criticized—than the colonial policies of France and Britain as a result of the Congo crisis. Administration of the Congo was unique in the early years because, by decision of the European powers and the Belgian government, Leopold II controlled the territory. The Belgian parliament passed legislation to provide that the Congo would be directly administered by Leopold as the chief of state and that the union between Belgium and the new state should be "exclusively personal." As a result of these decisions, the Congo has sometimes been referred to as Leopold's "personal playground." Leopold's primary concern in the Congo seemed to be its economic development and his resultant profit. He appointed an Administrator General for the Congo to oversee economic development. The country was divided into fifteen districts, each under the supervision of a commissioner who was directly responsible to the Administrator General. Chieftaincies were divided into zones and eventually into sectors, and the power of the chiefs was reduced. In 1891, rules for governing the native population were formulated. "Invested" chiefs confirmed by the government enforced the Administrator's rulings. Little attempt was made to study the native social and political structures, and the "invested" chief was not necessarily the recognized authority in the tribe.

Stories concerning abuses in the Congo began to circulate in the European capitals. Protests were raised over slavery, forced labor, and alienation of land. Britain led the demands for investigation of conditions and reform of any abuses. As a result of these charges and counter-charges the Belgian government finally annexed the Congo in 1908. Leopold's personal rule was ended. A Ministry of Colonies was created to succeed him. Immediate steps were taken to reform working conditions and native ownership of land. However, the new administration continued many of the structural arrangements already in existence. Policy was directed from Brussels. The country was divided into districts under Belgian colonial administrators. The *chafferie* was created as an administrative sub-division. The chief in the area performed a number of administrative functions for the state. He was invested by the district commissioner and could be removed by him. When *secteurs* were created, *secteur* chiefs were selected by the district commissioner, and their salaries were paid by the colonial government. Urban areas were governed by district commissioners. Native cities, such as Leopoldville, were headed by chiefs appointed and removed by the district commissioners. Sector and *chafferie* native authorities were not those who held customary power in the tribes in many cases. By 1919, *chafferie* members had grown to 6,095. The increase in *chafferies* necessitated the appointment of subordinates to the chiefs. In 1926, the colonial office recognized the problems arising from the appointment of "chiefs" who did not have customary power in the tribes. A study of the native system was undertaken and the number of *chafferies* was reduced. Proper native authorities were appointed where possible, and chiefs were to be acceptable to the tribe before appointment. Although Belgium attempted some form of indirect rule, native authorities were appointed and removed by the colonial government and received a salary for their services. In some cases, salaries were placed in native treasuries. These funds were used for tools, educational facilities, and medical care of the tribe.

Belgium did not attempt to follow the French policy of assimilation. There was little notion of introducing Belgian institutions or culture in the Congo. Belgian policy has been described as paternalism. Belgium hoped to avoid the "mistake" of the British and French in creating an educated elite that eventually spearheaded the drive for improved status and independence. Until 1950, elementary education was the highest level available for the Congolese. Secondary education was not provided, and there was little enthusiasm for its creation. It was feared that advanced training might encourage nationalism. Vocational and craft training was available to encourage development of a skilled labor force. A primary three-year course in teaching, clerical skills, or agriculture was provided. Higher education overseas was not permitted until the 1950's. As late as 1956, only three Congolese had been sent overseas for advanced training. Congolese women were afforded few educational opportunities until the 1950's when elementary education was opened to them. In the early years courses were available in sewing, cooking, and child care. In *Congo My Country* Patrice Lumumba criticized this policy. He concluded that when Belgium gave education to the males they educated one person. If education had been open to women they would have educated the family.

Lacking facilities and teaching staff, the colonial service turned to the Catholic Mission schools to provide education. In 1925, the colonial office agreed to give certain missions a monopoly of the educational funds in return for their services. Such schools received government subsidy, and their faculty was put on the government payroll. In return for the subsidy, the government regulated curriculum, and craft training was emphasized. Other missions were discouraged from entering the Congo. Although the mission schools administered the government's policies, they also introduced Christianity in the Congo. Christian Congolese played a role in the breakdown of the traditional system and the development of nationalism.

Belgian colonial officers argued that their educational policies were superior to those of the British or French. In the 1950's, about fifty percent of the school age children in the Congo were enrolled in classes. This percentage was higher than in British or French areas. However, this percentage was at the elementary level. Secondary and college levels were almost nonexistent. As a result of United Nations' pressure, a university was established in the Congo in 1954, and a limited number of Congolese were permitted to enroll. Degrees were offered in medicine, agriculture, and education. Law and political science were omitted from the curriculum since it was feared these disciplines might produce nationalistic leaders.

Belgian educational policy produced a significant number of skilled labor and technician graduates. The Congo does not face the extreme shortages of skilled labor that plague many African states. However, no professional class was trained to whom power could be turned after independence. The shortage of trained political leaders, civil servants, industrial management, and the professions has been critical in the post-independence period.

Belgian colonial officials concluded that the Congolese desired improved economic standards rather than intellectual development or political participation. A policy of increased economic rewards was instituted in order to discourage the growth of opposition elements. In 1949, a ten-year plan for financial investment in the Congo was adopted. Economic development was promoted by a system of special protections and incentives for business. For example, the *Comité Special* encouraged prospectors in Katanga. If exploitation became possible as a result of these efforts, the *Comité* received one-third of the profits and the government two-thirds. The scheme was similar to that used by Leopold II in promoting business development.

As mining and industrial activities increased, a shortage of labor developed. Congolese were induced to leave the villages for employment in the mines and in the factory. Prior to the 1950's little attempt was made to preserve or develop village life. Migration from the villages was pushed on the grounds that the Congolese would advance only as they became detached from traditional life. The colonial government limited the immigration of large numbers of Europeans to the Congo, and permanent settlement was discouraged.

Emphasis was placed upon training native technicians. Although discretionary or administrative positions were not open to Congolese, they were encouraged to seek skilled labor positions. This policy stimulated urban growth. Rubber plantation development was promoted, and Congolese also were urged to leave the village for employment on the plantations. The growing concentrations of native populations around European towns and settlements were organized into "extra-customary centers" administered by chiefs and advisory councils appointed by the colonial district commissioners.

The decision to encourage the exodus from the villages assisted in breaking down the traditional system. Tribal ties weakened among Congolese living in the urban areas or clustering around European settlements and towns. The Belgian policy of using chiefs as administrative officers of the colonial government undermined their authority. The division of tribes into districts and *secteurs* and the appointment of chiefs for each administrative level disrupted traditional levels of authority. Since the district commissioner controlled the appointment and removal of chiefs, traditional systems of selection were ended. After 1950, the disruption to traditional life was recognized and measures taken to stem the exodus from the villages. Tenant farming was extended and agricultural policies revised to encourage rural development.

The 1949 ten-year development program emphasized extension of transportation and communication to promote internal trade. Increased public services were undertaken including leisure-hour recreational facilities for Congolese workers. Programs of hygiene education and medical care were expanded. Proposals were adopted to provide adequate housing and slum clearance.

The economic development plan was designed to raise Congolese standards of living and prevent dissatisfaction over the colonial status. Although political activities and responsibilities were discouraged, labor unions and tribal kinship associations were permitted. These organizations grew in the urban areas. As the Congolese left the villages for employment in plantations, mines, or factories, they tended to group into tribal self-help associations. Since political parties and political participation were denied them, these associations became significant as a means for expressing desires and dissatisfaction. Although Belgium had attempted to insulate the Congolese from the independence movements growing in other areas of Africa, news of developments in British and French territories tended to filter into the Congo. Service in World War II had given many Congolese an opportunity to move around Africa and observe developments. Demands for greater freedom grew despite Belgian policies.

In 1959 rioting broke out in Leopoldville as a result of the banning of an ABAKO meeting. Although order was re-established in a short period of time, Belgium moved quickly to meet the demands for greater political freedom. Election of rural and municipal councils was promised immediately, and the suffrage would be given to all adult males. The colonial service proposed the gradual creation of a national assembly after a five-year, step-by-step liberalization of the colonial structure. Congolese leaders objected to the step-by-step proposal and argued for immediate political power. Surprisingly, Belgium yielded to this pressure, and the Congo became independent without the planned political tutelage period. The results of this decision are only too well known. Belgian "paternalism" had discouraged the development of a leadership elite, political parties, and electoral and civic responsibility. Advanced educational opportunities had been limited. Top echelon administrative posts were closed to the Congolese, and no serious attempt was made to train a Congolese civil service. When the Congolese undertook the job of running the Congo, chaos developed almost immediately. Colonial policy was a factor in the difficulty that the Congolese encountered in achieving a stable system in the immediate post-independence period. It is almost unbelievable that a country of 139,000 square miles and a population of thirteen million people would have relatively only a handful of college graduates at the time of independence.

OTHER COLONIAL POWERS IN AFRICA

Although this discussion of colonial policy is intended to center on the British, French, and Belgian systems, brief reference should be made to other colonial powers in Africa. Of these, the Portuguese have received the greatest international attention as a result of the unrest and open conflict in Angola and the flight of 300,000 Angolans to the Congo in search of sanctuary. Portuguese policy has been termed "Christian paternalism." Government statements list as policy aims the christianizing, colonizing, and civilizing of Angola, Mozambique, and Guinea. During almost 500 years of Portuguese rule, emphasis has been placed upon the overseas areas as an integral part of Portugal. Following the structure of a unitary state, colonial administration centers in Lisbon. The concepts of self-determination or commonwealth are rejected in favor of a single entity governed from the center. In 1951, the colonies were redefined as "overseas provinces," but little change was made in administrative policy or the unitary system.

Since the 15th century, Portugal has espoused the ideal of individual assimilation for Africans in its territories. Requirements for achieving this classification include the ability to read and write Portuguese, the abandonment of tribal traditions, and the acceptance of the "moral sanctions of Portuguese culture." Portugal considers its colonies to be in a "state of social degradation" and argues that its mission is to make the Africans "equal to us" and achieve a solidarity of brotherly love with its overseas territories. Africans who have not attained assimilation are considered wards of the state. Traditionally, emphasis has been placed upon the obligation to work; and contract labor systems, often involving abuses, have entered into the colonial system.

Government statements stress the unique cultural tradition of Portuguese policy. For example, in 1960, on the 500th anniversary of the death of Henry the Navigator, celebrations were held extolling the solidarity of Portugal with its overseas territories, attempting to stir popular support for the government program. Despite these claims, very few Africans have achieved assimilation status. Although estimates vary, the figures do not exceed five percent of the overseas population. Many Africans who meet the educational requirements do not bother to apply, since assimilation does not guarantee equal status. Education facilities also are limited, and few Africans have an opportunity for more than three years of elementary training. Literacy in the colonies is estimated at only three percent of the total population. In addition, complaints are heard concerning administration and processing of the applications. Officials check the homelife of the African applicant to be certain tribal traditions have been abandoned. In some cases, bribery is reported to have entered into the procedure. Portugal admits these deficiencies but argues that it will take centuries to achieve its cultural goals. In view of the unrest in its colonies, considerable doubt can be raised whether the overseas Africans are willing to wait or even accept these aims of solidarity and assimilation.

Until 1951, Spanish colonial policy was described as "unreconstructed paternalism," based on the unitary approach, but without the Portuguese emphasis upon assimilation or cultural solidarity. However, after 1951, policy was revised significantly. Present Spanish policy seems to hope for the peaceful decolonization of its overseas areas and for the eventual creation of a loose association with Spain. In preparation for independence, certain measures of economic and administrative autonomy were allowed in Spanish Guinea in 1963 and Equatorial Province was granted some degree of political autonomy. These steps suggest a move toward eventual independence in contrast to the continued Portuguese insistence upon a unitary system attached to Portugal.

Italian influence in Africa has been limited, since Italy entered the continent relatively late when few areas remained for expansion. Major policy changes came in the period of Fascist rule. The drive into Ethiopia was based in part upon the desire to expand overseas areas for exploitation by the home country in search of autarky. With the end of Fascism, these policies were abandoned. In 1950, Italy was made a trust nation over Somalia, which was placed under a United Nations trusteeship agreement. The Trusteeship Council spelled out detailed steps that were to be taken in assuring Somalia independence by 1960. Appraisals of the Italian administration conclude that, despite limited funds, a sincere effort was made to follow the agreement and achieve the goals prescribed by the United Nations.

German colonial policy was discussed above briefly in relation to Tanganyika. The broad outlines of the policy in Southwest Africa and Tanganyika centered around a direct-rule system paralleling to some extent a military occupation. In establishing control, little attention was given to local customs and traditions, and the assistance of the traditional authorities was not encouraged. German administration also emphasized self-supporting colonies with internal development carried on by private initiative. Despite this policy, sizable government investments were devoted to communication development, particularly in Tanganyika.

This brief discussion of colonial powers in other areas of Africa may illustrate additional similarities and differences in the policies that were followed. At the time of this writing, few colonies still exist; and Portugal appears to be the only colonial power still clinging to the notion of the unity of the overseas areas with the home country.

CHAPTER 2

Political Processes

ISSUES IN THE PRE-INDEPENDENCE PERIOD

THE AFRICAN NATIONALIST MOVEMENTS BEGAN AS A REVOLU-
tion against the traditional system, as well as colonialism, as a
result of colonial policy. The discussion in Chapter One indicated
some of the differences in colonial policies:

French assimilation policies produced a highly trained elite,
but left the great majority of the French subjects without adequate
academic opportunities. Assimilation tended to educate the elite
away from Africa. Service in the French parliament and French
cabinets afforded experience in parliamentary government, but
extended absence from Africa contributed to poorly organized
territorial parties.

Belgian paternalism discouraged the growth of an educated elite,
political parties and civic responsibility. The emphasis upon the
creation of a Congolese skilled labor force may prove significant
in the future economic growth of the Congo. However, the severe
shortage of an experienced managerial class, political leadership,
and career bureaucracy precipitated the collapse of the economic
and political system after the Belgian administrators pulled out.

British policy did not emphasize the training of the elite, and
greater educational opportunities were available to the masses. Assimilation was not encouraged. A Nigerian civil servant in commenting on British policy observed that Britain assumed "the
British were born and not made." Since parliamentary members
served in local assemblies rather than in London, more highly developed local party organization occurred. However, British indirect rule encouraged localism, regionalism, and tribalism, which

aggravated the problems of post-independence unification of the states.

The contrast in educational policies is illustrated by the figures on school enrollments. The French assimilationist approach kept percentages of school population low. In 1946, 11.6% of the elementary school age population in French colonies was enrolled. By 1953 the number had risen to 22.5%, but percentages varied from colony to colony. In Senegal 14.9% were enrolled, Dahomey, 18%; Niger 5.1%; and Guinea 6.3%. All of West Africa reached only 76.6% in 1953. In contrast, the Belgian Congo elementary enrollment percentages were 56.1 in 1946 and 59.1 in 1953. However, only 2.2% of the elementary population went on to the secondary level as late as 1959, and higher educational opportunities were restricted to seminary training until 1956. Kasavubu and Gizenga received advanced education in this way. British postwar policy aimed at eventual compulsory schooling for their colonies, but the school age children actually enrolled in classes fell well below this goal. Although the elementary enrollment figure was less than that of the Belgian Congo, a higher percentage attended the secondary level, and greater opportunities were available for advanced study.

Despite these differences in colonial policy, all three tended to have a similar impact—the breakdown of the traditional system. Tribal organization emphasized community and clan responsibility. A series of associations in a complex order of gradation existed among the members of the society, who were bound together by kinship and communal ties affording the members protection and security. The colonial systems introduced secular authority and outside rule, which gradually reduced the power of the chiefs and traditional leaders.

Christianity seriously weakened the tribal system by undermining African religious beliefs and the spiritual influence and position of the tribal chiefs. Christian missions introduced the "white shirt" as well as the Bible and often frowned upon traditional culture and mores. The tribal system broke down as monogamy was enforced among converts, equality of the sexes was introduced, and mission schools emphasized individualism rather than communalism. The introduction of Western education assisted in producing an African educated elite who found it increasingly difficult to understand or communicate with the traditional authorities. Some members of the elite began to look down upon African civilization and culture as archaic and outmoded.

Agriculture had been the center of traditional Africa, and village life was based upon the division of labor among the members of society. Introduction of new methods upset these arrangements. For example, the use of the plow brought men into planting, which had been a woman's job. The need for labor in mines and plantations pulled men out of the villages, with women and boys left to handle the agricultural chores. The encouragement of cash-crop production in the rural areas created new social classes and new buying habits, which broke down the self-sufficient village system. Plantation development and white settler migration resulted in alienating land and shifting African populations from territories that they had considered part of their tribal homeland. Cattle raising in some traditional societies had been a sign of aristocracy. The introduction of a money economy made it possible for anyone to buy cattle.

As Africans moved to the urban areas in search of employment and opportunity, the village agricultural system was further weakened. In some cases, the proportion of young men to young women was out of balance. The power of the traditional leaders was undermined as the young members moved out of their jurisdiction. Traditional practices, such as polygamy, were difficult to follow in the urban centers. Fathers had less authority over sons, and brides could be obtained on an individual basis. Money payment became a means to avoid performance of the traditional services system.

The colonial systems sowed the seeds of their own destruction. Urbanization, commercialization, and education created a new African who no longer paid deference or respect to the traditional authorities. This growing younger elite sought new ideas, goals, and status. The impact of Western civilization shook the foundations of the traditional system, but the weakened traditional beliefs and culture were not replaced by Western. This created a void that is not yet resolved. It was natural for the "detribalized African" to seek status and position in the colonial system. Having created the new African, the colonial powers could not bring themselves, at least until it was too late, to allow him equality and freedom. Refusing to return to the traditional culture, the new elite began to question the power and authority of the colonial system. Their pressures for equality heralded the beginnings of the modern independence movements.

THE BEGINNINGS OF THE INDEPENDENCE MOVEMENTS

The early organizations protesting colonial policies generally began after the World War I period. Various factors in addition to those mentioned above entered into their formation. During the war, greater contact between the African and European decreased or exploded, if it ever existed, the myth of white superiority. After the war, the ex-servicemen resented the return to conditions of limited opportunity and low economic standards. They had hoped their loyalty to the cause of the colonial power during the war would lead to greater freedom and status. In Senegal and Madagascar, branches of the French Socialist Party were formed to demand greater economic opportunities and expansion of citizenship status. In 1920, the Kenyan Government introduced a pass system, called Kiponde, that triggered discontent since it was required only of Africans. Responding to the protests, Harry Thuku organized the Kikuyu into a Young Kikuyu Association. These activities resulted in his arrest shortly thereafter, and the association was renamed the Kikuyu Central Association with Jomo Kenyatta as its General Secretary. Woodrow Wilson's Fourteen Points and the Versailles Conference's emphasis upon self-determination encouraged Africans to push for expanded political participation. The Gold Coast National Congress for British West Africa had as its goals self-determination and "no taxation without representation."

By World War I, a small intellectual elite, composed of lawyers, doctors, merchants, and civil servants, had evolved, largely as a result of mission school activity. The Nyasaland uprising of 1915, spearheaded by this elite, criticized participation in a "white man's war" and pressed for equality and dignity for Africans. Its leader, Chilembwe, received his early education in mission schools and advanced training in the United States. A Nigerian Youth Movement formed after the country was unified in 1914 was composed largely of educated Yoruba middle class families who demanded liberalization of colonial policies. The dislocation resulting from industrialization of Southern Rhodesia rather than the growth of an educated elite stimulated the formation of employees' associations whose purpose was to bargain collectively for higher wages and improved working conditions for the African laborer.

The twenties were relatively prosperous, and the nationalist movements ebbed briefly. Colonial policies were liberalized to some extent. More Africans were admitted to the civil service; educational facilities were expanded; colleges were opened in a few areas; and larger numbers of Africans were sent overseas for education. These developments quieted the protests.

In the thirties, the nationalist movements tended to flourish. Although commercialization and urbanization increased, the depression was felt in Africa, and prices for raw material exports fell as markets decreased. Governmental revenues declined, with a resultant cut in salaries and civil service positions, and unemployment became a pressing problem. Africans who had studied overseas or in Africa found economic opportunities limited and uninviting. A 1930 youth conference in West Africa provided an opportunity for the educated elite to protest a dark future.

World War II provided additional stimuli to the growth of nationalism and the desire for greater autonomy. The Atlantic Charter and Allied declarations emphasizing freedom and self-determination encouraged African aspirations. The United Nations Charter provisions for self-determination of peoples and protection of dependent areas reaffirmed these hopes. As a result some Africans refused to return to seclusion policies and the role limitation of colonial powers.

War service permitted further contact between African and European. Africans serving overseas became more acutely aware of standards of living and political freedoms in other areas. Troops stationed throughout Africa had the opportunity to observe colonial policies and to exchange ideas with Africans from other territories. American Negro servicemen receiving equal treatment and rights did not go unnoticed. The Indian success in achieving independence also spurred movements in Africa. In French areas, Hitler's racist policies were condemned, and the Free French received enthusiastic support. Vichy's repressive policies stimulated resistance movements in such areas as the Ivory Coast. North Africans had assumed that loyalty to France in the war effort would assure greater autonomy and freedom in the postwar period. The failure of France to respond to these demands precipitated the outbreak of hostilities. The news of North African conflicts also prompted leaders south of the Sahara to demand liberalization of colonial policies.

GROUPS IN THE INDEPENDENCE MOVEMENT

The educated elite played an important role in the independence movements. Mission schools generally provided the beginning opportunities for education. These schools were often subsidized by the colonial powers, because they could provide the needed facilities and teaching staff. For example, 93% of the Congolese school children were enrolled in mission schools as late as 1958. The influence of these schools in the development of the nationalist elite may be illustrated by a study of religious affiliation of the Ghanaian Legislative Assembly released in 1954. At that time, seventy-seven percent of the members were Christian. This figure is markedly higher than that for the entire Ghanaian population. Where advanced educational opportunities existed, there was a tendency for an African professional class to develop. In the postwar period, they gravitated into the colonial bureaucracy or became members of an urban middle-class professional elite. Although their numbers were relatively small, they spearheaded the independence movements. A breakdown by professions of the 1951 Gold Coast legislature indicates 15 members were chiefs, 4 farmers, 3 skilled laborers, 6 professional politicians, 18 professional men, and 14 teachers.[1]

The significance of the educated elite's role is emphasized by the educational backgrounds of the 84-member 1951 Gold Coast legislature. Sixteen had received advanced training in the United Kingdom and 4 in the United States. Nine were graduates of Achimoto. Secondary graduates numbered 15; and 36 had received standard VII certificates, which would be equivalent to the primary level. States such as Ethiopia provided limited educational facilities until the very recent period. An educated elite did not emerge as early as in other areas and forces of modernization and liberalization have been slower to develop. The elite has taken a more active role in the last few years. They led the unsuccessful 1960 coup that attempted to overthrow Emperor Haile Selassie and place his

[1] David Apter, *Gold Coast in Transition* (Princeton, Princeton University Press, 1955).

son on the throne. The elite hoped the son would resign eventually in favor of a republic.

Although Africans with advanced degrees provided leadership for the independence movements, the study of the 1951 Gold Coast Assembly reveals that the secondary and primary graduates also took an active part in the pressure for freedom. Certain tensions developed between the older and younger educated elite. The older elite had been taken into the colonial bureaucracy or elected to seats in parliament in the early period. They gained a prestige and status that the younger group resented. Their close cooperation with the colonial personnel branded them as "gradualists." Since the younger group was still involved in the struggle for status and position, the older elite tended to view their policies as too "radical" or "extremist."

A second group active in the nationalist movements was the urbanized African. There were virtually no cities in Africa before the arrival of the Europeans. Colonial policies encouraged commercialization and urbanization. For example, Leopoldville grew from 175,000 in 1939 to 350,000 in 1960. In the early period, the older urban families, professional elite, and merchants formed an economic middle class that pushed for liberalization of colonial policies and improved status. As time passed, larger numbers of Africans migrated to the cities to find improved economic opportunities. These immigrants were the younger members of the rural areas, generally under 40 years of age. Forming the semi-skilled and unskilled laboring class, they hoped to move up in economic and social status by ability.

As the urban African became dependent upon occupational specialization and urban employment, his tribal and lineage attachments weakened. Urbanization accelerated social mobility. Loss of the economic protection of the rural, self-sufficient community accentuated the insecurity of the laborer but encouraged the growth of individualism. The urban African had more opportunities for contact with Europeans and with Western culture and civilization. He also experienced European discrimination in jobs and position. More than the rural African, he felt the struggle for status and prestige. These factors contributed to the growth of a nationally-minded labor class.

However, urbanization did not always weaken tribalism. Urban policy varied from colony to colony. British and French West Africa permitted virtually unrestricted migration, and few if any regulations were placed on urban residence in relation to tribal affiliation. Northern Rhodesia and the Union of South Africa used residence controls to foster tribal grouping. Although these restrictions were designed to limit the disrupting effects of urban life, a side effect was the perpetuation of tribalism by the development of urban tribal associations. European settlers dominated the urban centers in central Africa and British East Africa, and controls were placed on the residence and activities of Africans. Where tribal segregation was enforced, tribal urban associations were stimulated. Even where residence restrictions were not adopted, there was a tendency for tribal unions and kinship associations to develop. These groups assisted in finding jobs and protecting tribal members. Kinship association also provided the African with a sense of belonging and security. States, such as Tanganyika, which were composed of a large number of relatively small tribes were able to amalgamate these tribal associations, thus broadening the base of the national independence movement. Nigeria and the Belgian Congo had more difficulty in unification, since a few large tribes tended to dominate them. This has been given as one explanation for the development of tribally based multi-party movements.

Antagonisms also developed between the older urban elite and the laborer. The professional class, older families, and merchants wished to protect their status and prestige. The laborer also resented the close cooperation of the former with the colonial administration, and feared domination by the urban middle class. Tribal welfare and kinship associations were one means to represent the wishes and desires of the lower economic levels of the urban population. The elite feared the loss of their status and influence to the laboring class if political suffrage was to be based on population alone.

Gradually, trade unions arose to represent the interests of the laborer. They became pressure groups seeking labor participation in government, no taxation without representation, and equal wages, hours, and working conditions with white labor. Where the unions were able to carry off successful strikes or demonstrations, their leaders became nationally known and politically significant.

For example, Joshua Nkomo gained prominence as the general secretary of the Rhodesian Railways African Employee Association. The unions also were used as a means to broaden the base of the independence party movement. The urban laborer, as the intellectual elite, tended to be nationalist in outlook and to have experienced inequality and discrimination firsthand. They were generally enthusiastic supporters of the independence drive.

With the growth of an urbanized nationalist movement, urban areas became the center for activity. In such states as Uganda, Tanganyika, and Sudan, where only one major city existed, the movement was united more easily. The drive was more dispersed and disunited in states such as the Belgian Congo, Kenya, and Southern Rhodesia with more than one major city, since several urban party groups developed.

Although urbanized Africans spearheaded the independence movements, they represented a minority of the population. A mass movement required the support of rural Africa since the majority of the population was found there. Rural Africa responded more slowly to the movement for liberalization, modernization, and independence. Traditional authorities still tended to dominate the rural areas and the self-sufficient community or a semi-feudalistic system existed in many areas. Tribal loyalties persisted and a sense of nationalism was not well developed. Western civilization had less impact on rural Africa, since there was less frequent contact between the European and the African farmer, educational facilities were limited, and commercialization developed more slowly.

As cash-crop production and a monetary system were introduced by the colonial powers, new social classes developed with new goals and higher standards of living. The self-sufficient community declined with a resultant weakening of lineage attachments and tribal loyalty. Coastal areas of West Africa engaging in cocoa and cash-crop production, developed a large number of small, independent cash-crop producers who responded enthusiastically to the independence movements. The cash-crop system did not become significant in Northern Nigeria until after the war, and an independent producer class did not emerge to challenge the power of the emirs or the feudalistic land system. Commercialization has not affected the present Ethiopian economy to any great extent. This may be a partial explanation for the perpetuation of the feudalistic land system and the status and power of the lord and church hierarchy.

In attempting to enlist rural support, the mass independence movements encountered opposition from the tribal chiefs and traditional authorities who had attained influence and status under the old colonial regimes, particularly the British. The urbanized elite was viewed as a threat to their position, since the elite had broken with the traditional system and was pushing for modernization. In the 1950's the influence of the traditional authorities improved when the suffrage was expanded to include greater numbers of rural voters. Rural Africans tended to remain more loyal to the traditional authorities and their African institutions. A few chiefs sensed the handwriting on the wall and responded to the urban elite's request for support. Others attempted to counter the independence movements or form opposition groups. After the achievement of independence, many governments took measures to reduce the power and influence of the chiefs. In some cases, they were taken into the party and given local administrative positions. In other states, the chiefs were stripped of all power, and governmental administrators took over their functions. Any attempt to revive tribalism or tribal authority was viewed as a threat to a united national movement and as a possible encouragement of secessionism, since the continued support of the rural areas was considered essential to the successful development of the state under the independence-party leadership.

The ex-servicemen were enthusiastic supporters of the independence drive. War service afforded them occasion to move around Africa and overseas areas. Upon return to their countries, the ex-servicemen expected improved status and greater political and economic rights. Frustrated by the slowness of change, they moved into the independence movements readily. Joining forces with the younger educated elite in protesting conditions, they formed what was considered the "radical" wing of the independence movements.

The professional army did not play the same role in the formation of the independence movements. The professional armies generally have been too small to exert controlling political influence. The lack of a feeling of professionalism may have deterred the motivation to take decisive political action, or the tendency for the ex-servicemen to move into the mass independence movement may have influenced the professionals to follow their lead rather than attempt a separate or distinctive position. In North Africa the professional army has played a more decisive political role. The Egyptian Free Officers Corps, for example, responding to the charges of governmental corruption and abuse, assumed responsibility for the overthrow of Farouk and the purging of the forces of corruption in the government. Although the FOC had intended originally to turn power over to the existing political parties, the unwillingness of their political leaders to bring about the reforms desired by the FOC resulted in the formation of a military government, the Revolutionary Command Council, composed primarily of FOC members. In Africa south of the Sahara, the professional army appeared to have accepted the principle of civilian control over the military during the period of the drive for independence. It saw itself as an arm of the independence movement, and under the control and direction of the civilian leaders. This does not mean, however, that the "Free Officers Corps Notion" may not gain support in the future. Many independent states are undertaking the training and building of larger professional armies. As the sense of professionalism develops, the army's view of its role in politics may alter. For example, the Gabon professional army took an active part in the attempted overthrow of the government and the liberalization of the dictatorship. The forced resignation of President Youlou of the Congo-Brazzaville also was precipitated in part by professional army action. These crises resulted from a series of complaints over the high-handedness of government officials, abuse of powers, and lack of action to stem unemployment. Governmental restriction of union activities also was condemned by the army. Differing from the Egyptian FOC example, the armies showed a tendency to return power to the civilian government after politicians of their choice were placed in office. The Ethiopian professional army has remained loyal to Haile Selassie, with a few exceptions to the present. In the attempted coup against him, it did not join forces pushing for a republic, and it has not taken action in response to criticism of the government's policies.

The year 1965 has brought a shift in the view of the military role in politics. Toward the end of the year, three bloodless military coups occurred south of the Sahara. On November 25,

General Joseph Mobutu, head of the Congolese army, seized power from President Joseph Kasavubu and had himself proclaimed president for five years. On December 22, Colonel Christophe Soglo, commander of the Dahomey armed forces, overthrew the government he had helped establish only a few months earlier. On December 31, Colonel Jean Bokassa, head of the Central African Republic 1,200 man army, removed the government of President David Dacko and proclaimed himself head of state. In each coup, the military leader maintained he had taken power in response to a growing sense of disillusionment with parliamentary squabbling and the politicians' inability to cope with internal problems. Each maintained that civil strife would have broken out had they not acted promptly. Contrary to earlier practice, there seemed to be little inclination to surrender power to the civilian leaders after stability was restored. However, it may be too early to draw conclusions.

A second reason given for the coups was fear expressed over the threat of internal subversion coming from "Peking-style" communism. Mobutu expressed concern over Kasavubu's attempts to woo the so-called militant socialist states of Ghana, Guinea, and Tanzania. Soglo opposed the actions of former President Apithy in breaking relations with Nationalist China and opening diplomatic ties with the mainland. Bokassa reportedly ordered all Chinese technicians out of the Central African Republic within 24 hours after the coup. A four million dollar grant from Peking, negotiated by former President Dacko was refused and a complete break of relations was anticipated. The Boumédienne unseating of Ben Bella in Algeria expressed a similar concern over the close relations of Ben Bella with the Soviet Union, China, and Cuba. Whether or not these explanations give an accurate picture of the factors precipitating the coups, it seems clear that the military is assuming a more active political role and will move when they disapprove of policies. The year 1966 brought further evidence of military power with the coups in Nigeria and Ghana. As a result, the military will be a force to reckon with in future African development.

The nonprofessional soldier has been significant in post-independence politics. He played a role in the riotings and lootings by the Force Publique in the Belgian Congo in the immediate post-independence period. The riots over salary scales in Uganda, Tanganyika, and Kenya also were led by the noncommissioned officer group. These uprisings according to some reports, came close to toppling or overthrowing the governments in Uganda and Tanganyika. The situation was considered serious enough to warrant the recall of British troops to restore order and stability. In the Togolese uprising, the assassination of Olympio was led by a group of noncommissioned servicemen who had been released from active duty in the French army in Algeria. Anger over the unwillingness of Olympio to pay their regular salaries triggered the attempted coup. The French decision to muster out additional African troops has caused concern in former French areas. They fear other coup attempts similar to that in Togo. In all of these cases, the role of the noncommissioned soldier has tended to be disruptive and potentially dangerous. The government's ability to maintain popular support and the professional officers' control and discipline over their men are critical in eliminating or regulating this potential source of instability.

Religious organizations generally have not played a decisive role in the African independence movements. One reason may be that many African states are pluralistic with a mixture of Islam, Christianity, and Animism. Since the population is so divided religiously, it is difficult for any one church or religious group to dominate. Ethiopia is also divided religiously, but the Coptic Church, as the state church, has been in a position to play a significant role in building support for the Emperor and the institutions of the state. Since the church views its function as an arm of the imperial structure, including the traditional feudalistic land system, it has opposed, to a large extent, modernization or liberalization. In the Belgian Congo, the Catholic Church also was given a favored position, but the Church used its powers to support the political policies of the colonial administration. Therefore, it did not become significant in the developing independence movement. The role of Islam in Northern Nigeria was discussed previously and as was indicated, the Christian Church was significant in training an educated elite that moved into the independence movements. However, the church itself did not play a decisive role.

The significance of the press in the stimulation of the nationalist movements varies to some extent from country to country. In the European settler areas of Africa, such as the Republic of South

Africa and Southern Rhodesia, the press did not play a significant part in the encouragement of African nationalism or the independence movements, although a highly developed European press and radio system evolved. The policy of the press supported white supremacy. Although criticisms of governmental policy might be found, the basic notion of European settler domination of government was rarely questioned.

In a few areas of Africa, such as Ethiopia and Liberia, an authoritarian press system existed in which the freedom of the press was strictly controlled and censorship limited criticism of the government. Since these states have a long history of independence, the question of censorship policies deterring the growth of an independence movement is not relevant. However, limitation of freedom of the press served to restrict the voicing of opposition to governmental policies and assisted in the perpetuation of the power of the ruling elite. One recent example of Ethiopian censorship policy was the barring of the sale of an American magazine that contained an article critical of the Emperor and the government. The press was reported to have been instructed not to make the ban known to the public. Despite censorship attempts, the issue was secretly distributed by student groups, and mimeographed copies appeared in Addis Ababa.

French and British West Africa placed few controls on press operations or ownership and an African-owned press developed. Agitational papers such as Azikiwe's *West African Pilot* became influential in stirring a spirit of independence and nationalism among Nigerian youth. Independence groups often founded papers to facilitate communication of their ideas and programs to the people. Since independence, these papers have continued to present the majority party position or have become government papers. Since they tend to air only one viewpoint, the governments are criticized for denying freedom of the press. This is not entirely accurate, since other papers also circulate.

THE MASS INDEPENDENCE MOVEMENTS

The leaders of the independence movements needed to mobilize all the energies of their people in the creation of a unified, highly organized independence drive. With the development of an educated elite, the acceleration of urbanization and commercialization, the resultant growth of an urban labor class, and the introduction of cash-crop farming, the scene was set for the push to independence. Political leaders faced the problem of organizing these forces into an effective movement. Division would permit the colonial power to play off one faction against another, thus delaying or preventing independence. The process by which this unification was achieved may be illustrated by a discussion of the independence movement formation in a few of the African states.

Blaise Diagne organized the Senegalese landowners, Muslim leaders, and French intellectual elite in 1914. They campaigned against encroachment of citizenship privileges in the communes. Diagne was elected to parliament in 1914 and served until his death in 1934. By the 1930's he was accused of being pro-French and protecting only the interests of the communes. A local branch of the French Socialist Party, the SFIO, was formed to campaign for expansion of privileges to all Senegalese. Lamine Gueye became its leader in the forties on a platform of full political rights for all inhabitants of black Africa and not just the communes. Since Gueye also served in French parliaments, he gradually became associated with a pro-French policy. Leopold Senghor broke with the experienced and honored Gueye on the charge that the sole purpose of the SFIO was to establish personal power for Gueye. When Senghor established the *Bloc Démocratique Sénégalaise* (BDS) in 1948, observers predicted that Senghor would meet his political demise in the 1951 elections against Gueye. Since the electorate was to be broadened in these elections to include a large percentage of rural votes, Senghor used the time from 1948 to 1951 to build support among the bush peasants. Despite his university education and his extended residence in Paris, he was able to convince them of his interest in their problems. Gradually the peasants looked to him for leadership and support. In the elections, Senghor and the other BDS candidate, Abbas Gueye, carried the electorate and Lamine Gueye lost his seat in parliament. The platforms of the two parties were similar but Senghor's appeal to rural Senegal spelled defeat for the SFIO.

The Guinea Socialist Party was headed by Diallo until his death in 1954. Diallo was a schoolteacher who led the drive for expanded political rights in French Africa. Mineral exploitation brought a rising economic growth rate and industrialization, with a resultant growth in urbanized labor. By the 1950's, unemployment plagued the youth concentrated in the towns, and dissatisfaction over Socialist Party programs grew. Sekou Touré criticized the lack of contact between party militants and the masses and charged that the intellectual leaders were using the party to serve their own interests. When Touré became Secretary General of the *Parti Démocratique de Guinée* in 1952, he moved to increase its popular base. Touré headed the labor movement and had gained national recognition from his success as a strike leader. He used this popular support and the labor organization to spearhead the growth of the PDG. As the size and strength of the PDG grew, the power and prestige of the older political leadership waned.

Félix Houphouet-Boigny had organized the Ivory Coast *Syndicat Africain Agricole* (SAA) in 1944 to protect the interests of the small farmers against the large French planters, lumbermen, and European commercial firms. He reorganized it into the *Parti Démocratique de la Côte d'Ivoire* in 1945. The party was a coalition of Europeans, coffee and cocoa planters, young intelligentsia, Muslim leaders, and laborers. The small farmer base of the party was important in contributing to its growth as a mass organization. Boigny's break with the French Marxists in 1949 tended to alienate the young intelligentsia and trade unionists, although they have not formed a successful opposition movement.

Dahomey did not succeed in creating a united movement since there was a gap in development between North and South. The South was more urbanized and commercialized, and greater educational opportunities existed. Three major parties developed. Ahomadegbe never served in French cabinets but gained prestige as a direct descendant of the Abomey kings. Although his strength was primarily regional, his alliance with the labor union movement brought him into prominence. As a follower of Houphouet-Boigny, he supported the *Rassemblement Démocratique Africain* (RDA) and De Gaulle's proposed French Community. These actions branded him as pro-French. Apithy was encouraged to enter politics by a Catholic priest and gained support from Catholic groups. Various Catholic associations protested the close cooperation of the RDA and the French Communist Party. In 1948, Apithy broke with the RDA and formed the *Indépendence d'Outre-Mer* (IOM). Maga, the son of a northern peasant, was a schoolteacher who became known for his work with youth groups such as the Boy Scouts. Becoming interested in politics, he formed the first political organization in the North, the *Mouvement Démocratique Dahomeen* (MDD). Since no unified movement developed, Maga and Apithy formed a coalition government with Maga as President and Apithy as Vice President. The *Union Démocratique Dahomeene* (UDD) became the opposition party.

Despite Belgian policies of insulation, a Congolese independence movement began among the *evolués,* the younger urbanized Africans who moved into the skilled and semi-skilled middle class. Urbanization permitted contact with Congolese from many areas and the discussion of mutual problems. Since political organizations were prohibited, social and fraternal organizations arose to represent the desires of the *evolués*. For example, Lumumba was a member of the *Amicale Libérale* of Stanleyville, and Cyrille Adoula the *Amicale Socialiste* of Leopoldville. The *evolués* protested the lack of advanced education available to them. In 1957, certain towns were permitted to elect their own community councils. All males over 25 were given the suffrage. Kasavubu was elected the *bourgemestre* of Dendale Commune and surprised Belgian officials by demanding full independence. Falling copper prices and soaring unemployment stimulated growing anti-Belgian feeling. Belgian officials permitted Patrice Lumumba to attend the all-African People's Conference in Accra in 1958. He returned full of enthusiasm for independence. De Gaulle's visit to Brazzaville and his proposal for autonomy within the French Community had a significant impact on the Congo. Numbers of Congolese were permitted to work at the Brussels World's Fair where they came into contact with many people and ideas. Nationalism grew as a result of these contacts. In 1959, an ABAKO (Association for the Advancement of the Bakongo) meeting was banned. When 30,000 unemployed Congolese decided to meet anyway, the police fired into the crowds and arrested Kasavubu as their leader. As a result of riotings, Belgium granted independence, although no unified movement had developed to which power could be handed. The seventy ethnic groups of the Congo, subdivided into many clans, were torn between national and tribal loyalty. The fraternal and social organizations tended to form many tribally based parties vying with each other for power. The lack of a unified movement aggravated the problems of instability after independence.

In Tanganyika, Julius Nyerere succeeded in creating a nation-wide organization for the Tanganyikan African National Union (TANU), although his efforts were limited by colonial governmental policies. In 1955, Nyerere resigned his teaching position to devote full time to political organization. TANU's greatest support came from the growing urban African middle class. Since this was an inadequate base to achieve a TANU majority party status, Nyerere concentrated on enlisting rural support by organizing rural branches. TANU also adopted a multi-racial policy prior to the 1958 elections to gain support from the European and Asian communities. By 1960, no real opposition remained, and TANU won the elections overwhelmingly.

The United Gold Coast Convention was formed in 1947 to work for eventual independence. The UGCC sent Dr. Danquah to London to invite Kwame Nkrumah to assume the secretariat of the party because of Nkrumah's proven abilities in organizing the African students in Britain and establishing the West African National Secretariat in London. In accepting the post, Nkrumah expressed his determination to organize a mass movement. After his return, demonstrations broke out in the Gold Coast protesting postwar shortages and high prices. Nkrumah was arrested along with other members of the UGCC but was released shortly. Responding to the protests, the British proposed a new constitution providing universal suffrage and African ministers sharing in government responsibility. Nkrumah objected to this constitution as falling short of full independence. He and the older elite of the UGCC split over the acceptance of the constitution and the creation of a party newspaper for mass communication. Nkrumah's opening of Ghana National College also widened the breach. The final break came as a result of the creation of a UGCC youth study group that Nkrumah organized under the name of the Committee on Youth Organization. The CYO represented the younger educated elite of Ghana, which had not achieved economic status or governmental position and resented the power of the older elite. When the CYO accused the UGCC leadership of compromising the drive for independence in order to preserve their position and status, the UGCC decided to remove Nkrumah as secretary. As a result of these tensions, Nkrumah broke with the UGCC in 1949. Using the CYO as a nucleus, Nkrumah formed the Convention People's Party and adopted the slogan of "positive action" and independence "now."

With the support of the youth movement, Nkrumah set about building a mass party. By bus, which was more notorious for breaking down than arriving on time, he campaigned throughout the countryside, enlisting support for the CPP. Nkrumah's success in building the party resulted in part from his organizational skill, from hard rural campaigning, and from his ability to convince the common man that he understood his problems. Nkrumah has been singled out as the first Ghanaian politician to eat with the common man, live simply and austerely and avoid status symbols such as limousines or luxurious homes. Although Nkrumah and several party leaders were arrested in 1950, the Convention People's Party (CPP) won the municipal election in Accra. Their success was attributed to the highly developed party structure. In 1951, the (CPP) campaigned in national general elections with the slogan of self-government now and won a clear-cut victory over its opposition. Nkrumah formed the new government and started Ghana on its way to independence.

The Nyasaland African National Congress was formed in 1944 out of a desire to improve conditions in the country. The younger generation demanded greater equality of opportunity and social, economic, and political advancement. Nyasaland servicemen who had been stationed in India and Burma during the war had been influenced by the independence movements in these states. Indian influence may have played a part in the adoption of the name "Congress" for the Nyasaland Movement. Its members were primarily government employees, since little industrialization or urbanization occurred, and the adult males often migrated to the Rhodesias to find employment in the mines and industry. The National Congress did not grow rapidly until the British proposed the creation of the Central African Federation. Fearing domination by the Southern Rhodesian white settler government, the Congress campaigned for the breakup of the Federation. They called for universal adult suffrage and for racial integration of schools, hospitals, and other facilities. Dr. Hastings Banda, in protest against the creation of the Federation, went to Ghana to practice medicine. He returned to Nyasaland in 1958 to spearhead the drive for independence, re-naming the movement the Malawi National Congress. Use of the federation issue and fear of Southern Rhodesian domination helped build a unified mass movement.

The Kenya Study Union, which was formed in 1944, was re-organized into the Kenya African Union (KAU) in 1946. Jomo Kenyatta became its president in 1947 shortly after his return from London. The Union had its greatest support among the younger educated elite and ex-servicemen. Kenyatta campaigned among the Kikuyu who were frustrated over urban unemployment and land shortage in the rural area. Through Kenyatta's effort, the Kenya African Union became increasingly Kikuyu dominated. The Mau Mau uprising brought about strict control of African organizations. Kenyatta was imprisoned, and the Kikuyu were barred from politi-cal activity during the emergency. Political leadership passed to Tom Mboya who had gained prominence as a trade union leader in the Kenya Federation of Labor. Since the Federation was not barred from political activity, it could speak for the African. Mboya as a member of the Luo tribe was not subject to the Kikuyu restrictions. The colonial administration permitted associations only at the local and district levels, and Mboya concentrated his efforts on these levels, first forming the Nairobi African District Congress and later the Nairobi Peoples Convention Party. Wishing to broaden the base of this party, he attempted closer cooperation with the Kikuyu by urging the lifting of controls on their political activity. The Kenya African National Union (KANU) was formed before the 1961 elections by a merger of the Kenya African Union and Mboya's Nairobi party. It was hoped that the Kenya African National Union would become a mass movement, but smaller tribes were reluctant to join, apparently out of fear of Kikuyu and Luo domination. The Kenya African Democratic Union (KADU) was formed as an opposition to represent their interests.

Northern Rhodesian opposition movements began in the 1930's as a result of urbanization and mining development. African wel-fare associations were formed to represent the educated elite, ur-banized labor, and the miners. Industrial unrest in the copper belt stimulated the organization of the African Mineworkers Union in 1949. Harry Nkumbula used the unions as a base for the forma-tion of the African National Congress (ANC), which campaigned for freedom and the breakup of the Central African Federation. Kenneth Kaunda led the more "extremist" young elite in a split with the African National Congress on the grounds of their close cooperation with the British and moderate policies, and the United National Independence Party (UNIP) gained control of the independence movement.

THE LEADERSHIP ELITE

The discussion of the formation of the independence movements indicates the significant role played by the national leaders of the parties. A brief survey of the backgrounds of a few of the leaders at the time of independence may illustrate some of the forces and factors that contributed to the development of a leadership elite. Since shifting and military coups have occurred after independence, these men do not necessarily hold the same political position currently.

Sir Abubakar Tafawa Balewa, the late Prime Minister of Nigeria, was born in 1912. He received his education locally and was granted a teacher's certificate from Katsina College. After teaching for a period, he went to the London University of Education for one year in 1954. He considered this year abroad as the most important influence on his life because he came into contact with "people who knew individual liberty." Upon his return, he became a Native Authority Education Officer and shortly thereafter was appointed to the Northern House of Assembly, where he became an advocate of regionalism and the protection of Northern rights. In 1951, he was one of the founders of the Northern Peoples Congress.

Dr. Benjamin Azikiwe, President of Nigeria, was born in 1904. He received his education at mission schools and worked as a government clerk in Lagos from 1921 to 1925. Going to the United States for advanced training, he took postgraduate work at the University of Pennsylvania, working as a coal miner and boxer to support himself. He became interested in journalism in the United States. Visiting London in 1934, he published a book on *Liberia in World Affairs.* Returning to the Gold Coast, he became editor of the *African Morning Post.* After his return to Nigeria, he founded a chain of newspapers and joined a series of youth movements. In 1944, he organized the Nigerian National Council which eventually developed into the National Council of Nigeria and the Cameroons (NCNC).

Dr. Hastings Banda, Prime Minister of Malawi, was born in 1902. He began his education in mission schools and worked as a clerk in the mines of the Union of South Africa for a period. He attended the Wilberforce Academy and the University of Chicago and received a Doctor of Medicine degree in Nashville in 1937. From 1945 until 1953 he practiced medicine in London where he came into contact with other African leaders. He became politically active when the British proposed the formation of a Central African Federation and returned to Nyasaland in 1958 as the head of the Malawi National Congress (MNC).

Félix Houphouet-Boigny, President of the Ivory Coast, was born in 1905. He began his education at Bingerville and attended medical school at Dakar, practicing as a medical assistant for a period of years. Boigny was elected a member of the French National Assembly where he helped organize and became president of the RDA. Serving as a minister in the French cabinet he helped prepare the *loi cadre.* Although he was active in support of the French community, he sued for independence after Mali was granted independence.

Jomo Kenyatta, President of Kenya, received his early education in mission schools. He served as an inspector of water supplies for a period after graduation. He became interested in journalism and published a Kikuyu newspaper in the 1920's protesting the white highland policy. He went to London in 1929 to testify on this issue. Returning to London in 1931, he studied English and anthropology until 1945. During this period he traveled in Europe, studied briefly in Moscow, and became active in the Pan-African movement.

Tom Mboya, General Secretary of KANU, was born in 1930 and falls into the younger educated group of Africans. He was educated in a Catholic mission school, but did not complete the requirements for a primary certificate because of lack of funds. He worked for the municipal council in Nairobi after 1951 and became active in Nairobi political movements. Interested in the trade-union movement, he became General Secretary of the Kenya Local Government Workers Union and the Kenya Federation of Labor. He traveled in Europe and India as a union representative and won a scholarship to study industrial management at Ruskin College in 1956, also traveling in the United States and Canada. He won the Nairobi seat in the elections of 1957. He played a significant role in the formation of KANU, and held various cabinet posts in the independence period.

Kwame Nkrumah, President of Ghana, was born in 1909. He received his early education in Catholic mission schools. After receiving his teaching certificate from the Government Training College in Accra in 1926, he taught until 1935, when he went to the United States to major in economics at Lincoln University and take postgraduate work at the University of Pennsylvania. In this period he became president of the African students organization of America and Canada. Going to London in 1945, he became active in the African Student's Union and the Pan-African movement. In 1947, he returned to Ghana as the General Secretary of the United Gold Coast Convention (UGCC).

Leopold Sédar Senghor, President of Senegal, was born in 1906. He was educated at the Catholic school in N'Gasobil, at the *lycée* in Dakar, and did advanced work in Paris. He taught at a *lycée* in Paris for a period. In World War II, he served in the French army. In 1945, he was elected as a deputy from Senegal to the French assembly. In 1948, he formed the *Bloc Démocratique Sénégalais* and defeated the SFIO in the 1951 elections. Although Senghor is considered an intellectual and a gifted poet, he has made a strong appeal to the bush peasant of Senegal.

Sekou Touré, President of Guinea, was born in 1922. He received a few years of education in the French technical school in Conakry but was expelled for leading a food strike. He was employed for a period by a business firm, and showed an early interest in the trade-union movement. In 1952, he became Secretary General of the PDG, leading a movement to break the ties of the Guinea labor movement with the French CGT, the French Communist Trade Labor Federation. He was active for a period in the *Rassemblement Démocratique Africain,* an inter-territorial party, but broke over the question of independence and led Guinea to a *"non"* vote on the question of membership in the French community. He has been active in the Pan-African movement and in the support of political federation of Africa.

This brief survey of the backgrounds of African leaders represents only a handful of those who could be discussed. However, it illustrates various factors that seemed to have been significant in the creation of the African leadership elite. The leaders are relatively similar in age with the exception of Mboya and Touré. Mission school education played a part in their development. After completing their early education, many of these leaders served in administrative posts or in the professions. Most of them became urbanized and gravitated toward political movements in the cities. They all had some opportunity for overseas experience. Some served in the French assembly and cabinet; some were college students; some served in a professional capacity. In commenting on their backgrounds, they mention the contacts they had with other African students and with American movements such as Garveyism. Several consider their overseas experience as the most significant factor in the development of a spirit of nationalism and the drive for independence. Service in World War II was not common to all and would seem to have been a less significant factor. Their backgrounds reveal opportunities for the development of political skills. All of them may be classed as experienced and able politicians with a special talent for organization. This skill was valuable in building a mass party. The leadership elite generally succeeded in organizing effective and unified mass movements. Having achieved the goal of independence and freedom, they faced the problem of governing their states and consolidating their power.

ONE-PARTY DEMOCRACY

African political structure and processes are in a state of transition. There has been shifting from multi-party systems to one-party systems, and in a few cases, political parties have been abandoned in favor of a military junta or "guided democracy." Stabilized political structures have not developed, and the systems that will evolve finally are difficult to predict. The African states do not have identical political histories or experiences, and the period of time for observation of party procedure and process is relatively brief. Recognizing these elements of transition and dissimilarity, certain common patterns of party structure and process have emerged, which the following discussion will attempt to analyze. However, the student is urged to investigate the political systems of individual African states in order to become familiar with significant differences and to avoid oversimplification or overgeneralization of African political development.

The mass independence movements that were put together prior to independence encouraged the growth of one party systems having overwhelming popular support as the groups credited with ending colonialism. Governments foster the one-party pattern to achieve the highest degree of unity possible in the period of consolidation of power. African parties describe themselves as one-party democracies. Democracy is defined as a people's government whose basic characteristics are freedom, equality, and discussion. Freedom and equality are considered necessary if there is to be "valid discussion." African leaders, as Julius Nyerere, Kwame Nkrumah, Jomo Kenyatta, and Sekou Touré emphasize that these three factors of democracy are the essence of the pre-European political system. Kenyatta states that traditional African society revolved around the family tree, blood brotherhood, the clan, and the tribe. Traditional authorities were advised by the elders and all members of the tribe participated in the discussions. Nyerere and Touré often refer to the pre-European governmental process in which members of the village arrived at policy by discussion among themselves with deliberation continuing until agreement was reached. At the point of consensus, the chief pronounced a decision which all would abide by without further debate. Kenyatta concludes that when the people obeyed their tribal councils they "obeyed themselves and their true will."

The supporters of one-party democracy maintain that the one party structure is a re-establishment of this traditional system. All citizens in the state are to be members of the party and given equal opportunity for participation and debate. The party leadership has the function of enforcing the consensus that is achieved. In abiding by the decisions of the party, it is argued that people are following their own will or the general will as in traditional practice. Opposition parties are not considered essential to a democratic system, but are viewed as an artificial device adopted by the West to promote discussion. This Western institution is rejected on the grounds that no reasonable opposition can exist for each issue, and that no basic division of opinion is found in the African states, since all members of society are in agreement with the basic goals of the mass party. Rather than a loyal opposition serving as a check on the mass party, opposition and debate occurs within the one-party structure. Kenyatta points out that "constructive opposition from within" was not an alien concept in African traditional society and plays an important part in the one-party process.

African leaders recognize that the village discussion system will require modification, since the government of the nation cannot be conducted efficiently by direct popular participation and must rely upon a system of representation. Representative democracy is considered to depend upon freedom of individual discussion, but periodic elections also must be provided in order that the citizen be given an opportunity to express his choice of representatives. As long as the mass party is open to all, permits freedom and equality of discussion, and choice among candidates, an organized opposition is not considered essential to the maintenance of a democratic system. An analysis of the structures and procedures of a few of the African parties may assist in illustrating their interpretation of the one-party pattern.

PARTI DÉMOCRATIQUE DE GUINÉE

The PDG was formed in 1952 with Sekou Touré as Secretary General. Touré was critical of existing party organization and accused the intellectual elite of using the party structure to preserve their position and status rather than promoting the needs of the people. He pointed out that parties were organized prior to election campaigns, but after the election the organization tended to disappear, and no permanent contacts with the masses were maintained. Since the professional classes had received French education, Touré concluded that they had become more French in outlook than African. He urged that the PDG work for a reconversion from "colonial culture" to an authentic "African mentality" that would be representative of the village peasant and not the French-trained intellectual. Touré's expulsion from school after a few years of primary education may have encouraged a greater degree of resentment toward the French trained elite. A noticeable anti-intellectualism has developed in PDG organization as a result of Touré's views. Although the intellectual elite was brought into the party after the achievement of independence, there has been a tendency to exclude them from inner party circles. Since Touré used the trade-union movement, which he headed, to expand party membership and build a mass party, he turns to the skilled laborer or to trade-union leaders as representatives of "true African mentality." Consequently, the PDG was developed under their leadership rather than a minority intellectual elite as occurred in some African states. Although France tried to control elections by hand picking members of the assimilated elite as candidates who were considered more favorable to France, by 1956 the PDG had become the undisputed majority party.

Touré states that the PDG is not modeled after traditional European political parties. Rather it is a "movement for African emancipation" whose goal is anti-colonialism and progress. Touré also maintains that the PDG cannot be classed as a one-party system because it is "the regime of the state." The constitution of Guinea and the party platform provide that the PDG is to be the supreme organ of the state and superior in role to the institutions of the government. The role of the cabinet and parliament is to "apply the decisions and *mots d'ordre* of the party." The legislature serves as its ratifying arm and the cabinet as the executive arm. Independence of the bureaucracy has no relevance since the ministers and administrative staff are expected to follow party directives except on "matters of detail." The party controls the selection of candidates who run for office, and the elected president of the party serves as head of the state. The party also is to direct communication media in order to mobilize opinion in raising the standard of living and promoting national unity.

Seven thousand village and urban committees, which are responsible for carrying party directives to the membership, form the basic unit of the PDG. An Executive Committee heads these village and urban organizations. It is composed of ten members, including representatives of the local women's and youth groups, who are elected yearly by the members of the local constituency. In theory, elections are open to all eligible voters, but only those who have paid party dues and hold party cards are permitted to participate. A week prior to the elections, a list of party members is prepared by the committee, and only those on the list may vote.

The village Executive Committee is required to meet at least once a week to discuss affairs of local and national concern. A large percentage of the discussion time is devoted to directives that are sent to the villages from the National Political Bureau.

Discussion of party policy is designed theoretically to permit everyone (party members) to participate in the decision-making process. The Executive Committee is responsible for expressing the concerns of the local branches of the party to the upper echelons of the party.

The next level of party organization is the Section. The village committees are grouped into forty-three Sections. The ten members of each village Executive Committee within the Section form the Section Congress, which meets twice a year. At the head of each Section is a fifteen-man committee, the *Comité Directeur,* which is elected by the Section Congress from among its members. Two representatives of the regional youth group also sit on this committee as ex-officio members. Each member of the *Comité Directeur* is assigned a specific function, such as finance, organization, or administration. A semi-annual Regional Conference brings together the members of the Section *Comités Directeurs* for further discussion of party policy and program.

At the top of this pyramid is the National Party Congress, which is to meet every three years and is responsible for adopting national policy. It receives reports from the lower levels of the party, the government, and the Political Bureau, which are to be considered in deciding party programs. Once PDG policy is agreed upon, it is understood that the lower levels will implement it without further discussion. The National Congress also elects the Political Bureau, which is the supreme organ of the party and the state. The majority of its members are government ministers. The others hold key positions in the National Assembly, armed forces, or the bureaucracy. Sekou Touré is the Secretary General and President of the party. Below him are a political secretary, three organizational secretaries, and a treasurer. The Bureau is divided into three major committees, organization, finance, and conflicts. The members of the Political Bureau tend to be young, their average age being under forty. They generally come from the secondary-certificate holder group rather than the educated elite, but the majority had experience in the civil service of the French Colonial Administration.

The Political Bureau is responsible for the direction and development of party programs and serves as the decision-maker and administrative director for the government. Technically, all party and government programs are funneled through it. These responsibilities present the Bureau with a veritable flood of decisions and paper work, which has resulted in jam-ups on decisions. Many questions have been deferred because of the impossibility of handling them quickly and efficiently. Inability to handle its responsibilities swiftly may result in governmental immobility.

Associated with the party are the Women's Organization of Guinea; the Youth Group, which permits members to the age of twenty-five; the Pioneers, which takes youth to the age of fourteen; and the trade union movement. These groups assist in representing and organizing all interests in the state.

The organization and structure of the PDG appears to draw heavily from the Leninist model. The supremacy of the party over the state is considered necessary to mobilize totally the energies of the people. It is argued that the Marxist-Leninist emphasis upon collective action is more compatible with African tradition than the Western concepts of individual initiative and multi-party organization. Sekou Touré maintains that collective living and social solidarity are an integral part of African life and that the African conceives of political organization in relation to his family, village, or clan. The Guinean political system attempts to blend the procedures of the traditional village council meeting with the Leninist concept of the supremacy of the party over national life.

The PDG contends that its structure of government and party organization promote a democratic system. Membership in the party is theoretically open to every citizen, and all members of society may participate in the political process. Officials of the party are to be elected at every level and are to represent their constituents' interests. Of course, a question may be raised concerning how much control the Political Bureau exercises over the choice of candidates for office and whether every voter actually is a party member and does participate actively in elections and policy discussions.

Popular participation is essential if the PDG is to live up to its claim that the party is the repository of the popular will because of the continual debate and criticism carried on within the party over programs and policy. According to PDG theory, the common will derives not from the summit of the party pyramid but from the base in the village committees. The popular will expressed in the villages theoretically moves through the party pyramid to the Political Bureau where it is enforced. At this point the PDG may draw upon Rousseau and the concept of the General Will as well as the "democratic centralism" of the Leninist model.

Several problems may enter into the ascertaining of the common will. One is the actual relationship of the village constituencies and the Political Bureau on policy decisions. Almost of necessity the Political Bureau will have to adopt administrative rulings and enforcement procedures that may be significant. Even if it is assumed that the base of the party has the authority to set the broad outlines of policy, there are problems of assuring that village wishes actually are sent to the top through the machinery of the party. Those individuals who express village consensus to the leadership and those in the pyramid who are responsible for sending information to the top can become important power centers. The Political Bureau's ability to state and enforce the general will of the villages is dependent also upon the makeup of the Bureau itself. In addition, there is the danger that the Political Bureau may become so bogged down with administrative responsibilities that it will lose contact with the people.

THE TANGANYIKA AFRICAN NATIONAL UNION

TANU was created in 1954 by the reorganization of the Tanganyika African Association. Following its formation, Julius Nyerere appeared before the United Nations Trusteeship Council to ask for support in speeding independence. Since TANU membership was centered among urban commercial employees, it faced the problem of building mass support. After 1955, Nyerere devoted full time to the problems of organizing the party, but his activities were restricted by the British Colonial Administration's refusal to register TANU branches in the rural areas and by close supervision of the financial operation of the party. Since the opposition, the United Tanganyika Party, concentrated its efforts on organizing the urban economic and intellectual elite, Nyerere shifted TANU emphasis to the village and rural areas. By 1960, TANU strength was so well established that the party was unopposed in 58 out of the 71 seats of the national legislature. Nyerere has proposed that two TANU members may run against each other in legislative races to provide wider choice for the voter, but few candidates choose to follow this suggestion.

Although TANU philosophy does not espouse the supremacy of the party over the state as in Guinea, it has adopted a party pyramid structure similar to the PDG. Membership in the party is open to any African who pays a two-shilling fee. The basic organization of the party is the Branch in each village. The next level is the District and over the District is the Province. Each of these levels is headed by an elected executive committee that is responsible for the enforcement of party directives. Each level holds an annual conference to set party policy and select the members of the executive committees. At the top of the pyramid is the Territorial Annual Conference. This conference is composed of two representatives from each of the sixty districts of the state, three delegates from the ten provinces, and the members of the party's Central Committee. The Annual Conference elects the party President and adopts national party policy.

Assisting the President of the party is the Central Committee, whose members he appoints. Although the Central Committee is responsible for the administration of TANU, the policy body of the party is the National Executive, which meets four or five times a year and advises the President on party platforms. Since these meetings are closed to the public, the procedures and operation of the National Executive are difficult to determine.

The District level of the party is the key link between party headquarters and the people, since TANU found the Branch too small to be effective. The District has a full-time paid secretary and a part-time president who have the responsibility of interpreting party policy to the people and transmitting local views to the upper echelon of the party. TANU operation has been hampered by a shortage of trained leaders. District levels of the party often are headed by young men in their twenties with varying degrees of educational and organizational background, thus restricting the district's ability to perform its functions effectively.

Party philosophy stresses belief in the dignity and rights of the individual and in the equality of the members of society. Nyerere argues that TANU has established a true democracy based upon the

Greek tradition of government by discussion among equal members of society. An organized opposition is not considered necessary for the maintenance of open and free discussion, since TANU attempts to include possible opposition elements in the party. Representatives of the Tanganyika Federation of Labor, the cooperatives, and the TANU Youth League participate in party conferences. Nyerere argues that TANU philosophy is a continuation of the African tradition of "talking until you agree." The problems of maintaining "free discussion among equal members" are similar to those of the PDG.

Several areas of possible division or opposition exist in TANU. One group supports African traditionalism and opposes the equality emphasis of the party. This group tends to favor a return to tribal structures and traditional authority, while the TANU majority opposes this view as a possible threat to the unity of the party and the state. A second group within the party appears to encourage some degree of racialism. For example, they urge Africanization of the civil service. The majority of the party still support the multiracial position of Nyerere, since the adoption of an "African only" policy might affect the mass-party status of TANU. A third group, composed of the younger party members, occasionally express opposition to Nyerere's "moderation." Ntemvu broke with TANU and attempted to pull the left-wing elements with him, but he was defeated overwhelmingly in the 1962 election. Although these groups have not yet gained significant electoral support, they may become important in the future.

Since TANU has not adopted the Leninist pattern of party supremacy over every aspect of national life, party influence in government comes through personal contact between the party and the government by the overlapping of personnel. For example, the president and cabinet ministers are also members of the National Executive of TANU. There are several cases where governmental officials have refused to follow TANU policy. The bureaucracy has shown the greatest degree of independence and TANU has accused some of its members of having "neo-colonialist" leanings because of their reluctance to follow TANU directives. Recently Tanganyika and Zanzibar have federated to form the state of Tanzania. This federation may bring revisions in the TANU organization and procedures in the future.

THE CONVENTION PEOPLE'S PARTY

The Convention People's Party of Ghana was formed in 1949 from the nucleus of the Youth Committee organized by Nkrumah. The CPP also faced the problem of building mass support. By enlisting rural members the CPP developed into the mass party in a short period of time.

CPP structure and organization is very similar to that of TANU. The basic organization is the Branch in every town and village with large cities subdivided into wards. The Branch meets once a month to discuss party programs and matters of local interest. Its executive is elected annually and consists of a chairman and vice-chairman, a secretary and assistant secretary, a treasurer, a finance secretary, a propaganda secretary, and five executive members.

The next level of the party is the Constituency. Its annual conference is composed of two delegates from each branch. The Constituency Executive is selected by the conference and consists of a chairman, vice-chairman, finance secretary, treasurer, and eight elected members. The secretary and propaganda secretary are full-time paid personnel who are responsible for supervising and organizing the Branches within the Constituency and implementing party directives. The Annual Regional Conference is composed of two delegates from each Constituency in the region. The Regional Executive is elected annually, and its officers are similar to the Constituency Executive, including a full-time secretary and propaganda secretary.

The highest level of the party is the Annual National Conference, which is composed of six delegates from each constituency, six delegates elected by the women's section, six delegates elected by the Youth League, and delegates elected by each affiliated organization. The ex-officio delegates include the national officers of the party, the members of the National Executive, the Central Committee, and party members in the Legislative Assembly. The National Conference adopts national policy and hears reports on party activity.

The National Executive Committee is charged with the responsibility for carrying out party programs, organizing and supervising the work of the lower levels of the party, and approving candidates for governmental elections from nominating lists prepared by the

Regional and Constituency Executive Committees. It meets twice a year and is headed by a life chairman, Kwame Nkrumah, who is not elected periodically as is Nyerere. The other members of the National Executive are the national officers of the party; the chairman of the standing, finance, and staff committees; the members of the Central Committee; and one representative elected by each Constituency at its annual conference. Since it is a large body, the Central Committee, which is composed of the party leader and eight members selected by him with the approval of the National Executive Committee, serves as its directorate. Special members may be appointed with the approval of the National Executive Committee.

The CPP also provides for a Tribunal of Justice to handle questions of party discipline. It consists of three or more members appointed by the National Executive Committee and is responsible for investigating and reporting on cases of expulsion. A CPP parliamentary committee is also provided, composed of all the party members in the Legislative Assembly and any additional members appointed by the National Executive Committee. It is under the direct supervision of the party leader who appoints its chairman and supervises its policy decisions.

The Women's League is an integral part of the CPP. It may organize women's sections in every Branch or Ward of the party to carry on projects of special interest to women. However, the section is to be a "part and parcel" of the Branch or Ward and no separation of women's activity is to occur. The CPP Youth League also is integrated into the party. Membership is open to youth between fifteen and thirty years of age. Each Branch of the party appoints a member to serve on the Branch Youth League Executive, and the Central Committee appoints members to serve on the National Youth League Executive. There is also a Pioneer's Movement for those under fifteen years of age. The inclusion of the Youth League in the party may be a carry-over from the CYO, which Nkrumah organized and which became the nucleus for the CPP when he broke with the UGCC.

There has been opposition to CPP policies. The United Party operated for a period as a legal opposition. It tended to draw support from the economic and intellectual elite of the old UGCC, the Ashanti chiefs, and large cocoa planters who were opposed to

Nkrumah's economic policies. Opposition has now been outlawed, and Ghana has moved to a formal one-party status although the United Party never polled a large percentage of the electoral vote when it was allowed. In the 1960 elections, it received 124,000 votes to Nkrumah's more than one million.

Nkrumah agrees with Nyerere that a two-party system is not an essential characteristic of a democratic government and is alien to African tradition. He also argues that Ghanaian opposition movements have used unorthodox and apolitical methods in attempting to gain power. A number of the leaders of the United Party were arrested for plotting the assassination of Nkrumah. Investigation of the plot revealed some truth in the charges and may substantiate Nkrumah's claim that they do not play according to the rules. The ex-members of the defunct United Party continue to represent one area of opposition to the CPP.

A second area of opposition may exist among the economic and social elite of the CPP. In May of 1961, Nkrumah announced new rules for CPP members. These included limits on their property acquisitions and requirements against luxurious living. Nkrumah indicated that party members should serve as examples of socialism and the Party's aim of "building of a socialist pattern of society." Some members of the CPP have expressed their resentment over these restrictions. When the wife of Krobo Edusei purchased an expensive gold-plated bed on a trip to London, Nkrumah protested that her action did not set a good example of CPP socialism. Shortly thereafter Edusei was removed from government office for a period, although he was later reappointed to the cabinet.

In 1962, Nkrumah announced a five tier structure for the Ghanaian economy that emphasized state enterprise and joint state and private ownership. These economic policies caused further opposition from members of the business community. The bomb threats against Nkrumah that preceded the declaration of a state of emergency in September 1962 are considered by some observers to have been led by members of this economic elite. Other observers conclude that the threat came from the left wing of the CPP who are angry over Nkrumah's moderation. The "radical wing" viewed the reappointment of Krobo Edusei to the cabinet as an indication of a return to moderation. Opposition wings in the party presented Nkrumah with a problem in maintaining CPP unity. Adoption of policies too far left or right could alienate important segments of the party and a middle of the road policy seemed unacceptable to anyone.

Opposition to Nkrumah's policies came to a head in 1966 when he was en route to Peking for a state visit. A combined paratroop-infantry attack engineered by the army succeeded in overcoming the presidential security guard after limited fighting. Lieutenant General J. A. Ankrah, who had been removed several months earlier on the charge of plotting Nkrumah's overthrow, was appointed Armed Forces Commander. Ankrah announced that parliament was dissolved, that the CPP was outlawed, and that a National Liberation Council would rule until a new constitution was written. Ghana Radio stated that "gross economic mismanagement" had pushed the state to the brink of bankruptcy. The National Liberation Council appealed for a $50.4 million loan to assist the economic crisis and pay for urgently needed foodstuffs. Nkrumah had run up a billion dollar deficit before his overthrow and foreign currency was virtually nonexistent. The Council moved quickly to review the inflation, wage freeze, and tax structure. Hoping to limit government expenditures, overseas embassies were reduced, Ghana Airways operation was curtailed, and projects such as an olympic games complex planned by Nkrumah were cancelled. Ankrah promised that the government would be turned over to civilian leaders as soon as a new constitution was written and the crisis passed.

At the March 1966 meeting of the Organization of African Unity, Guinea, Mali, and Tanzania walked out in protest over the seating of the military government since they supported Nkrumah as the legitimate head of the state. Sekou Touré appointed Nkrumah the honorary President of Guinea, and consultations were held aiming at the return of Nkrumah to Ghana. In a radio broadcast to Ghana, Nkrumah threatened he would return with a military force and that all coup leaders would be killed. The Liberation Council has uncovered a number of special military camps that Nkrumah had planned to use in case of a coup attempt. Although Guinea, Mali, and Tanzania continue to support Nkrumah as the legitimate head of Ghana, they may be reluctant to supply the troops necessary to return him to power.

THE PARTI DÉMOCRATIQUE DE LA CÔTE D'IVOIRE

The PDCI was originally organized by Houphouet-Boigny to represent the interests of the small African farmer against the French planter and businessman. Boigny expanded this rural base in creating a mass movement. Differing from parties discussed above, labor unions and urbanized Africans did not play a major role in PDCI formation. Boigny affiliated the party with the French Marxists in the early years of its existence, but in 1950 the PDCI broke with the Communists and adopted policies oriented toward closer cooperation with France and the West. By 1956, the party polled 87 per cent of the votes in the general election, with the remaining 13 per cent divided among a number of opposition groups.

The PDCI is organized on a hierarchical pattern similar to that of the CPP or TANU. In the early period, dues were required for party membership, but after 1950, the base units of the party were de-emphasized and membership dues were no longer required. The Subsection of the party became the key to party activity. The Subsection Bureau and its Secretary General served as the main link between the party upper echelon and the base of the party. During the colonial period, the French used the Secretaries General as one of their administrative arms, thus increasing the power and prestige of the office. The PDCI adopted the procedure of requiring that all requests to the party be channeled through the office of the Secretaries General in order to use them as a deterrent to the growth of opposition elements. Since the Secretaries General were in a position to influence French decisions on appointments and assistance programs, their powers were not without significance. Opposition elements could find it difficult to get their needs communicated to the French Administration or the PDCI if the Secretary General was unfriendly to them or their viewpoint.

Since ethnic diversity is greater in the Ivory Coast than in some African states, the PDCI faced a more difficult problem in building a united movement. As government posts were increased immediately before and after independence, the PDCI used these positions as one means to build popular support. The party provided deliberately for the appointment or election of a number of representatives from the various ethnic and economic groups. The immigrant as well as the native population receives appointments. Older party members were balanced by the selection of a percentage of the youth. Although trade unions had not played a primary role in the formation of the PDCI, a number of their representatives were selected to serve in various posts. By this process, Boigny hoped to bring all elements into the government and control opposition. This policy gained new adherents for the party, since the appointment or election to government office carries with it economic gain and higher social status. The increase in the number of officeholders also permitted the party to further de-emphasize party membership on the lower levels of the party pyramid. Each officeholder is required to pay a percentage of his salary to the party, assuring the PDCI a steady source of income for organizational needs and campaign expenditures.

The Secretary General at the Subsection level of the party is still a key in the PDCI structure. He enforces party policies and supplies information concerning developments in his area. The PDCI has continued the policy of requiring that all communications to the party must be channeled through the Secretary General. This policy strengthens the position of the Secretary General, since he may refuse to send requests to the top, and there is little appeal from his decision. He is appointed by the party and is responsible for his position to the PDCI rather than the people in his area to assure that he will serve as a party check on the growth of opposition elements. The PDCI tends to avoid the appointment of Secretaries General who are residents of the area they serve in order to guard against a Secretary General's becoming too committed to his area or influenced by members of his community. In nominating candidates for elective office, the party leadership avoids selecting Secretaries General. Since candidates standing for election are dependent upon the Secretary General to get out the vote in his district, nomination of candidates other than the Secretary General tends to promote greater party control over campaigns. If conflict and tensions develop between a candidate and the Secretary General, the upper levels of the party may step in to mediate the conflict, thus assisting top echelon control over both posts.

In maintaining mass support, the PDCI tends to emphasize the accomplishments of the party rather than the issues of nationalism,

colonialism, and neo-colonialism. Since the PDCI policy statements endorse close co-operation with France, constant denun-
ciation of colonialism or neo-colonialism is somewhat awkward.
Tax reform for farmers and small business was undertaken in the
immediate post-independence period to encourage rural adherence
to the party, and these accomplishments tend to be stressed in
campaigns.

Opposition to the party and to Boigny in particular has arisen
among trade union members and student groups. The trade-
union leadership is critical of Boigny's policies as primarily
oriented toward small farmer interests. Members of the student
groups, especially those who have received training in France,
objected to the break with the French Marxists and view Boigny
as too conservative. Co-operation with France is criticized for
encouraging neo-colonialism and detracting from the goals of Pan-
Africanism and African nationalism. Both groups are angry that
they have not been given a higher percentage of governmental
posts and protest that the conservative PDCI members dominate
the government. Boigny decided to bring a larger number of these
opposition elements into the parliament as PDCI candidates in the
hope of silencing their criticisms. Their inclusion in the legislature
is considered dangerous by some observers who feel Boigny will
not be able to control them.

Boigny describes the one-party structure of the Ivory Coast as
democratic. He has stated that as long as "the masses trust us"
there is no need for a legal opposition since democracy is preserved
when the government is freely elected. Boigny agrees that there is
room for opposition within the party, but no group that questions
the regime will be tolerated. The Ivory Coast constitution re-
enforces this view by providing that there shall be freedom for
all groups that respect "democracy, the community, and the
republic." This provision has been interpreted to deny freedom to
those who oppose the regime since it is the "embodiment" of the
community and the republic. Not only is opposition outlawed in
elections, but voting abstention is considered an unfriendly act
and frowned upon. Preventive detention is used if opposition goes
beyond the limits in criticism of the government.

The PDCI structure differs from that of TANU and the CPP in that
the base of the party and mass party membership are not stressed.

Voting support is the key to party membership. Local party branches meet infrequently and government by local discussion does not receive primary attention. Democracy is defined as free choice by the electorate over government officeholders rather than "talking until you agree." However, free election choice is not practiced within the party, since party leaders are not elected frequently at each level of the party, and the central party leadership appoints key officials to assure loyalty to the party and its policies. Patronage and party nomination controls are key levers in maintaining unity.

The PDCI interpretation of one-party democracy may be open to greater abuse of power than those of the CPP or TANU since its structure permits fewer opportunities for popular check on party policies and programs. Power tends to concentrate in the hands of a few key party leaders. The primary popular check on the government is the election process, but the electorate votes for only one slate of candidates. Even though there is an attempt to balance representation among interest groups, the distribution is worked out by the party leadership rather that the voters.

These examples of one-party structure indicate some of the structural similarities and differences. One-party systems generally center around a complex hierarchy or pyramid, based upon village branches, that is claimed to be democratic, since popular opinion moves from the base through the hierarchy to the highest level of the party for enforcement and implementation. Certain problems arise in regard to the operation of this structure. One question is whether the party is actually open to all on a voluntary basis. If party membership is restricted, or if it is not voluntary, the democratic label is debatable. Complaints have been raised in many states over the discrimination in appointments and scholarships that is felt by those who are not party members or who do not take active roles in support of party policies. There is also the problem of the continuing recruitment of leadership from the ranks of the party, since the party must remain sensitive to the desires of its members and open to new ideas and leadership if it hopes to keep mass support. The returning overseas college graduate and the growing number of college and high school graduates trained at home are beginning to protest the "entrenched," "moderate," and "unresponsive" party leadership. The degree of control that is exercised over nominations for party and governmental offices by the top levels of the party also is significant. When key men, as in the PDCI, use their positions to control selection of candidates for office, the operation of the base of the party in preserving mass participation is virtually destroyed. In some of the states which have adopted this party pyramid structure, certain levels of the party have not been developed. The PDCI was one example and another is the Senegal UPS, which has not created regional levels throughout the state. If the pyramid structure is incomplete, the discussion-funneling approach may not function effectively.

Intra-party debate is the key to the maintenance of "democratic free discussion," which the one-party structure is intended to assure. The actual operation of intra-party debate may not be studied easily, since party deliberation frequently is secret and the divisions of opinion that may exist at various levels of the party are difficult to observe. However, criticism of party operation is heard in many states. It is contended that political consciousness is poorly developed and that the masses tend to look to traditional leaders in their villages for guidance and direction. Party officials at the various levels of the pyramid also have considerable influence over policy and programs. Although this may suggest the development of power centers or a leadership group, many studies of opinion formulation in traditionally democratic societies also point to the tendency for policy elites to form.

Many African leaders describe themselves as monists on the question of the role of groups or institutions within the state. The monist position emphasizes that all institutions and groups have a central institutional focus in society and believes in the homogeneity of the people, the institutions, and the state. The mass political party serves as this focal point, and all groups are free to operate within or in relation to it. However, not all one-party states insist on this monist view of the role of pressure groups within the state. For example, the Kenyan labor movement maintains its separate existence and is not considered an arm of the party. Leaders as Nyerere and Senghor view monism as a necessity in the immediate post-independence period but do not rule out the possible growth of a multi-party system in the future. Touré and Keita see the monist approach as good in itself and do not foresee the movement to multi-parties or pluralistic pressure groups.

Considerable effort has been devoted to the attempt to categorize African party structure. Since the structure and organization of the parties is still in transition, efforts at final classification may be premature and the use of traditional Western classifications may not necessarily be suitable for the African systems. One model suggested is the Leninist or neo-Leninist. Among its characteristics are the concepts of party supremacy in the state, an elitist minority party, and a complex structural hierarchy based upon the local cell or branch but controlled by the top echelon of the party, sometimes termed democratic centralism. African parties may have borrowed from this model in varying degrees. The Guinean PDG comes the closest to the neo-Leninist model since it accepts the supremacy of the party although it rejects top echelon control over the party membership.

TANU, PDCI, and the CPP do not fit the neo-Leninist classification, since they reject the concept of an elitist minority party with supremacy over the government. These parties might be described as pluralistic, since they attempt to build a mass movement representing all of the interests of the society, with organized interest groups included in the party structure itself or affiliated with the party. Interchange of ideas and conflict of opinions are to occur within the party rather than between parties or interest groups.

Attempts also have been made to classify the African parties as democratic or authoritarian. Since many African leaders define democracy as "talking until you agree," multi-party systems, the loyal opposition, separation of powers, and other concepts are considered unnecessary for a democratic regime. Using this definition of democracy, the question of whether the one-party system may be classified as democratic centers around the operation of free discussion among equal members of society. The structural pyramid that has been created appears to be open to freedom of discussion at the base of the party, but it also may be subject to control over policy- and decision-making by the top echelon or leadership. Actual practice in regard to free discussion may vary among levels of the party and from state to state.

Certain characteristics that are often attributed to authoritarian or totalitarian party systems are lacking in many present African systems. For example, the parties have not established complete control over the lives of their citizens or over all organizations functioning in the society. State ownership of every economic resource has not been adopted and is not necessarily considered a desirable goal. Although preventive detention acts have been passed, the parties have not moved to terror or police methods to assure unity and conformity. Parties have organized party press, and varying degrees of control or censorship over mass media exist. However, government management of all communication media is not a usual practice and nongovernmental papers circulate freely in many states. Aggressive or expansionist ideology is sometimes considered a characteristic of authoritarian regimes. Although anti-colonialism might be classed as an "aggressive issue," there has been an observable trend for the African states to reestablish trade and aid ties with former colonial powers and to deemphasize anti-colonialism in party propaganda, particularly in former French areas. The task of final categorization of the African one-party democracy system remains for the future when the trends and patterns which have been discussed have solidified and stabilized.

PARTY PLATFORMS

African parties generally do not have clearly defined platforms. In achieving independence, it was necessary to build a unified, disciplined mass movement that could exert pressure upon the colonial powers. It is this pluralistic coalition that faces the problem of governing after independence. The parties have avoided the adoption of clearly outlined programs or platforms because of the divergency of interests represented in the party. The so-called "radical" group finds it difficult to accept the "moderate" position. Urban and rural interests are not necessarily similar. The goals of the intellectual elite differ from those of unskilled labor. Governing parties, therefore, minimize divisive issues and attempt to postpone unpopular decisions until a greater degree of stability is achieved. It is feared that detailed platforms might split the coalition and weaken their power in the state. Since the party members were united on the goal of independence, the issues of anti-colonialism, neo-colonialism and freedom have been used.

One result of the party's emphasis upon the issues of nationalism, loyalty to the state, and anti-colonialism has been to concentrate attention upon the state, thus placing the party in a subordinate position to the government. Guinea is an exception to this pattern. In addition to the emphasis upon the national interest, party platforms endorse industrialization, greater educational opportunities, and equality of the members of society. The methods that will be used to achieve these goals are generally left vague to avoid splitting the coalition of interests that the party represents.

The parties, also have turned to various weapons that they could use in building long-term loyalty. Among these are patronage, the extension of party control by the reorganization of local government, and the "hero" status that parties have been accorded by the achievement of independence. This hero aura attaches particularly to the party leader who serves as a symbol of independence and freedom. Many African mass parties are headed by charismatic leaders who are seasoned political organizers and have campaigned extensively throughout their states. Since the leader has become the "father of the country" in the minds of the people, he may perform the important function of serving as a focal point for the party and the state. The cult of the leader is used in varying degrees by African states to emphasize an area of cohesion within the party that may overcome the divisiveness within one-party ranks. The tendency toward extension of personal power and concentration of power in the hands of the leader may be explained in part by the need for a focal point.

THE ROLE OF THE OPPOSITION

African leaders wish to maintain the one-party pattern that has evolved. The growth of strong opposition parties is discouraged, since they would decrease the executive's ability to control the other branches of government. Centralization of power and unity of direction are considered absolute necessities in the promotion of stability. Not having to counter an organized opposition permits government officials to devote more time and attention to development problems. Campaigns are less expensive and may be used to build enthusiasm for party platforms, check on voter opinion, and observe party structure in operation. Many states have moved to legal one-party status. Even where an organized opposition is permitted to operate, it tends to be weak.

In the period of the formation of the PDG, TANU, and CPP, one area of opposition came from the tribal chiefs who objected to the loss of their traditional power to party leaders and a centralized governmental administration. Detribalism was pushed by Sekou Touré on the grounds of promoting national advancement since Touré argued that feudalism lived on in Africa in the person of the chief. In 1957 he initiated legislation requiring the election of all chiefs, and a 1958 governmental decree provided that all non-elected chiefs be suppressed politically. Little reaction followed these actions. Since the chiefs had been used by the French as administrative tools of the colonial system, the chiefs were viewed as lackeys and popular antagonism existed to their enforcement of colonial policy. In Tanganyika, a number of tribal chiefs opposed TANU on the grounds that its platform was too radical. TANU used several techniques to discourage tribalism and restrict the authority of the chiefs. One was to create TANU organizations on the local level. A second was the appointment of career bureaucrats to take over local administrative functions. Finally, in 1960, TANU discouraged the continued existence of tribal associations and attempted to integrate such groups into the independence movement. Despite TANU efforts, elements of tribal voting were evident in the 1960 election. The CPP confronted similar opposition from the traditional authorities. Accentuating the difficulty was the outbreak of violence in Ashanti led by the chiefs and other opposition elements including former supporters of the UGCC. The CPP first attempted to bring the chiefs into the party, which was successful in a few cases. Nkrumah also stripped the chiefs of power by creating governmental and party organizations on the local level.

One reason traditional authorities have had little success in their efforts to counter independence party strength is that a platform advocating the return to the traditional system does not seem to rouse enthusiasm in a continent in a hurry to achieve industrialization, economic growth, and increased social welfare. Many traditional authorities also dragged their feet on the question of independence, since the colonial period provided them political and social status. Gradualism on independence did not promote mass support. The educated elite and urban African who broke with the traditional system tend to view any attempt to re-establish the power of the tribal authorities as a step backward. In a few states the older educated elite joined forces with the traditional authorities in opposition to the mass movement, but their numbers were still too small to be effective. When they were thwarted in their attempts to overcome the independence party majority, a number of the traditional authorities moved to open revolt, attempted coups, or assassination in a vain attempt to regain power. Preventive detention, security trials, and imprisonment have followed such action. It is doubtful whether a return to the traditional system will hold much attraction to the Africans in the future. If not, this area of opposition will decrease in importance.

Additional areas of opposition may develop within the independence parties themselves. The heterogeneous coalition, which was built prior to independence, will be more difficult to maintain as the government moves ahead with development programs. The parties use of anti-colonialism, nationalism, and independence as issues to promote unity cannot be continued for an extended period of time, since they tend to lose their luster after attaining independence. The parties, in governing, must make decisions concerning economic and social policy for the state that may antagonize certain interest groups.

It is perhaps inaccurate to speak of the existence of an African middle class. However, some members found among the older educated elite, urbanized African and secondary certificate holders achieved a higher standard of living than the laborer or rural African. Spearheading the independence drive, they hoped their support for the independence movement would further raise their standard of living or at least protect their status. Where the independence party has adopted programs designed to redistribute the resources of society, provide greater economic equality for every citizen, and promote increased governmental controls over the economy, grumbling has been heard from members of the economic elite. One example is Nkrumah's proposed program of socialism and redistribution of income.

The attempted plot to overthrow Nkrumah found some support among these elements in the CPP. Their reaction to his proposals

for "socialization" illustrates the disenchantment that can occur as
the independence party undertakes economic development measures. Although the economic elite agreed with the mass party goals
of freedom and independence, they are not necessarily enthusiastic
about the ideal of equality or communalism. Protests similar to
those heard in Ghana have also appeared in Tanzania and Guinea,
where the goal of economic equality has been pushed by the mass
party. Although this opposition is latent at present, a group may
form that could become significant in the future. If the mass party
pursues "equality measures," it is possible this elite may break
away as a conservative opposition party.

A second possible area of opposition within the ranks of the
mass party is found among the younger educated elite, particularly the recently returned overseas-college graduate. This group
is in a hurry to achieve reform and modernization, and tends to
support greater state controls over the economy as the means to
these ends. The PDCI of the Ivory Coast held a special conference
attempting to reconcile differences in viewpoint between the youth
and the government leadership. The party statement calling for the
conference concluded that the PDCI did not liberate the country in
order that a split would develop between the youth and the older
party members. The party statement expressed the belief that the
growing lack of understanding resulted from the youth's being
overseas and losing touch with the problems of the state. The fact
that the PDCI felt it necessary to call a conference to reconcile
differences in viewpoint within the party indicates the seriousness
of the split. Resentment over the older elite may be encouraged
in states where the returning overseas graduate encounters an older
party elite entrenched in the bureaucracy or elected officers and
limited private economic opportunities. Since the youth may have
less at stake in the status quo, they are more inclined to favor "radical" measures that will push them ahead more quickly. The older
elite, having achieved some level of economic and social status or
security is less enthusiastic to try measures that may "rock the
boat" or upset the system. If the independence party follows a moderate course, which does not produce rapid economic gains in the
short run, the younger groups could break with the party in favor
of a more "radical" solution. The discussion of the membership
of the PDG, TANU, CPP, and PDCI indicates that liberal or left-wing

groups exist in each of the parties and that dissatisfaction with party programs is not uncommon. If the left wing should break away from the mass party in the future, it is difficult to predict what economic philosophy it might adopt, since opinion within this group covers a broad spectrum from democratic socialism to Marxism.

Although Communist influence and support may be found in the African states, its significance is not easy to assess. Where the one party structure is followed, communists operate within the party rather than as a separate organization. Since intra-party debate is closed to study and analysis, the numbers of communist supporters cannot be determined accurately. The discussion of the radical wings of the one-party structure indicated possible areas of communist support particularly among student groups and younger members. A few organized groups exist. For example, the PRA-Senegal is more Marxist in outlook than the UPS, but its movements have been restricted and public meetings are banned by the government. Communist influence in such groups may become significant in the future, particularly if the left wing of the mass party breaks away. Some observers of the African political scene have concluded that the mass party itself is strongly influenced by communist philosophy. African leaders deny that they are Communist controlled or dominated. In attempting to hold the party coalition together, the mass party has adopted an economic philosophy that is described as "African Socialism." An analysis of this philosophy may assist in comparing or contrasting it with Communism.

AFRICAN SOCIALISM

Although economic philosophy differs among African parties and leaders, there is agreement on a number of concepts. African Socialism generally rejects the capitalistic approach as unacceptable since private capital in the African states tends to be concentrated in the hands of foreign investors and business, which are associated with colonialism and discredited in the public mind. Governments plan to gradually remove their influence by Africanization of the economy. Capitalism is viewed as a system that divorces wealth from its true purpose, that is the satisfaction of needs. It is argued that capitalism encourages luxury production and creates *have* and *have not* classes. Finally, the capitalistic system is accused of using its wealth to gain international power and prestige and promote colonialism and neo-colonialism.

Africans say that their socialism will avoid the pitfalls of capitalism since its sole purpose is to banish poverty and prevent class development. Once needs are satisfied in a given area, no further production will be permitted. African Socialism is said not to concern itself with developing international power or gaining international prestige, since its only goal is to satisfy needs and raise the standard of living.

It is claimed that African Socialism is particularly suited to the African scene. Traditional African society is described as communal or as a "community of brotherhood" that rests upon the solidarity of the kinship group. African leaders wish to build upon this community solidarity in creating modern states. Nyerere refers to it as a "communitary" society and Touré terms it a "communaucracy." Senghor calls it an "assembly of individuals" emphasizing group solidarity and communion rather than individual autonomy. The description of African life as communal refers to rural rather than urban life, since in the cities a more individualistic system developed. Touré maintains that urban life was influenced by colonialism and that "true" African civilization is found in the village kinship society. In order to build upon the kinship pattern, co-operatives are fostered to replace it with a modern system promoting agricultural advancement.

It is argued that the co-operative movement will permit Africa to escape the class struggles of the European industrial revolution. African leaders claim that classes do not exist at present and that their growth should be avoided. Touré describes Africa as composed of one class, "the dispossessed." Others, as Senghor, describe it as "social groups struggling for influence." African Socialism considers the doctrine of class warfare meaningless, and maintains that society exists for the individual and that the individual fulfills himself through service to society. It stresses belief in communal values and views the government's role as service to the whole nation rather than to one group or class. The Communist emphasis on the proletarian revolution is rejected in favor of national revolution. Senghor argues that the "Dictatorship of the Proletariat" requires a proletariat and a capitalistic system at war. To accept this doctrine would be just "gargling a formula," since the Senegalese labor movement represents only 10 percent of the population, while the mass party includes 85 percent. Rather than class warfare within a nation he sees a global struggle between *have* and *have not* nations.

African Socialism contends that the primary means of production, exchange, and social service should be the responsibility of the people, or the government as their representative. However, states differ on the degree of governmental control and state ownership that should be undertaken. Where land is privately owned, no government has moved to extensive nationalization, although the cooperative system is preferred. African Socialism might be described as pragmatic on the question of public ownership and direction, since the degree of state control appears to have evolved with experience and in response to economic pressures. There was little emphasis upon the public sector in the early period after Ghanaian independence, but controls were instituted to meet a revenue decline caused by the fall of cocoa prices on the world market. In Guinea, state control and government monopoly were clearly stated as goals in the early post-independence period, and governmental control of exports and imports was instituted. The operation of state trading had such a disastrous effect upon the Guinean economy that governmental controls gradually were relaxed and a less centralized system was permitted. This pragmatic approach may explain the variance in the degree of state ownership from state to state.

African leaders maintain that African Socialism differs significantly from Russian or Chinese Communism. African leaders also are critical of Communism or Marxism as anti-religious since they disapprove of the negation of the existence of God. African leaders praise the lack of violence in the African revolution. The achievement of independence without open conflict is considered a substantiation of Gandhi's theory of non-violence and a refutation of the Communist doctrine of violent revolution. African Socialism does not view the party as a vanguard of the proletariat, but as a mass party open to all members of society. Labor unions shall conform to party policy rather than serving as the leadership of the proletariat. They shall pursue the same goals as the majority party to prevent groups from hardening into antagonistic classes. The African states also reject the concept of the withering away of the state. For these, as well as other reasons, African leaders argue that African Socialism is unique and distinct from communism or any other "ism."

However, many leaders term themselves Marxists and almost all agree that Marx has had an influence on their political philosophy. Marx is credited as the source for the ideal of economic equality of the members of society. The concepts of communal living, state control over the distribution of wealth, and the imperialistic nature of capitalism found in the writings of many African leaders are admittedly adapted from Marxism. Maoism also has influenced African political theory because of its emphasis upon the agricultural or peasant base of the revolution. Many African leaders believe that agriculture will condition all other development projects in their states. Since they feel the Chinese Communists understand the role of agriculture in an underdeveloped economy, Maoism has gained some adherents. African leaders admit that Marxism and Maoism may have influenced the development of African theories of government, but deny Communist leanings or Communist control of their revolutions, although Russian and Chinese support of various party leaders and groups is well known. Their intervention in the Congo is one example. The African leaders deny Communist domination on the grounds of their desire to maintain the independence and freedom of their states. They argue that they do not intend to substitute a new form of imperialism for the old colonialism that they fought to end. Although some observers of Guinean politics concluded that the state had fallen under Communist control in the early post-independence period, Sekou Touré upset these theories when he demanded the recall of the Russian diplomatic staff from Guinea on the grounds of internal subversion. Touré stated he did not intend to lose Guinean independence to a new form of outside control. The Russian representatives in the Belgian Congo also were forcibly ejected on a charge of an attempted plot against the state. One Russian diplomat was escorted to the airport in the middle of the night and was not even permitted to take time to put on his shoes before being placed on a plane leaving the Congo.

Peking has been seeking a foothold in Africa and apparently concluded that Burundi, which is situated on the Congolese frontier, would be an ideal center for propaganda and shipment of arms to the Congolese revolutionary forces. The assassination of the Burundi Premier Pierre Ngendandumwe triggered the rupture of Burundian diplomatic relations with Communist China and the ending of all Chinese activity in the capital, since the investigation of the assassination revealed Chinese involvement in the plot. The expulsion may have caused Chou En-Lai to reassess his statement that "the revolutionary situation is excellent" in Africa. A similar setback was suffered in Niger. At a Communist conference in Hanoi, Red China had disclosed its interest to depose the "pro-Western leader" Hamani Diori. The illegal opposition party, Sawaba, led by Djibo Bokary, was given Chinese support and a small number of Niger *emigrés* in Ghana were sent to China for Commando training. A few also received training in Algeria. Bokary hoped to gain support from Haoussa tribesmen who resented Diori's Germa tribe affiliation. Contrary to the plan, the Haoussa refused Bokary any support after he crossed into Niger, and the government crushed the attempted revolt. In response to this threat, Diori created "vigilance committees" and "self-defense groups" to guard the country's leaders and protect the villages. Diori also joined with Houphouet-Boigny of the Ivory Coast in spearheading a drive against Chinese activity in Africa. A similar attitude toward extension of Communist influence was revealed in an interview by Kenyan Finance Minister James Gichuru. He commented that any attempt to introduce Communism into Kenya would be strongly opposed both by the government and the people. He concluded that "the tradition of our people" cannot accommodate Communism as it is interpreted in Russia or China.

These cases may indicate the leadership's desire to avoid control or dominance by any bloc. However, a number of the younger members of the independence parties do not necessarily feel as strongly about the differences between African Socialism and Communism. They argue that classes will develop, an elite will evolve, and industry will become more important than agriculture. Those differences that have been stressed as distinguishing African Socialism from Marxism may be considered less important in the future, when this younger element gains control of the parties. On the other hand, industrialization and economic development may stimulate the growth of a middle class favoring a moderate or conservative turn in party philosophy. Although present party systems espouse one-party democracy, African Socialism, and centralism, it may be asked whether mass support for these approaches will hold in the future as the economic issues that divide the wings of the party become more intense. It is impossible at this point to predict whether a split will occur, when it might occur, or if party philosophy will move right, left, or remain the same.

CHAPTER 3

Governmental Processes

INTRODUCTION

A SURVEY OF THE DEVELOPING CONSTITUTIONAL PROVISIONS and processes should include an analysis of the formal and informal power patterns and relationships that may be found in the new states. Of the two, the formal structural relationships are more easily discernible and materials more readily available for study.

The formal constitutional relationships may be used as a baseline for the study of the governing process. The formal structures may serve as a focal point of order in the chaos of the still-evolving political relationships. The constitutions may reveal what political institutions and techniques states have adopted in attempting to build effective governments. The formal constitutional structures also may reflect a minimal institutional consensus that exists in the state. They may suggest whether consensus centers on the political traditions of the colonial system, the tribal system, historic precedent, or whether they represent a radical break with the pre-independence period. The formal constitution also may mirror the contemporary political traditions of the state and serve as a partial indicator of political compromises and power alignments in the community. Structural compromises and their causes may be significant. Finally, comparison of the formal constitutions of the emerging African states permits general classification and analysis of formal structural differences and similarities.

However, it should be recognized that the study of the formal constitutions alone will not provide a well-balanced picture of the political relationships that are developing. African constitutional structures are still in the process of transition and evolution. In several states, the original constitutions have been amended significantly. The constitutional structures that may emerge finally are uncertain. Even if the formal constitutional structure is not abandoned or amended, political developments and constitutional interpretation may modify structural provisions and procedures. The power patterns and political relationships that evolve may be significantly different from the formal provisions.

Informal relationships are more difficult to trace or analyze. Since the states have achieved independence only recently, information and materials concerning informal power patterns is limited or often unobtainable, and African politicians seem reluctant to discuss them. Some students of government suggest that informal power relationships result from the issues facing the society. Since issues change, no one locus of power may exist. If this approach is accepted, informal power patterns may be discussed in relation to the dominant political issues facing the African states. These issues differ from state to state, but the need to provide unity, direction, and stability tend to be critical questions for every state. Although the formal constitutional provisions may camouflage informal power patterns, they also may reveal institutional consensus and political compromise attempting to resolve these issues. The following discussion will center upon an analysis of the structural and institutional provisions of the formal constitution in the hope that they also may shed some light on the evolving informal power patterns.

A survey of the constitutional provisions and structural procedures of the newly independent African states reveals similar patterns in forms of government; the role of the executive, legislative, and judicial branches; and the division of power between the central and local governments. These patterns appear to be drawn in part from Western models. A more detailed examination of the constitutions may indicate whether the borrowing from the West is more apparent than real.

CONSTITUTIONAL MONARCHY PATTERN

Ethiopia and Morocco are examples of African states that have adopted the constitutional monarchy form of government. Both states have a long historical experience with the institution of a monarchy, since they claim a status of independence or existence as nations for over one thousand years during which the Emperor or Sultan has been a significant governmental institution. In the traditional system, the position of the emperor derived in part from his spiritual role in the state. He was considered the "anointed of God" and was given special responsibilities for defense of the faith. The spiritual role of the monarchy may explain in part the autocratic tradition of the institution and the virtual divine right of kings concept attached to it. In both states, the monarch's power of final decision was not to be questioned, but discussion and debate could occur prior to his imperial decree or pronouncement. However, the monarchy was not the only locus of power in the state. In practice, authority in the traditional system was divided or balanced among the monarchy, the religious hierarchy, and the lords. The monarchy defended the faith in return for its promotion of respect for and obedience to him. For example, religious ceremony stressed his spiritual power and position. The lords were given protection and lands by the monarch in return for collecting taxes and supplying troops in cases of national emergency.

The adoption of a constitutional monarchy is an attempt to blend the best of the traditional rules and procedures with a modern system patterned primarily after the British model. The historical experience with and popular support for the institution of the monarchy may prove a distinct advantage for these states, since they have a common political tradition to which they may turn in the modern period. This institution may serve as a focal point of unity and stability in the movement to modernization. The problem of achieving a balance between stability and change may center less around the creation of stable and effective governments than around the modernization and liberalization of the traditional autocratic system.

Since the traditional system basically involved a balancing of powers among the throne, the clergy, and the feudal lords, it was difficult for any one of the three to assume dominant control. Under the new constitutions, the monarch is given authority to create new political institutions that may replace gradually the functions of the clergy and the lords. For example, the provision for a centralized administrative structure permits the government to collect taxes without relying upon the assistance of the lords. The adoption of a modern army system reduces the government's need for troop supply by the lords. The development of provincial administration and services may undermine the position of the lords if the people gradually look to the government for health, welfare, or other services. The introduction of a state-controlled monetary system also tends to lessen dependence upon the lord by his tenants. The establishment of state supported educational systems decreases the reliance upon the church administration of schools and may contribute to a weakening of the influence of the clergy in the state.

Liberalization of the traditional structure is necessary if the government is to respond to the pressure for change and modernization. It would be difficult to carry out a land-reform program, for example, if dominant political power remains in the hands of the feudal landlord. However, modernization of the traditional autocratic system requires limitation of the powers of the monarchy as well as the lords and the church. Rather than liberalizing this institution, the adoption of the new constitutions may tend to strengthen the position of the monarch in relation to the lords and the clergy, since the monarch may use his constitutional power to check and limit the role of the other two. The monarch can assume a dominant legal position, since he is not checked as in the traditional system. The controls on the power of the monarchy that are provided under the new constitutions are found in the legislative and judicial branches and the bureaucracy. Political parties provide an additional force to check the monarchy in Morocco. Ethiopian political parties have not yet developed. Since these institutions were not part of the traditional power structure, their role and status in the governmental process is still evolving and developing. There is uncertainty on the part of the members of the branches of government and parties of their proper function in the governing process. The institution of the monarchy has popular support and a tradition of obedience is attached to it, and there has been a tendency for the monarchy to dominate the other branches of government. Although the problem of limiting the powers of the monarchy is central to the creation of a "true" constitutional monarchy, this liberalization is dependent upon the ability of the other branches of government and the political parties to assume significant political power in the state.

An examination of the functions and powers of these branches of government may assist in assessing the present effectiveness of the new check-and-balance system. A bicameral parliament was created in the 1955 Ethiopian constitution. The lower house, the Chamber of Deputies, is now directly elected. Article 93 provides that the country be divided into electoral districts each containing 200,000 inhabitants, or as near that figure as possible. Each district shall have one deputy and one additional deputy for each additional 50,000 inhabitants. Deputies shall be twenty-five years of age, residents of their districts, and property owners. Deputies serve four-year terms and may be re-elected. This represents a revision of the 1931 constitutional provision for indirect election of the lower house and indefinite terms of office. The upper house, the Senate, is appointed by the Emperor for a six-year term, one-third to be appointed every two years. Under the previous constitution, life terms were provided. The Senate shall not be larger than one-half the size of the Chamber of Deputies. Qualifications for Senator require the candidate to be thirty-five years of age and a prince or dignitary of the Empire. Legislative proposals passed by both houses are transmitted by the Prime Minister to the Emperor who may sign them or return them to either house with his comments or proposals for substitute legislation. A bill may not become a law without the Emperor's signature. Article 92 authorizes the Emperor to proclaim decrees "consistent with the constitution" in cases of emergency and when parliament is not in session. Such decrees require the approval of both Houses when they meet in their next regular session.

The ministers of the state are appointed and dismissed by the Emperor and are individually responsible to him. The ministers form the Council of Ministers, which advises the Emperor. The Prime Minister heads the Council and presents to parliament the Council's proposals for legislation after receiving the approval of the Emperor. Although a Prime Minister is provided for in the Constitution, the position has gone unfilled periodically since the Prime Minister's office involves little actual power and is dominated by the influence and decision-making power of the Emperor. The ministers of the government are appointed and removed by the Emperor, which restricts the Cabinet's willingness to oppose his views. Haile Selassie apparently removes those who disagree with him or who become too influential. These individuals often have been sent to the provinces or to overseas posts where their influence would be politically less significant. The Emperor does not eliminate rival factions and groups within the state. Rather he uses the principle of divide and rule in attempting to control them. His appointments appear to be based more on achieving a balance of power among factions than on the policies or abilities of the men. This procedure encourages a rapid turnover of governmental personnel and helps to deter the growth of permanent factions. The Emperor has indicated that he opposes the development of political parties, since he contends that they are not necessary for the proper operation of the constitutional monarchy system. His policy of playing off rival factions against each other and rapid turnover in governmental appointments restricts party development, since it is more difficult for permanent groupings to organize. As long as the Emperor retains the power of final decision-making on legislation, administrative policy, and appointments, political activity will tend to center around gaining and retaining his favor rather than political party development.

The Emperor's appointment and removal powers have contributed to the development of a personal patronage system that government officials resent. However, fear of the Emperor and suspicion of fellow governmental officials has limited the development of open revolt against the system. In response to the grumblings, an Imperial Ethiopian Institute of Public Administration was created, and a few independent agencies have come into existence in which Western civil service practices are followed.

In his relationship with parliament, the Emperor has tended to follow the same divide-and-rule technique. Although parliament is accused of being a rubber stamp, it has shown several indications of attempting to limit the control of the throne. For example, the Chamber of Deputies insisted that the various ministers defend their budget requests before approving the 1959-60 budget. The Emperor found it necessary to bring considerable pressure on individual members of the Chamber to get the budget accepted.

These few examples of the operation of the government under the 1955 constitution indicate that the provisions for a constitutional monarchy may serve more as a possible proposal for the future than as an accurate description of the present governmental system. The power and personality of the Emperor tend to overshadow the role and position of the cabinet, parliament, or administrative personnel. Areas of discontent and dissatisfaction exist in the system as it now operates. The attempted coup of 1960 and the discussions of a coup attempt when Haile Selassie dies point to the possibility of a violent revision of the imperial institution in the future.

Although North African states are not generally included in the scope of this study, Morocco will be discussed since it illustrates another constitutional monarchy form. The operation of the Moroccan system of checks and balances is similar to that of Ethiopia. Immediately after independence was granted, the institutions and procedures of the administrative system of the French protectorate were followed because the traditional pattern had been outmoded by the administrative changes introduced during the protectorate period. Under the independence agreement of March, 1956, the king retained all sovereign powers. A royal cabinet was created to manage the king's personal and ceremonial functions. A Secretary General was formed to serve as the monarch's personal administrative agency, coordinator, and planner. The Council of Government (Cabinet of Ministers) supervised the various agencies of government such as police, army, communications, and other services. Special commissions were created to prepare plans for the Royal Army, economic affairs of the state, social welfare, and the revision of legislation. In this period of adjustment and change-over from French administration, the independence party, Istiqlal, acquiesced to several procedures that tended to reinforce the position of the monarchy. For example, decisions on governmental programs and policy were cleared with the palace, thus establishing a precedent of the monarch's veto over governmental proposals. Few objections or questions were raised when the monarch announced the alteration of certain institutional structures in the state. Therefore, the traditional pattern of the monarch's having final power over such questions was perpetuated. Istiqlal was faced with a dilemma. If it merged its policies with those of the king, it might lose its political identity. Since its pre-independence campaign had used the monarchy as a symbol of nationalism and unity, Istiqlal leaders found it awkward to do an about face and refuse support to the monarch's wishes. Istiqlal placed itself in an unenviable position, since Mohammed V upon occasion used the party as a scapegoat for failure in policies and programs.

The role of the monarchy became a critical issue in the governmental crisis of 1958. Istiqlal pressed for a new constitution defining the legal rights and functions of governmental bodies. Mohammed V issued a Royal Charter that provided for the eventual adoption of a constitutional monarchy and statutes defining the powers of the ministers in the Council of Government, but he withheld provisions for legislative powers. In January, 1959, Istiqlal split into two factions. One grouping, which was primarily conservative in outlook, continued to go by the name of Istiqlal and was led by Al-Fassi and Ahmed Belafrej. The second group, more radical in outlook, was led by El-Mehdi Ben Barka and adopted the name of the Union of Popular Forces. It was allied with the trade-union movement. During the period of the party split, Mohammed V moved to consolidate more political power in his hands.

With the unexpected death of Mohammed V in February, 1961, Hassan ascended the throne. Hassan moved quickly to designate himself as Prime Minister and to adopt many of the policies and slogans of the Union of Popular Forces, thereby stealing some of its thunder. For example, he began a national mobilization of the unemployed, forming a labor corps for public works reconstruction. Other areas of economic planning, such as land reform, also were undertaken and pushed. Finally, Hassan submitted a constitution to a referendum by the Moroccan people. This constitution was overwhelmingly approved by 84.8% of the voters.

The new constitution created a "democratic, social, constitutional monarchy" for Morocco. In his speech of transmittal, Hassan II stated that in order to assure the proper functioning of the new institutions of government, the king would remain the guarantor of the constitution and "be able at all times to control and follow state affairs." With the consent of the people, the king would be responsible to "triumph, as in the past, over obstacles which could arise before us." The retention of final decision-making power by the monarchy is very similar to the Ethiopian constitution. However, no provision in the Moroccan constitution makes the cabinet ministers directly responsible to the monarchy. Article 35 of the constitution gives the monarchy emergency power. It provides that in cases of threat to the "integrity of the national soil" or "interruption in the course of action of the constitutional institutions," the king shall have the right to declare by decree a state of national emergency. In the event of such action, the king shall assume the responsibility for taking measures to meet the emergency, which shall be terminated by royal decree. It is left to the discretion of the king to decide when a threat to the state or an interruption of constitutional procedures exists. This power could be used to check parliament and the cabinet. The emergency powers article is limited to some extent by the requirement that parliament declare war or a state of martial law and that martial law may be proclaimed for a thirty-day period only. New legislation is required to extend it beyond this limit.

Since the present constitution of Morocco has come into effect only recently, it may be too early to trace evolving patterns or trends. The constitution provides for a complex check-and-balance system with powers divided among the monarchy, cabinet, parliament, and various special councils, commissions, and boards. The effective operation of these checks and balances will depend upon whether the parliament, cabinet, and political parties develop their powers and clarify their functions in relation to the monarchy. The position and influence of the monarchy has been strengthened by Istiqlal's policy of extolling the leadership of Mohammed V in the independence struggle and by the monarch's moves to consolidate his power in the period of the split in the party. Although limitation of the role of the monarchy is central to Moroccan political liberalization, the new constitution does not necessarily clarify this issue. Widespread student riots have occurred in protest over Hassan's conservatism. The leaders were hung by Hassan on the charge of attempted overthrow of the monarchy. These events may point to a violent revision of the monarchy system in the future similar to the pattern of Ethiopia.

Despite the limited materials upon which to make a judgment, operation of the new constitutions in both states seems to indicate that a key to the establishment of a constitutional monarchy system is the liberalization of the monarchy. The institution of the monarchy can perform the valuable function of providing order and cohesiveness in the period of transition from the old to the new. On the other hand, the same institution may become a force impeding the development of an effective democratic system. The struggle is between the forces of tradition and modernization. The institution of the monarchy, therefore, may help solve the problems of stability but hinder the government's ability to respond to the pressures for change and liberalization.

PARLIAMENTARY PATTERN

A second pattern of central governmental organization that has been incorporated in the constitutions of the emerging African states is the parliamentary form. The British system of government has been used as one model, since it is primarily the former British areas that have adopted the parliamentary system. Many former French territories have shied away from the parliamentary model because of their fear of creating weak governments. During the colonial period many of their leaders served in the French *Chambre* or in French cabinets. They observed cabinet instability and recurrent government crises first hand. They concluded that France was unable to make the parliamentary system work effectively and that the adoption of the parliamentary form might result in similar cabinet crises and dead-center government in their states.

In their negotiation with the British Government prior to independence, many former British areas accepted constitutions that paralleled rather closely the Westminster model. The Nigerian Constitution may be used to illustrate this pattern. The constitution provides for a two-house federal parliament, with the upper house, the Senate, intended to represent regional interests. The twelve Senators from each region are elected by Regional Legislative Houses upon the nomination of the President. Four additional Senators represent the Federal Territory, and four National Members are selected by the President on the advice of the Prime Minister. Senators are not permitted to serve in the lower house or in the cabinet, and they may be removed if they lose their citizenship, are convicted of a serious crime, or are adjudged insane or incompetent.

The lower house, the House of Representatives, is composed of 312 members who serve a term not to exceed five years. Nigerian citizens who are 21 years of age may run for a House seat with the exception of the North where only male citizens are permitted to stand for office. Representatives serve single-member districts, which are created by dividing the number of House seats into the total population of the state. Redistricting is to occur every eight to ten years.

All legislation must pass both houses. Following the British model, however, power is concentrated in the lower house. For example, money bills must originate in the House of Representatives. If such bills are presented to the Senate at least one month before the end of the parliamentary session and are not passed without amendment within a one month period, they may be sent to the President for his approval without Senate action. Bills that do not involve appropriations may not be delayed longer than six months by the Senate before being sent to the President for promulgation.

Executive power is vested in the President who is the representative of the British monarch in Nigeria. He is the commander in chief of the state, convenes and dissolves parliament, makes all appointments, and performs ceremonial duties. In order to limit patronage and political pressure in the appointment and removal process, a judicial service commission, a police service commission, and a public service commission are created to advise the President on appointments and removals of civil service personnel. In practice all powers vested in the President are exercised with the advice of the Prime Minister. The *de facto* executive power is exercised by the Prime Minister who is a member of the lower house and the leader of its majority coalition. He appoints his cabinet, which operates on the basis of collective responsibility. Emergency power may be voted by the legislature on the advice of the Prime Minister. This provision was used in the Action Group crisis discussed in the last section of this chapter.

Differing from the British system, the constitutional courts are specifically accorded the power of judicial review. This power may be used in cases of dispute between the federal government and the regions, between two or more regional governments, or in cases concerning the constitutionality of the acts of the federal government. Sufficient time has not elapsed since the adoption of the constitution to arrive at definite conclusions concerning the operation of this power in practice.

Although the Nigerian constitution differs to some extent from the British model, its basic provisions tend to be patterned very closely after the British. Other British areas also began independence with similar constitutions, but several of these states have abandoned or modified the Westminster model and moved away from the parliamentary system. For example, Kenya, Ghana, and Tanzania completely revised the original constitution because of the difficulty which they found in making it work effectively. Contrary to the policy of many former members of the French area, Senegal attempted to follow the parliamentary system in the immediate post-independence period but abandoned it as unworkable.

It may be helpful to examine possible reasons for the difficulty that the African states seem to encounter in following the parliamentary pattern. Since British areas have been more inclined to adopt this model, the discussion will center on the British system. The British form is based on the principle of parliamentary supremacy. This principle is one that developed slowly from the period of the Middle Ages. The 1600's brought limitations on the power of the monarchy and acceptance of the principle that the monarchy should act through parliament. The 1800's saw the expansion of the franchise and the gradual establishment of the dominance of the House of Commons over the House of Lords. By the early 1900's the monarchy was divested of all real power and the democratic parliamentary system was based upon the principle of political freedom. Persuasion and argument rather than indoctrination and force were the means used in carrying out governmental programs, and change occurred gradually as consent and consensus was reached on policy questions.

This governmental form evolved and developed in response to power realignments and popular pressures in Britain. The African states have not experienced this historical evolution of the principle of parliamentary supremacy, and political alignments and pressures in the African states necessarily are not identical with those of Britain. The degree of popular understanding and support for the principles of parliamentary supremacy may not be as high as in Britain, and the British model may not meet the criteria of having popular acceptance as the governmental form by which the state is to be governed.

The processes and procedures of the parliamentary system are considered somewhat cumbersome and complicated. In order for the system to run effectively, a knowledge of parliamentary law, of the rules of debate and voting, of the role of the party leaders and whips, and of the functions of committees is necessary. Such knowledge is not well developed in Africa. A small percentage of the African population participated in parliaments prior to independence, and African M.P.'s served a relatively short period of time prior to independence. It is not unusual for a high percentage of the M.P.'s now serving in African legislatures to have had no prior parliamentary experience. These M.P.'s complain that the parliamentary process is confusing and see little point to all the maneuvering or deliberation and debate. Since Africa is in a hurry to reach its goals of economic and social improvement, slowness of action is not considered a virtue.

The relationship between parliament and the cabinet is significant in the operation of the parliamentary system. In the British model, parliament is the supreme organ of authority, and no other institution in the state is competent to override its decisions. Theoretically, parliament has the power to legislate on any matter it chooses or to repeal any action of a former parliament. The cabinet functions as the administrator of legislative decisions and the executive committee of parliament, maintaining continuous consultation with the M.P.'s on matters of policy. The British cabinet is collectively responsible to parliament. Ministers are expected to resign if they lose support of the majority of the House of Commons on a confidence issue, or they may seek to reverse the opinion by asking the monarchy to dissolve the parliament and hold new elections.

In practice, policy proposals come to parliament from the cabinet. The cabinet has become the initiator as well as the administrator of policy. Votes of no confidence are rare. One reason is that much of the decision-making is done behind the scenes. In meetings with the committees of parliament and the party, the cabinet attempts to resolve disagreements over legislative programs and persuade M.P.'s to accept a united policy position. The cabinet attempts to anticipate criticisms and tailor its proposals to gain needed support. The behind-the-scenes maneuvering is important if the government is to be able to operate effectively without cabinet instability. African knowledge and experience with these extra-legal procedures is limited, and they find it more difficult to make the system operate smoothly.

In the parliamentary system, the cabinet operates on the basis of collective responsibility. Consensus is assumed to be oriented toward basic issues rather than a charismatic personality. If consensus on basic goals and procedures has not been achieved, it is more difficult to maintain support for the principle of collective responsibility.

The British parliamentary model also depends upon the operation of an effective two-party system. The cabinet becomes, in effect, the executive body of the majority party in the House of Commons. Party discipline, the party platform, the need to win elections, and the desire to present a united front to the voters help assure the cooperation of the cabinet and the majority of the House of Commons in preventing dead-center government and cabinet crises. African parties tend to be carry-overs from the independence movement rather than political parties in the British sense. Since party structure, party discipline, and party platforms may not be as well developed, the independence party may find it more difficult to perform the majority party role effectively. In Nigeria, regionally based parties have evolved and coalition governments are essential to prevent secession. Such divisive tendencies place additional stress on the system.

The role of the opposition party is important since the parliamentary system provides no external check such as separation of powers. The loyal opposition is an internal check on the system, and criticism by the opposition is important in limiting or moderating majority party power. The ability of the opposition to create sympathy for its views and gain public support in winning seats in Commons represents a constant threat to the majority, since the opposition can become the majority party in the next election if the present government gets too far out of line with popular wishes.

An effective two-party system does not exist in most African states. In the majority of African states, the independence party holds overwhelming power and the possibility of overcoming its majority is remote. A weak opposition is no electoral threat to the majority. If it has no real chance of becoming the majority, its protests and policies may not be taken seriously. Facing over-whelming party numbers in parliament, the opposition may become frustrated in performing the loyal opposition role. A number of opposition leaders have complained that it makes little difference whether their party members are in parliament or not since they cannot control voting results. There is a trend in many African states to outlaw opposition parties completely and to adopt the principle of one-party democracy. One-party rule eliminates the opposition and prevents the operation of the internal check func-tion.

Finally, the British system has the institution of the monarchy, which helps to personify or symbolize the unity and identity of the nation. The Queen performs innumerable ceremonial functions which assist in humanizing the government and relieve the Prime Minister of many time-consuming duties. African states do not have similar institutions to perform these functions. Several states, as Nigeria, have created Presidential or Governor-General offices as a substitute for the Queen. Although they perform ceremonial duties, they do not necessarily symbolize the state in the minds of the people.

The above discussion indicates some of the reasons for the movement away from the parliamentary system in Africa. Several African states, such as Nigeria, Uganda, Sierra Leone, Malawi, and the Belgian Congo continue to follow this form. However, members of the leadership in these states have expressed their preference for the presidential system. The present military govern-ment of Nigeria has indicated a new constitution will be written. The parliamentary pattern appears to be most firmly established in those states with a significant white settler population such as the Republic of South Africa or Southern Rhodesia where the politi-cally dominant white settler population may have greater under-standing and support for the principle of parliamentary supremacy.

White settler domination in these areas has been a major issue in African politics for a number of years. The Rhodesian prob-lem reached crisis proportions by the fall of 1965. White settler domination was encouraged by electoral requirements adopted dur-ing the period of British South Africa Company rule. Company policy provided that all "civilized men" should have the right to vote. In 1898, a common roll was adopted and all male citizens who could meet the income, property ownership, and knowledge of the English language requirements could be registered. In practice, these qualifications eliminated most Africans from the roll. In 1912, income and property requirements were raised to limit African registration. When the constitution of 1923 was adopted, the common roll policy was continued with requirements of annual income of £100 along with knowledge of English. Income and property requirements were raised in 1944 and 1951 to further restrict African registration.

Under British urging, a Central African Federation was formed in 1953 composed of Southern and Northern Rhodesia and Nyasaland. Britain hoped that the Federation would assist economic development of the three areas and provide a lever to liberalize European dominance of Southern Rhodesia. A number of African seats were guaranteed in the Federation parliament to assure greater African participation. However, qualifications for electors were set by each territory, and Southern Rhodesia was able to continue limitation of African participation. For example, only 429 non-whites in Southern Rhodesia voted in the Federation elections of 1953.

African objections to the Federation began even before the federal constitution was completed. Leaders in Nyasaland and Northern Rhodesia were concerned that the Federation might permit Southern Rhodesia to spread white settler domination throughout the three territories. As a result of their pressure and protest, Nyasaland was granted independence in 1963, becoming the state of Malawi. In 1964, Northern Rhodesia, taking the name of Zambia, followed suit. Both states adopted the principle of "one man, one vote," and African majorities assumed power. Southern Rhodesia also began to demand independence, but Britain indicated Rhodesian electoral provisions should be liberalized before independence would be accorded. A new constitution was adopted by Southern Rhodesia in 1961 which made little change in the basic parliamentary form of 1923, but provided for an A and B roll for voter registration which virtually created the separate roll system avoided in the earlier constitution. The A roll elects 50 constituencies or seats in the one-house legislature and requires property, income, and English knowledge qualifications. The B roll elects 15 special electoral district seats and lowers the property, income, and educational requirements. In constituency elections, the B roll is counted as ¼ of the total A roll vote if the B vote exceeds this figure. In electoral district votings, the A roll is counted as ¼ of the total B vote if the A vote exceeds this number. The system is designed to give Africans 15 electoral district seats with the Europeans dominating the 50 constituency seats.

In the negotiations over independence, Britain indicated that the 1961 constitution was unacceptable and should be liberalized to assure a gradual increase in African participation with an eventual move to "one man, one vote." On November 11, 1965, Southern Rhodesia issued a Unilateral Declaration of Independence taking the name Rhodesia. Britain condemned this action as treason and instituted economic measures designed to bring about the fall of the government. African states, particularly the members of the Commonwealth, have urged military action, but Britain has avoided military sanctions arguing that the economic boycott will force the Rhodesian Government to negotiate in the near future. The situation remains precarious, and if economic measures do not have the desired result, it may become explosive.

PRESIDENTIAL PATTERN

A third pattern or form of government which has been incorporated in the constitutions of the newly independent African states is the presidential. This form seems to have found the widest support of the three discussed and has been adopted by the largest number of states. Those states which have abandoned the parliamentary system have turned to this model. The members of the former French areas of Africa generally adopted some form of the presidential pattern after rejecting the French parliamentary system as unsuitable for them. In examining the apparent enthusiasm for the presidential system, an analysis of some of the characteristics of the Gaullist constitution may be helpful, since it has served as a model for many of the former French areas and other African states have borrowed from it in varying degrees.

The Gaullist constitution attempted to reconstitute the authority of the French Republic under a strong presidential system. The principle of parliamentary supremacy was abandoned and parliament was no longer considered dominant over the executive branch. Since the president is not responsible to parliament, he does not stand or fall on its votes of confidence. These provisions are designed to eliminate cabinet instability and crises. Presidential authority includes the power to dissolve the assembly on any issue at the president's own discretion. This permits a presidential check over parliamentary reluctance to support his programs. This power is limited only by the requirement that the assembly cannot be dissolved twice in the same year. An additional control over parliamentary recalcitrance is the president's power to bring issues directly to the people by referendum. If the people approve the proposal, the parliament is bypassed. The president also is granted emergency powers when the integrity of the nation, its independence, or the execution of its laws are menaced. In such cases, the president is empowered to assume the powers of government until the emergency is ended, the determination of which is left to his discretion. The only limitation on this power is that the assembly may not be dissolved during the state of emergency.

In order to place the president on a different political plane from the members of parliament, the president is directly elected by an absolute majority of the popular vote. The provision for a presidential mandate that has a broader base than that of the members of parliament is intended to remove the president from the influence and pressures of the multi-party system.

African states have adopted many of these features in their new constitutions, particularly the concentration of power in the hands of the president and the emergency powers article. These provisions seem to attract the African states, because the Gaullist model centralizes power in one hand or one branch of the government. In contrast to the collective responsibility of the parliamentary system, the concentration of powers in the hands of the president may permit greater centralization of direction and encourage greater uniformity and speed of action. The presidential system may promote unity, since the president serves simultaneously as symbolic head of the state and chief executive authority. Present African governments often center around one man who is the leader of the independence movement and has achieved a kind of hero status in the minds of the people. This leader normally campaigned actively before independence and is generally well-known throughout the state. It may be natural that power is given to him after independence. It also may be easier to obtain popular support for a governmental program or policy if, as president, he is associated with it and is responsible for its administration.

The presidential system avoids some of the problems of dead-center government. In periods of presidential-parliamentary clashes, the president may use his powers of dissolution or appeal to the people over the heads of the parliament by means of the referendum. Since the president is the symbol of unity and a national hero, it may be easier for him to rouse popular support. His popularity also may permit him to overcome opposition or criticism from parliament. Finally, in cases of uprising, civil unrest, or governmental crisis, the president may resort to emergency powers and take over direction of the government.

Although concentration of power in the hands of the president may promote more stable and effective government, it also may create problems in the maintenance of democratic freedoms in the state. In order to assure diffusion of power, the African states have adopted varying forms of separation of powers following the American model. Separation of the executive, legislative, and judicial branches is designed to prevent one branch from dictating to the others and to provide a check and balance system. However, the separation of powers structure adopted by the African states differs from the American model in that the three branches are not presumed to be coordinate. The supremacy of power in the hands of the president limits the ability of the other two to serve as real checks on executive power. For example, the threat of dissolution, the referendum, and the emergency powers can be used to whip the legislature into line and assure adoption of presidential policy. Therefore, the Gaullist model of a "rationalized" legislative branch, while assisting the cause of stability, may result in overconcentration of power in one hand and a potential danger of a dictatorship.

Having looked at the general patterns of government in the newly independent African states, a more detailed examination of the powers and functions of each branch of government may assist in tracing the informal power patterns developing under these systems. Since the majority of African states have adopted a presidential pattern, the following discussion will center on its operation.

EXECUTIVE BRANCH

The African constitutions generally provide that all executive power or authority of the state be vested in the president, and he is responsible for seeing that the laws are properly executed and administered. The president acts on his own discretion in executive questions and is not obligated to follow advice tendered by any other person or body.

The president is given direction over the civil service and authority to appoint the members of the bureaucracy, which permits control over the men and their viewpoints. The appointment power generally is not limited by constitutional requirements that the legislature consent to selections. The president also is responsible for final decision on promotions within the civil service and for removal of members of the service. In the Tanzanian constitution, the removal power is qualified by the requirement that the president take such action only in cases of malfeasance in office or of high crimes and misdemeanors against the state, but the decision on what constitutes malfeasance or high crimes is generally left to his discretion. The appointment and removal powers give the president an important patronage lever that may be used to strengthen his political power and position. Most constitutions do not provide for agencies to regulate and administer merit procedures for the civil service. Tanzania provides for a Judicial Service Commission to advise on appointments to the judiciary. The Nigerian constitution provides for special commissions to advise on all civil service appointments and removals and to administer promotions.

In his relationship with the cabinet, the president has the authority to appoint and remove ministers at any time and on any issue. Legislative approval is not required generally, and cabinet members do not have to be members of the legislature. The cabinet is under the direction of the president and is directly responsible to him. This encourages unity of policy on executive programs.

The executive branch of government is given important grants of legislative as well as executive powers. In some states, the president is empowered to initiate legislation and set the agenda for legislative deliberation and action. In such constitutions, the legislature only proposes amendments to bills introduced by the president, thus being placed in a rubber-stamp position and under virtual control of the executive.

Although the majority of constitutions do not follow this pattern, they permit presidential initiation of legislation. There is generally an article providing for a yearly presidential state of the union address to the legislature in which the executive program is detailed. The president also may address parliament at other times that he deems advisable. In many cases the president prepares the yearly budget and oversees the auditing of the accounts of the state. Since the president supervises administration and execution of policy, there is a tendency to turn to him for detailed information concerning legislative proposals and for expert assistance. The executive branch tends to become a center for information, planning, and operational direction of governmental programs, since the president has expert staff at his disposal. This is not unlike many Western governments that exhibit a similar tendency toward executive initiation of legislation.

Most constitutions provide that all statutes must receive the assent of the president before going into effect. In a number of African states there is no provision for legislative overturn of a presidential veto. The Tanzanian constitution provides that the assembly may return a bill to the president for his assent within a six-month period after his first veto, provided two-thirds of the members repass the bill. The president must assent within 21 days of receiving it, unless he has dissolved parliament in the meantime. Since Tanzania has a one-party parliament, there is less likelihood of getting a two-thirds vote in opposition to the executive, thereby helping to assure presidential dominance over public policy questions and legislation.

A third check on the legislature is the referendum. Most African constitutions authorize the president to go over the head of the legislature in case of delay or opposition to executive programs and take the issue directly to the people. A majority vote brings the legislation into effect without further parliamentary action. The threat of a referendum is a lever in getting proposals through parliament.

A fourth check on the legislatures is the power of the president to call parliament into session at regular and special sessions and to dissolve parliament at any time. In some cases, the president may dissolve at will and call for new elections. His power is limited in some states by the requirement that dissolution may be ordered only after a no-confidence vote by an absolute majority of parliament. As a check on presidential abuse, a few constitutions provide that both the parliament and the president stand for re-election after dissolution. Most constitutions contain the limitation that this power may not be used twice in the same year. In spite of these checks on abuse of power, the threat of dissolution is an additional weapon of the executive.

As a final check on legislative recalcitrance, the executive is granted emergency powers in most constitutions. In some states, emergency powers may be used only in case of war or threat to the independence of the state. In many former French areas, the emergency powers provision is almost a carbon copy of the article in the Gaullist Constitution. Other states grant special powers to meet any "state of emergency." In Ghana, special powers were granted only to the first president. Although there is a wide variety of forms of the emergency power article, most constitutions leave to the discretion of the president to decide when a state of emergency exists. After such a declaration, the president assumes control of the government and is empowered to appropriate funds, legislate by decree, and declare martial law. Some constitutions limit his powers by requiring legislative approval after the end of the emergency. Others prohibit the dissolution of parliament during the emergency. These provisions do not represent significant limitations on the president, since the legislature does not have the power to check action during the state of emergency.

Presidential powers also include the direction of foreign affairs. He is empowered to appoint ambassadors, to negotiate treaties, to conduct national policy, and to command the armed forces. In several states the commander-in-chief power is limited by a requirement that parliament declare war.

Election provisions and procedures for the office of president vary among the African states. In most states, the president is chosen by direct national popular election. In these cases, an absolute majority of all votes cast is required for election. In other states, the president is chosen by a majority of parliament similar to the procedure used in selecting a prime minister. Some states, such as Chad, provide for indirect elections by an electoral college composed of Parliament, local officials, and special categories of chiefs. Most constitutions provide for a five- to seven-year term of office. A few permit removal of the president by an absolute majority vote of the parliament. In the case of Ghana, parliament proposed that Kwame Nkrumah be appointed for a life term, but Nkrumah condemned this legislation as undemocratic and a five-year term was followed. Despite the variety of provisions, all the constitutions attempt to give the president a broader electorate than the members of parliament in order that he may claim national mandate and representation.

In surveying the operation of the presidential system, it may be helpful to refer to an article written by Julius Nyerere, President of Tanzania, in which he expresses his interpretation of the role of the presidency in Africa.[1] Nyerere points out that there are two forms of the presidential system that could be adopted. One is the "President of a Republic." This type involves only ceremonial and formal powers similar to a constitutional monarchy. The second type is the "Executive President," whose powers are both formal and real. Nyerere maintains that the Executive President type is required by the history and experience of the African states for a number of reasons. One is that the people need political systems that they understand and support. The institution of monarch or president is respected and understood in Africa because of the authority and responsibility of the office. A ceremonial or formal institution is not acceptable since "symbolism" is not part of the African tradition. Nyerere indicates the people of Tanzania look to the responsibility of a "person" for authority. This person may be held accountable for his actions to the people or to the party, but he should not be hampered by them in his ability to lead. The executive president must bear responsibility for governmental actions, but he also must have the power necessary to carry them out. This view of the role of the presidency in the state supports the principle of executive supremacy found in the Gaullist pattern.

Nyerere also discusses the concept of parliamentary supremacy. He states that the parliament should be supreme and that the government should operate under a rule of law, but he rejects the American system of separation of powers and equality of the

[1] Julius Nyerere, *How Much Power for a Leader* (Tanganyika, 1962), also printed in *The Observer*, June 3, 1962.

branches of government because he feels that the lines of authority become blurred in the American system of checks and balances. When conflicts occur between the president and the parliament, ultimate power and responsibility should lie with the president. Nyerere admits that a check-and-balance system is an "admirable way of applying the brakes to social change." However, he argues that Tanzania does not need brakes but "accelerators powerful enough to overcome inertia." A check-and-balance system is impracticable if the executive is to be able to function without being hampered at every turn. Nyerere recognizes that the Executive President form contains potential dangers of dictatorship, but he concludes that African governments face an "overriding need to provide leadership." The dangers of a dictatorship must be risked in order to provide the needed "accelerators."

Many of Nyerere's views on the role of the executive would be supported by other African leaders. Emphasis is placed on the need to provide direction, unity, and speed. Centralized power in the executive branch is viewed as the most effective means to achieve these goals. Although legislative supremacy is paid lip service, it is subordinated to executive authority in practice. It is interesting that Nyerere equates the role of the president with the traditional role of the chief. This might appear to be an appeal to an autocratic tradition that would counter the attempts to establish democracy. However, the chief's authority was limited by the necessity to sense the consensus of the community and to act only after an issue had been thoroughly discussed and deliberated. The institution of the chief provided centralization and unity, but it also permitted discussion and criticism. The chief was a mediator as well as an enforcer of the will of society. There may be a tendency to adapt this tradition to modern systems. In present African systems, power is centered in the executive and controls over the population are more severe than might be found in Western democracies. At the same time, discussion of issues and criticism of proposed policies and programs are permitted and debate of governmental action is carried on with vigor. Occasionally executive policy is altered. Although proposals may be deliberated when a program is under consideration, once the executive has reached a decision no further criticism is anticipated. At the point of consensus everyone is expected to obey. Refusal to abide by consensus has been equated with subversion. Prior to the decision on policy questions, debate is curtailed only when it exceeds certain limits. Beyond the limits are the political institutions of the state, the basic goals of the majority party, and unity of the state. If these limits are exceeded, measures of suppression follow.

Most African states have passed preventive detention acts that provide for imprisonment without charge or trial for varying periods of time—generally three months. This legislation has been used on occasion against opposition party members prior to an election in order to restrict campaigning. It also is enforced against opposition elements who follow tactics designed to undermine the president or to stir up tribal loyalties that threaten the unity of the state. The governments justify the use of preventive detention in these cases by arguing that such persons represent "destructive opposition." In other cases, deportation has been used. For example, Ghana expelled Bishop Roseveare for criticizing the deification of Nkrumah and the "Godless aspects" of the Young Pioneers movement. The Bishop also opposed the government's view of the proper relationship between church and state. After a few months of expulsion, the Bishop was allowed to return by President Nkrumah. Some states, such as the Ivory Coast and Upper Volta, have created Courts of State Security to deal with crimes against the state committed by governmental members and deputies. These types of suppressive legislation are designed to prevent certain categories of opposition from operating. Its use indicates a fear on the part of the African leadership that violent overthrow of the government or civil uprising may occur during the transition period. For example, Tanzania used preventive detention to restrict two union leaders who were encouraging mass strikes. President Nkrumah of Ghana invoked preventive detention and emergency powers to put down strikes against the government. Both states were concerned that the strikes for higher wages might get out of hand and lead to open revolt and crisis.

Emergency powers also have been invoked in cases of civil unrest. The Cameroons used this power in the immediate post-independence period in order to put down a civil war. Senegal invoked emergency powers after the Mali Federation split and again in the period of the struggle for power between Prime Minister Mamadou Dia and President Senghor. As a result of this latter struggle, Senghor assumed control and Senegal abandoned the parliamentary system. In the 1954 uprising in Ashanti, President Nkrumah invoked emergency powers to put down the revolt of the Ashanti chiefs in opposition to the government's economic policies. He again resorted to emergency powers after bombings in Ghana and attempts to overthrow or assassinate him. In response to these threats, Nkrumah reshuffled the cabinet and arrested the Minister of Information, the Foreign Minister, and the Executive Secretary of the CPP as the ringleaders of the plot. He then assumed direct control over the civil service and the party. Following the Berber uprising in Algeria and the clash with the Moroccan troops on the Algerian border, Ben Bella invoked emergency powers and dissolved parliament. These examples indicate that presidential emergency powers are used to protect his position and authority.

The presidential appointment, promotion, and removal power over the administrative branch has been used to assure that the men under him share his viewpoints and are loyal to him. Julius Nyerere has said that the notion of the neutrality of the bureaucracy has no meaning in the Executive Presidential system. He charges that Western ministers use "unconstitutional pressures" to assure that they get men in office with whom they can work.[2] Since African constitutions vest the control over appointments in the president, no "unconstitutional" pressures are necessary. A survey of the practice of the African executive branch would indicate neutrality of the bureaucracy is not prized or sought after. Cabinet reshufflings and removal of members of the administration occur periodically as the president moves to maintain an administration sympathetic to his policies. Charges of corruption, disloyalty and plotting to overthrow the government enter into these reshuffles, removals, and arrests.

The referendum power also has been used to strengthen presidential position and authority. In the struggle for power between Mamadou Dia and Senghor which was mentioned above, Senghor used the referendum as a means to gain popular backing for the move to a presidential system, since the legislature was split in support for him and the proposal. After an overwhelming vote in

[2] *Ibid.*

support of Senghor's plan, a presidential system was established. Mamadou Dia was expelled, and the office of prime minister was abolished. Nkrumah used the referendum to establish the one-party system in Ghana, although there was no real opposition from parliament, in order to show popular enthusiasm for his leadership.

Presidential responsibility for the initiation of legislation has been taken seriously. Presidential program for budget, fiscal policy, economic planning, social welfare programs and national defense and security are prepared for the legislature. The president uses his powers of persuasion, his threats of dissolution, and his national position and popular support to assure passage of his measures. Legislative debate over presidential proposals is lively but when conflicts have arisen between the legislature and the president, the president normally has come out victorious. Legislative objection has caused the administration to alter proposals, but these cases are the exception rather than the rule. Legislative compliance with the wishes of the executive results in part from ultimate presidential authority. It also stems from the fact that the president and the bureaucracy are more likely to have the details, information, and facts concerning a given issue. The executive staff is better equipped to prepare complex legislative proposals and to compile necessary statistics and data. In addition, legislative members, as well as the populace, look to the president as the independence leader and national hero.

It may appear that presidential potential for control of the legislative branch is unlimited. Such a conclusion would ignore the role of the independence party. The legislature is generally composed overwhelmingly of representatives of the independence party. It is in the one-party councils that policy debate occurs. The president is the leader of the party in most cases and is respected and looked to for leadership. However, he must stay in step with party wishes and desires. Following the tradition of the role of the chief, he is expected to mediate and sense party consensus. If the president loses the confidence and support of the party elite, his authority in the state may be threatened. Debate over policy occurs in party circles, and agreement is reached on basic principles before the executive acts. Since the legislature is composed largely of the one-party group, it is not surprising that bitter debate does not arise over presidential proposals. The party caucus has already performed the discussion function and some form of consensus has been achieved. Bitter debate in parliament would be more likely to come from the opposition party. Since the opposition parties are small and poorly developed, if they are allowed to compete at all, the opposition is not able to perform its role effectively. This may help explain the limited parliamentary role in policy decision.

THE LEGISLATURE

According to the African constitutions, the legislative power of the state is vested in parliament. The constitutions generally do not state specifically the principle of parliamentary supremacy, but they adopt the principle of separation of powers of the three branches of government. However, a check-and-balance system based upon the creation of three equal branches is avoided to prevent dead center government in periods of executive-legislative clashes. Justin A. Domadegbe, Prime Minister of Dahomey, has described the legislature as "only an aid to the executive at all levels of the life of the nation." Although the executive branch tends to overshadow the legislative branch in power and prestige, it would be a mistake to conclude that the legislature has no influence. Executive-sponsored legislation is not approved without questioning, and government programs have been defeated occasionally through this process. Legislative committee meetings often produce more lively criticism than floor debate. Committee sessions are used by legislators to reshape executive programs to correspond more closely to their viewpoints. Legislative members sometimes resort to extra-legal techniques to express their opposition to administration-sponsored programs. For example, a number of Senegalese parliamentary members objected to the government's Four-Year Plan because it excluded certain projects such as schools, hospitals, and roads that they had promised their constituents. The Assembly President adopted the technique of neglecting to sign the bill for several months, which prevented its publication in the official journal and served to emphasize the opposition of the deputies to the presidential position. Despite such extra-legal techniques, anti-government votes are infrequent. For example, in the 1959 Ivory Coast parliamentary session, the vote in opposition to government-sponsored legislation never exceeded three at any one time.

African parliaments are composed largely of government- or

independence-party candidates. The size of the government majorities may be indicated by the returns from a few of the most recent elections. The Cameroons majority party received 70% of the vote cast. The Mali election gave 99.42% of the vote cast to President Keita's *Union Soudanaise* party. In Somalia, the SNL government party captured 69 seats, and the seventeen opposition parties won only 37. In Gabon, a stronger opposition exists, and the government party polled only 55.38% of the votes, with the opposition groups capturing 44.57%.

African Governments have attempted to encourage the election of majority-party candidates by the use of various electoral devices. Originally many of the constitutions provided for the election of the members of parliament from single member districts or constituencies. Districts were formed by dividing the number of parliamentary seats into the total population figure. Districts were to be as nearly equal in population as possible. Nigeria used this system. Other states abandoned the single member district when they discovered that it tended to encourage the election of opposition party legislators, or those who represented local interests, or in some cases tribal groupings. In some of the former French areas, Guinea for example, a single list system was adopted that permits the electorate to vote for the president and a slate of deputies by means of one check. Since the president is well known and commands popular support, the single list system assists the election of the entire slate. The single list also may discourage legislative members from forming attachments to a district and feeling responsible for the promotion of its interests. Since legislators do not owe their election to a district in this system but to the president or government party, there is a tendency for them to follow presidential wishes rather than those of a given district.

A second procedure decreases the number of constituencies but increases the number of legislators who serve the district. Dahomey, Togo, and Gabon have made of the country a single constituency with a national slate of legislators. Unlike Guinea, however, the president and legislators do not run on one list. Mauritania divided the state into two constituencies. Both systems encourage the election of government-party candidates since local groups have less influence in a national slate. A third technique continues the single member district system but permits a candidate to stand for election in any constituency whether he is a resident or not. This procedure permits the selection of "safe" districts for government candidates. Another system, adopted by Kenya, Ghana, and Tanzania, for example, is to outlaw the opposition party and provide that all organizations and candidates run under the banner of the independence party. This assures the government-party control over the selection of candidates in any given district and the make-up of the legislature.

While these devices foster the election of independence party majorities in the legislature, they operate against the representation of local interests. The executive branch seems to feel that representation of local viewpoints would be detrimental to the national interest, and that "localism" might upset the stability of the state. The executive branch is concerned that national programs be adopted that permit rapid economic and social development. Local interests may run counter to the over-all needs of the state. For example, a local area may pressure for a hospital while the central government plan calls for emphasis on communication development. Localism, regionalism, or an organized parliamentary opposition are considered unnecessary devices of disunity that retard adoption of government programs and deter the government from making rapid progress. African leaders contend that minority representation is a luxury that only a developed nation can afford.

Although opposition parties are not well developed, the president and a small elite do not force their will upon the members of the majority party. The independence party or the single-party structure is a coalition of interests. Selection of the candidates for the legislature often involves hard bargaining and careful balancing of interest groups in order to promote party unity and harmony. The interest groups forming the one-party coalition were discussed in Chapter 3. The necessity to preserve the party coalition checks the executive. The president cannot risk actions that would split the majority-party coalition, since his power and position are dependent upon it.

Information concerning the background and experience of parliamentary members is difficult to obtain, but certain general patterns may be indicated. Parliamentary members tend to come from the secondary-school graduates. A large number are rural teachers with secondary education certificates. Former Civil Service employees from the clerk levels of the bureaucracy also form a significant percentage of legislative members. Farmer or peasant representation is limited, and a small number of professional and business men are found in the legislatures. The overseas college graduates do not gravitate to parliamentary positions in large numbers. One reason is that they are used to meet the shortage of trained personnel available to the civil service. The college graduates also seem to prefer a career in the bureaucracy to the legislature, since administrative careers avoid the necessity to stand for election and to campaign. In addition, some members of the educated elite prefer to remain out of government and politics entirely and pursue private careers. Many young college graduates also find it hard to break into politics when they return home, because they are not well known in their districts and older politicians already control the constituents.

Members of parliament have had a wide variety of experience for their legislative positions. Since the size of the parliaments was increased in the immediate post-independence period (in some cases it was doubled), a significant number of legislators have not had prior legislative experience. Committee chairmen, floor leaders, and other parliamentary officials sometimes are selected from those who served in the colonial parliaments and who have had longer periods of tenure. However, those associated with the colonial period are classed as "gradualists" by some governments and by-passed for leadership positions because of doubts concerning their support for the party program. These positions also are filled in some cases by the party elite who were involved in the pre-independence struggle and who have had practical organizational experience. On the other hand, some states have adopted policies to discourage political leaders from holding legislative seats. Nearly half of the members of the Cameroon parliament were not returned to parliament in the last election because of a government directive against their holding elective positions. The adoption of this policy encourages the election of those who have had no prior parliamentary experience. The government apparently felt it would be easier to control those with less experience. Such policies tend to limit the effectiveness of the parliamentary operation.

The average age of members is lower than in Western parliaments. A larger percentage of African M.P.'s fall in the 35 to 50 age group than might be true in the West. For example, the average age of the American Congress is between 55 and 58 years of age. In the Ivory Coast 39 out of the 54 member legislature were between 39 and 50 years of age. One explanation for the lower average age is that the secondary-educated elite generally come from the younger members of society. Since the secondary-educated elite often began their education in mission schools, a relatively large number of legislators are Christian. In some states, this percentage is as high as 75%.

Parliaments are empowered by their constitutions to set their own rules of procedure. The internal structure of parliaments is similar to that of the West. Standing committees, committee chairmanships, party leaders and whips, the party caucus, and rules on debate and voting procedure are part of the pattern. M.P.'s without previous parliamentary experience often express their confusion over these rules and question the logic of the process. After service in one session of parliament, many members have returned to their village to belittle the parliamentary procedure as slow and cumbersome. These legislators seem to evaluate the parliamentary system on the basis of the quantity of legislation passed and the speed of its production. The deliberation, debate, and questioning that has taken place on any given piece of legislation tends to be regarded as irrelevant. Performance of parliamentary functions is sometimes ceremonial or perfunctory because of confusion over procedure and lack of commitment to the process. Limited experience also prevents legislative members from participating actively in the deliberative functions of parliament. These problems may offer an additional explanation for the limited legislative debate on executive proposals.

Western legislators have discussed at length their dilemma in regard to the representative function. They question to what extent their own integrity and knowledge should enter into their votes or whether they are bound to follow the wishes of their constituents. If they attempt to pursue the latter course, they face the problem of ascertaining what the wishes of their constituents are at any given time on any given issue. African legislators face a similar dilemma. Their problem often is complicated by a less vocal and informed constituency. If the representative does not hear from his constituents, it is almost impossible for him to know their wishes on a given piece of legislation. Majority-party platforms and campaign promises may not help him. It is difficult to feel a "mandate" from the voters on specific measures when the platforms are vague and generally espouse the principles of freedom, economic advancement, and anti-colonialism. It may be questioned whether "peace and prosperity" are more helpful to the American congressman.

Multiple lists, larger constituencies, and nonresidence in the district aggravate the problems of representation. If he does not serve a given district, the legislator will feel less responsibility to it and the channels of communication between the people and the representative may be blurred. Or a legislator may serve a district about which he has little knowledge or experience. For example, an urbanized African may have difficulty understanding the problems of the rural farmer. As was indicated, the executive branch tends to discourage legislators from taking strong stands to protect local or regional interests and desires.

The majority party has certain powers that it may use to control or regulate legislative action. M.P.'s who do not show sufficient enthusiasm for the government's proposals or who insist on defending a policy contrary to the government's position may not receive party endorsement in the next election or be denied party funds. Political office can be extremely significant to the M.P.'s since their parliamentary office may have liberated them from a lower economic status, rural life, and possibly tribal controls. These factors limit the legislator's willingness to take a strong stand against executive wishes.

Some governments have shown their disapproval of divergence from the governmental position by virtually equating opposition to the governmental policy with subversion. Legislators who become too vocal in their criticisms of the executive program have been arrested under preventive detention acts as "destructive opposition" and have been removed from legislative membership. For example, Houphouet-Boigny took such action to remove certain M.P.'s from the National Assembly. The Ghanaian preventive detention act was revised to permit restriction of movement for a five-year period without trial or charge. This can be used to control unapproved political activity. Such government attitudes aggravate the legislator's problems of representation.

There have been reports of bribery and corruption entering into the operation of the representative function. "Dash" is not unknown in African society. Some constituents have offered the payment of a fee in return for a service they desired a legislator to perform. One explanation may be that the constituents are not clear about the legislator's functions and responsibility. The abandonment of the single member district and the government's de-emphasis on local interest also may have encouraged lack of commitment to the district or the constituency. Where fee payment has occurred, legislators may come to regard their parliamentary position as a means to personal gain and as a stepping stone to increased economic status.

It would be inaccurate to create the impression that all legislative members are poorly informed on parliamentary procedure, are ignorant of the issues involved in legislation, or are unconcerned about their function of representation. Able members of parliament who are committed to the parliamentary processes are not difficult to find in each African state. Their present influence can be important, since key positions may be filled by such men. In the future development of the legislative role in the African states, these men also may play a leadership role. Although the legislature is overshadowed by the executive at this point and commitment to the parliamentary process is not high, future developments may alter this picture.

THE JUDICIARY

African constitutions provide for independence of the judiciary under a separation-of-powers system. Judges are removed from undue political party influence by not being required to stand for election. Provisions for appointment of the judiciary vary, but generally the executive is given this power. Since there is often no requirement for legislative approval to presidential appointments, he has virtual control over the make-up of the judiciary and the viewpoints of the men appointed. Presidential power is greater in the immediate post-independence period when a large number of judges are selected to serve in the courts created by the newly independent governments. Several states have adopted the practice of appointing special courts for trial of plots against the state. This permits the president to select the justices who serve on each case. The constitution generally does not prescribe qualifications for the individuals appointed to the bench. The question of the competence of the nominees is left to the discretion of the president. However, criteria may be enumerated in subsequent legislation.

To protect the independence of the judiciary, judges receive life appointments. In some states, compulsory retirement age is set at 62 or 65. In others, tenure continues during good behavior, and no set age for retirement is specified. Judges may be removed for malfeasance in office or for high crimes and misdemeanors. The meaning of these terms is not defined in the constitutions, but the legislature is not prevented from passing statutes to clarify the intention of the framers of the constitution. Removal power also is vested in the President. A few states require the approval of the legislature before removal of a judge. The Ghanaian constitution provided that the president may remove the Chief Justice without check, but until a recent amendment, removal of judges of lower courts required a two-thirds vote of the assembly. Since the parliament operated under a one-party system, the president's ability to obtain a two-thirds vote for a removal action was greater than in a multi-party system. President Nkrumah upon occasion has used the removal power when decisions he did not approve were handed down by the judiciary. For example, he took removal action when the court did not convict the three CPP members accused of plotting to overthrow him. He revoked the appointment of the Chief Justice when Information Minister Adamafio was freed. In March, 1964, he also revoked the appointment of three Supreme Court justices under the provisions of the new constitutional amendment. A special court was appointed to re-hear the case, and judges were selected to serve for the case. A jury of twelve men was appointed to assist in the decision. After a four-month trial, the five defendants were convicted and sentenced to death despite the earlier court decision of insufficient evidence. Those sentenced included Foreign Minister Ako Adjei, Information Minister Tawia Adamafio, and the Executive Secretary of the CPP, Coffie Crabbe. During the trial the Attorney General Kwaw Swamzi charged that the five had the ambition to assassinate President Nkrumah and become the "Stalin of Ghana." Nkrumah's actions caused the International Jurists Commission to condemn him for interfering with the independence of the judiciary. The Commission charged that justices were dismissed at will and that arbitrary imprisonment was occurring without the protection of an impartial trial. Their statement also accused the government of interfering with instruction and legal education in order to indoctrinate students in the government's views. All students entering the three universities of Ghana were required to attend a two-week orientation course at the Kwame Nkrumah Ideological Institute as a prerequisite to admission. The Commission expressed fear that the principle of the rule of law had been abandoned by the recent constitutional revisions and by arbitrary government policy. Similar special courts have been created in the Cameroons, Ivory Coast, Nigeria, Senegal, and Dahomey in cases involving threats against the government.

Constitutions vary on the number and types of courts provided. Provision is made for a Supreme Court, whose jurisdiction and powers generally are enumerated and the number of judges is prescribed. The lower courts are not always specifically named and their jurisdiction is not spelled out in great detail. In some cases, the superior courts are authorized to establish the functions and powers of lower courts. In other cases, the legislature is empowered to make these provisions.

Judicial review is not included generally in the constitutions. Tanzania and Nigeria are exceptions, since their constitutions provide that the supreme court has final power to interpret the constitution. In the other states, legislative supremacy is the rule, and parliament technically has the power to override court decisions by subsequent legislation. This power has been used on occasion to overrule unfavorable decisions. Since governmental majorities in the legislature are very large, it is not difficult for the executive to muster votes overturning a judicial ruling. The ability to invoke such action acts as a check on the independence of the judiciary. Despite constitutional provisions for judicial review, an example of the use of legislative action to overrule a judicial decision came in the Action Group crisis in Nigeria. This crisis arose over a split in the leadership of the Western Region involving Chief Awolowa, the head of the Action Group, and Chief Akintola, the Prime Minister of the Western Region. The Prime Minister was removed by the Governor, and a contest occurred over the control of the office. During the crisis, the question of the legality of the Governor's action was taken to the Privy Council. The Judicial Committee of the Privy Council ruled that the Governor, Sir Adesoji, had the legal power to remove Prime Minister Akintola. The crisis centered around the Governor's removal power as provided under section 33(10) of the Western Region Constitution. Seven months after the removal, Chief Akintola resumed his office as Premier despite the removal act of Sir Adesoji. Following the Privy Council decision, the Federal Government proposed an amendment to section 33(10) providing that the governor could remove the prime minister only after a resolution of the legislature. Since the governor had acted without legislative action, the amendment, in effect, permitted an overruling of the Privy Council decision. Commenting on this action, the Nigerian Prime Minister Abubakar Tafawa Balewa issued the following statement:

> I have given the issues raised by the judicial committee of the Privy Council most anxious thought and I have reluctantly come to the conclusion that of the alternative courses of action open to the Federal Government the most expedient is for it to give support to the constitution of Western Nigeria amendment law.[3]

He concluded that the national interest required the Federal Government to take all steps necessary to assure national unity and the continuance of the federation. A special session of the Federal House of Representatives approved the amendment action by a vote of 242 in favor and 18 against. After the crisis cooled, the Nigerian Parliament passed additional legislation to restrict appeal of cases to the Privy Council. This was done apparently to guarantee greater governmental control over judicial decision.

Although other examples could be used, the Action Group crisis illustrates the executive and legislative ability to go over the heads of the judiciary. The comments of Sir Abubakar indicate the emphasis placed upon national unity and stability as overriding considerations rather than concern for the independence and impartiality of the judiciary. The use of the amendment power brought the constitution into line with actions that were considered favorable to the government's position.

Many constitutions have a bill of rights providing for protection of freedom of speech, press and religion. However, procedural

[3] *The Times,* June 2, 1962.

protections receive less prominence in the African constitutions than substantive rights. Using the same Action Group crisis as an example, the government brought charges against the leaders of the Action Group for treason, felony, and conspiracy against the government. One of the individuals charged was Chief Obafemi Awolowo, the leader of the Action Group at the time of the crisis and the opposition party leader in the Nigerian parliament. Chief Awolowo sought defense counsel from Britain. When the two men who had been requested to represent him arrived at Lagos Airport, they were refused admission and were instructed to return to London on the next plane. The government wished to prevent any non-Nigerian counsel from participating in the case. A similar limitation upon the choice of counsel was followed in the case of Chief Enahoro who was another of those accused of treason, felony, and conspiracy. The refusal to admit these commonwealth attorneys aroused concern and criticism in the British Parliament. M.P.'s questioned whether right of counsel was being denied. Members of the Action Group charged that they were denied adequate defense by this action. Another illustration of the seeming lack of emphasis upon procedural protections is the statement of Mr. Tom Mboya, Justice Minister of Kenya, commenting on the new constitution. He indicated that trial by jury was foreign to Africans and could not be operated if it were open to all races. A third example may be the action taken by a few courts in cases involving questions of evidence. In several cases, the courts have indicated that when issues of evidence arose, the court would presume in favor of the government. In the same Awolowo trial, Judge Sowemino made such a ruling.

Some scholars in the field of law have suggested that a system of justice that stresses due process and procedural protections assumes that individuals restrain themselves in acting with regard to the government. The African governments' seeming lack of concern with procedural protections may result from the belief that such restraint does not exist in their states. The overriding emphasis is placed upon the protection of government stability and reflects a fear of violent overthrow, subversion, and conspiracy. The large number of treason trials suggests that elements of instability exist in these states justifying the fears of violent overthrow and offering a partial explanation for the presumption in favor of the government in such cases.

The apparent willingness of the executive and legislative branches to take action to override unfavorable judicial rulings and procedures; the attempts to control decisions by means of removal and special court appointments; and the emphasis on political rather than legal considerations severely limit the independence of the judiciary. The concept of the judiciary as a check or limit on governmental abuse of power is not given primary emphasis. In demanding unanimity of support for the executive's position, governments move dangerously near a rule of men rather than a rule of law.

In the discussion of the legislative branch, it was suggested that the parliamentary process may not have been well understood in African traditional society. Some scholars of African political systems have concluded that the legislative function was the least developed, and the judicial function was the most clearly defined. They point out that traditional law was based upon hereditary rights and customary procedure that were not changed radically or continuously. The chief function of tribal government was the adjudication of conflicts arising out of these customary rights. If this thesis is accurate, it might be concluded that the adjudicative process is well understood and supported by the mass of the people. Although understanding may be high, there seems to be little support for judicial independence, procedural protections, or the rule of law.

THE BUREAUCRACY

The career bureaucracy in Western societies is considered a possible force for governmental stability. The career civil service may provide continuity of policy and administration, since its membership normally does not change constantly or drastically. Career civil servants may give valuable assistance to political leaders because of experience in and knowledge of governmental bureaus in which they have served for a long period of time. Career bureaucrats may check policies that are unrealistic or poorly conceived, provide detailed information concerning a given problem, or draft practical and workable programs. In the period of the fourth

French Republic, the French bureaucracy was credited with supplying continuity of policy and administration despite recurring cabinet instability and governmental crises. It was viewed as an important element of stability in the French political system. Since the problem of stability receives a great deal of attention in the African states, the performance of a similar role by the African bureaucracy would be significant in the governmental process.

One current problem facing the bureaucracy is the shortage of trained personnel. All African states complain about inadequate numbers of expert and experienced civil servants. For example, land-reform programs have been delayed because of lack of trained administrators. Health, education, insurance, agricultural expansion, and other programs face similar difficulties. Part of the explanation for this shortage lies in the rapid movement to independence. Colonial powers had not undertaken, in many cases, a training program for an African career service. Africans were admitted to the colonial bureaucracy, but their numbers were small and their service was comparatively brief. It has been charged that a visit to any East African colonial secretary office prior to independence would have revealed uniform practices: Europeans at the desks, Asians typing, and the Africans serving tea. Whether or not this is an accurate picture, there is little question that the top posts were held by colonial personnel. The experience of the African in the key discretionary, policy implementation, and administrative positions was limited. For example, in East Africa there was only one African district commissioner as late as 1959. In West Africa, the transfer of power came rapidly in a period of ten years. The colonial powers had originally considered twenty-five years as the minimum necessary for proper preparation and orderly changeover. Africans were admitted to the civil service in large numbers in the ten years prior to independence. However, their length of service, experience, and training for top posts was limited. As a result of this rapid changeover, Ghana and Nigeria have shortages of skilled administrators. In Guinea, three months after the referendum vote, every French official was withdrawn.

Not only is expert personnel in short supply to fill top administrative positions, but there is a shortage of trained secretarial and clerical personnel. Use of inexperienced staff at this level encourages confusion and inefficiency, since policy decisions are not

well implemented. It is not unusual to have difficulty in finding
filed materials, in delivering messages, in verifying appointments,
and other routine matters. The lack of trained personnel at this
level hinders the efficiency of the top echelon of the bureaucracy
and limits their ability to perform their functions effectively or
speedily.

African leaders also complain of the lack of commitment to their
jobs of some staff members of the bureaucracy. An *esprit de corps*
among all members of the service is not necessarily well developed.
This sometimes results in perfunctory performance of a task without concern for efficiency or the end result. Since an administrative
appointment can mean improved status and economic advancement, many Africans seek positions although their understanding
of the functions and responsibilities of the position is limited. The
former colonial service inadvertently created the impression among
some uneducated Africans that a bureaucrat drives a big car, ar-
rives at the office at ten and leaves by eleven, and spends most of
his time at the club. When such individuals are appointed to the
service, the results can be disastrous. It is a common complaint
that some staff members leave unattended important matters of
detail simply because "it's five o'clock."

The Foreign Service of the newly independent states faces a
particularly difficult problem in regard to trained personnel. Since
the foreign affairs of the states were handled directly by the colonial
power during the pre-independence period, foreign ministries were
not maintained in Africa. The foreign office must be created and
built as a totally new department of government.

The problems that arise may be illustrated by the Togolese
experience. Upon becoming independent, the Togolese Government decided to abandon French procedures in the foreign office,
since they were viewed as a continuation of colonial influence. The
members of the Togolese Foreign Ministry were not experienced,
however, in handling the details of filing systems, protocol procedures, or form letters. They finally called upon the American
chargé d'affaires to assist them with these problems. Another illustration of the shortage of trained and experienced personnel
may be seen in the African delegations appointed to the United
Nations. A number of the delegates have graduated only recently
from college and are twenty-two to thirty years old. Several have

had little or no previous experience in the foreign service. The British protocol officer in Kenya indicated a similar problem in creating a trained foreign service for that state. Eighteen months prior to independence, a training program was undertaken. Because of the shortage of time, the Africans were being instructed only in foreign-policy questions of immediate or critical concern to Kenya. Eight individuals were selected to receive intensive training. It was presumed that they would form the backbone of the staff in the foreign office and the overseas embassies of Kenya after independence.

The discussion of the shortage of trained personnel may create the impression that all members of the civil service are inexperienced and untrained. This picture would be inaccurate, since the civil service has able and dedicated members serving in all branches. However, their effectiveness and efficiency is reduced by the necessity of relying on poorly trained personnel to fill positions where there are shortages of experienced reserves.

African Governments are making every effort to correct the problems of shortage of personnel left by the transition from colonial to independent status. One solution has been to undertake recruitment programs for recent college graduates of African universities or students returning from study overseas. Although these young graduates lack experience, they often have a more extensive background than members already in the administrative staffs. The appointment of these young graduates to key posts and the resultant bypassing of older career members has caused tensions and morale problems within the bureaucracy.

A second solution to the problem of the shortage of trained personnel has been to continue colonial civil servants in their positions after independence. The British government has offered to pay full allowances over and above local salaries after independence to encourage British civil servants to remain on the job. Despite these policies, a substantial number of these overseas personnel preferred to return home in the immediate post-independence period. One stimulus for this exodus was the popular demand for Africanization of the civil service. The retention of colonial officers is viewed by many African nationalists as a "vestige of colonialism." Africanization is pushed also to permit more Africans to hold such positions. Africans also voiced concern over the loyalty and commitment of colonial personnel to the new programs and policies. The overseas personnel, for its part, expressed doubts about the integrity and ability of African personnel and the standards of administration that would be followed after independence. A second factor in the unwillingness of some overseas personnel to remain in their posts was the change in their economic and social status that occurred with the ending of the colonial system. The lowering of status was a difficult adjustment for some of the colonial personnel to make and caused a desire to return home.

The significance of the expatriate-officer exodus may be illustrated by a recent governmental report from Uganda. Out of a total of 1100 expatriate officers in service in Uganda, 546 had requested permission to retire from the service. Two hundred positions in the civil service were being offered to candidates from the United Kingdom, since no local candidates could be found. The minister of state, Mr. G.B.K. Mayezi gave a "national emergency message" over Uganda radio. In his address he termed the shortage of technical and professional cadres in the civil service "alarming." It was pointed out that the situation would become more serious, since additional expatriate officers planned to retire in the near future. Despite the recurring demands for Africanization of the civil service, expatriate officers continue to be used to fill vacancies and to train African staffs for various bureaus and offices. In order to calm demands for Africanization of the service, they sometimes work in inner offices where they are not as noticeable to the public. However, the expatriates desire to return home, and the demands for Africanization of the service make the use of such officers only a temporary solution to personnel shortages. The demand for Africanization of the service can have serious political repercussions. For example, anger over the slowness of Africanization by Prime Minister Banda brought open conflict in Malawi. Banda found it necessary to suspend six ministers from the party after accusing them of leading a plot against him and being guided by "avarice and ambition." At his request, Parliament unanimously passed a detention act that permits the Prime Minister to imprison without trial, to dismiss members of Parliament, and to veto applications for citizenship. Banda also undertook a tour around the state to rebuild enthusiasm for him and his leadership after the coup had failed. He traveled to remote areas reminding the villagers that he had led them to freedom. Although he retained power, the coup attempt indicates the problems that can develop if Africanization is not carried out with reasonable speed.

Many governments have undertaken training programs for the civil service. In Uganda, this program is given top priority over all other educational needs. Government scholarships are awarded to outstanding students for training at home or abroad. As students graduate from these programs, the shortage will begin to correct itself. At present, the shortage of personnel limits the bureaucracy in its function of providing expert information and continuity of policy. It may not be in a position currently to serve as a center of stability in the government. After the period of transition is passed, this picture may be altered.

The neutrality of the bureaucracy is a concept that is found in many Western political systems. States, such as Tanzania, that have adopted a one-party system have emphasized that no "artificial distinction" should be made between politicians and civil servants. It is argued that this distinction makes sense only in a multi-party system where continuity of administration is significant because of constant changes from one party to another. Julius Nyerere has observed that in a one-party state such changing back and forth is not a problem, and that continuity is provided by the one-party system rather than the bureaucracy. According to this approach, civil servants properly should participate actively in political affairs of the state, and neutrality should be dispensed with as a principle of governmental procedure. Emphasis upon the political activity and policy position of the bureaucracy may be indicated by the number of removals of civil servants whose views differ from those of the party or the executive. Career service and long tenure in office is not guaranteed by this approach. The civil servant remains in office as long as he shows enthusiastic commitment to and agreement with governmental programs rather than neutrality. The bureaucracy as a center for continuity and stability is weakened by the African view of its role in government. As executive policies alter or governments are overthrown, the bureaucracy faces the possibility of complete overturn of its membership. The building of an experienced and expert civil service is made more difficult under the circumstances. Although the problems of shortage of personnel may be corrected in the near future, the role of the bureaucracy as an arm of the executive would appear to operate against the development of a neutral career service providing continuity and stability.

INTERNAL DIVISION OF POWER

Most African constitutions provide for a unitary rather than a federal system. The unitary form is preferred for a variety of reasons. It may promote stability, since it does not involve a division of powers between the central government and regions, as does the federal. Centralization of power avoids deadlock or clash between two levels of government. In the unitary system, governmental policies and programs do not face possible conflict with reserved regional powers from which federal action is excluded. Since the unitary bureaucracy is under the control and supervision of the central government, uniformity of enforcement, interpretation, and administration is encouraged. In order to de-emphasize local interests and tribal loyalties, some states deliberately have drawn administrative districts to overlap tribal lines. It is hoped that cutting across tribal lines may stimulate the development of a national point of view and loyalty. The unitary system also assures uniformity of electoral procedure and suffrage requirements, which generally are designed to favor the election of national parties or the government party. Centralization of power also permits a single court system and avoids possible conflicts arising from dual courts and jurisdiction. The unitary system not only lends itself to centralization of authority and greater uniformity of policy and program, but it avoids duplication of governmental institutions and personnel. The shortage of trained personnel would be aggravated by the establishment of dual levels of governmental institutions. The cost of a federal system also enters into the preference for the unitary system, and smaller states particularly are critical of this approach as involving excessive administrative units, overlapping of functions, and waste of funds. Finally, since some colonial systems, particularly the French and Belgian, were unitary in structure, colonial practice has served as a precedent for the new states.

Not all of the African states have turned to the unitary system, however. Notable exceptions are Nigeria and the Congo. An analysis of the possible reasons for adopting a federal system may shed light on the power structures and political processes of the two states. The Nigerian federal system stems in part from the British colonial structure. British influence in Nigeria began in the 1860's when Lagos was occupied. By 1886, Nigeria consisted of three divisions: Lagos and its territory under a British governor; the oil coast protectorate under a consul general; and the hinterland administered by the Royal Niger Company. By 1900, the Niger Company's authority was ended and the protectorate of Northern and Southern Nigeria was created. Finally, in 1914, Nigeria was unified under a governor general responsible for the whole area and assisted by lieutenant governors in each region. In practice, the system was decentralized and the lieutenant governors administered each region autonomously.

After World War II, a series of new constitutions recognized the three regions and created regional councils in each. In the North, a House of Chiefs and a House of Assembly were provided. In both the Eastern and Western Regions, a single House of Assembly was instituted. No uniform practice was reached by the regions on electoral procedures and suffrage requirements. For example, the North gave the franchise only to males over twenty-five. In the East, all citizens over twenty-one were allowed to vote. Western universal suffrage provisions had additional property or taxation qualifications. In 1951, regional elections were held for the central parliament. The legislature was to be composed of ninety-two representatives from the North, forty-two for the Western and the Eastern Regions, two from Lagos, and six from the Southern Cameroons. The National Council of Nigeria and the Cameroons (NCNC) considered itself to be the independence party and hoped to win a clear majority. The North formed the Northern Peoples Congress (NPC) to stop any inroads by the NCNC into the North. The Western Region organized the Action Group from the nucleus of a Yoruba cultural organization, the Egbe-omo Odudua. The election results produced no majority party, and strong tribal voting tendencies were evident. The NCNC polled heaviest among the Ibo, the Action Group among the Yoruba, and the NPC in the Northern Hausa-Falani area. The Federal Council of Foreign Ministers under the constitution was to include four representatives from each region. The election returns necessitated the creation of a coalition cabinet composed of the three parties.

During the election campaign the Action Group and the NPC accused the NCNC and its leader Azikiwe of attempting to foster Ibo domination of Nigeria. Statements made by Azikiwe at an Ibo conference in 1949 were used against the NCNC. These statements referred to the Ibo destiny to lead the children of Africa from bondage. Azikiwe had intended apparently only to stir the Ibo to action by his remarks, but the leaders of the other regions used them as evidence of Ibo aggressiveness, which roused tribal suspicions and loyalties. Since the election showed the importance of tribalism as a basis for gaining political power, the continued use of tribal rivalry as a political issue was encouraged with a resultant diminution of emphasis upon national unity. However, regionalism had been discussed prior to this election campaign. For example, in 1947, Chief Awolowo, the leader of the Action Group, commented that "Nigeria is not a nation. It is a mere geographic expression. There are no Nigerians in the same sense as there are Englishmen . . ." [4] Sir Abubakar, the leader of the NPC also concluded that: "Since 1914, the British Government has been trying to make Nigeria into one country but the Nigerian people themselves are historically different in their backgrounds, in their religious beliefs and customs, and do not show themselves any sign of willingness to unite." [5] Although the NCNC moved for a unitary form of government in order to counter the "divisionist" tendencies in the state, it was defeated and the regional system was adopted.

Since the political leaders have used the cultural, historical, and religious differences of the people of Nigeria in election campaigns, a brief survey of the three regions may be helpful. Nigeria illustrates a state that was carved out by a colonial power with its boundary lines having little relation to African political organization prior to the colonial period. In the Northern Region, an authoritarian political structure tended to dominate. By the fifteenth century, the Moslem religion was firmly entrenched in the North, and political and religious powers centered in the emirate and the theocracy of Islam. These leaders tended to be conservative, sup-

[4] *Path to Nigerian Freedom* (London, 1947), pp. 47-48.
[5] *Legislative Council Debates* (Nigeria, March 4, 1948), p. 227.

porting a rigid class hierarchy and political subordination of the masses. Islam was used to build support for the system, since loyalty to the social and political institutions tended to be equated with proper Moslem belief and devotion. During the colonial period, various British policies reinforced the emirate system. The indirect-rule approach perpetuated the political power of the traditional authorities and their dominance in the North. The Emirs administered the school system and controlled appointments to the bureaucracy, which assisted in producing an elite loyal to Islam and the emirate system. Western education was not widely adopted, and exposure to Western political thought was limited. Until 1945, no Northern Nigerian students were sent overseas for study. The British administration limited Christian missionary activity in the North, which also encouraged the entrenchment of the political system attached to Islam. A cash-crop economy came into significance in the North very late, and the land distribution pattern and class hierarchy system were not disrupted significantly. Many Southern Nigerians view the North as backward and autocratic and fear its domination of Nigeria. Since the North represents a majority of the population of the state, this concern is intensified.

The political tradition of the Ibo of the Eastern Region of Nigeria differs from that of the Northern peoples. The basic political unit of the Ibo was the family. Ibo political organization placed less emphasis upon age and status, and youths of ability could be elevated to political power over the elders. Ibo political procedures did not involve excessive respect for authority, and more individualism was allowed. Since Iboland was faced with problems of overpopulation and land pressure, Ibos tended to migrate to urban centers or other regions of Nigeria in search of employment. Scattering of members assisted in the breakdown of tribalism and reliance on the clan. The Ibo showed enthusiasm for Western education as a means to achieve new employment and status, and Christian missionaries were welcomed in Iboland as a source of such education. These characteristics and influences played a part in the Ibo tendency to become more Westernized than the Northerners and to be attracted to radical or militant nationalistic organizations. For example, the Ibos have dominated the NCNC and the Zikist movement. The de-emphasis on tribalism in Ibo history may have contributed to this nationalist and Pan-Africanist viewpoint.

In contrast to the political system of the Ibo, the political organization of the Yoruba involved a kingship structure. It was not an absolutist system, however, and the kings were responsible to councils of hereditary titleholders and could be removed for abuse of power. The system did not permit the individualism of the Ibo, since age and status were more respected in Yoruba society. One characteristic of Yoruba culture was the existence of a significant Yoruba consciousness that stemmed in part from a concept of common origin and an all-tribal political unity. Although differences of political and religious practice existed, the emphasis upon Yoruba self-consciousness persisted. The Action Group appealed to this tradition in its struggle to gain control of the Western Region. Campaigns emphasizing the threat of domination by the Ibo or the Hausa-Falani, revived the Pan-Yorubanism that had existed historically and facilitated the growth of a strong regional party while hindering the development of a Nigerian national movement.

This brief discussion of the three regions indicates some of the areas of diversity found in Nigeria and of the difficulty encountered in building a united state. As a result of British policy, historical development, tribal differences, and campaign tactics, Nigeria moved to the federal system when the present constitution was adopted. The federal system may have represented the best possible compromise, since no national party had developed, and political power and leadership tended to be regionally based.

In the Nigerian regional system, powers are divided between the central and regional governments following Australian or American precedents. The Federal government is a government of delegated powers including exclusive jurisdiction over foreign affairs, defense, fiscal policy and banking, communications, commerce and taxation, and the affairs of Lagos. Powers reserved to the regions include health, agriculture, and education with the exception of higher education. Article 66 provides for federal use of emergency powers in regard to a region. An emergency powers act was passed in 1961 giving the government, during a legally defined emergency, control over arrests, detentions, deportations, searches and seizures, and requisition of property for a twelve-month period. The exercise of these powers is subject to parliamentary revocation, and to a two-thirds vote of the parliament is required before the executive may assume these powers. A state of emergency was declared in the Action Group crisis in the Western Region. When a minority group of Akintola supporters refused to accept the governor's removal of Akintola, rioting broke out at a meeting of the regional parliament. After a special session of the federal parliament, the Prime Minister declared a state of emergency and appointed a federal administrator to govern until the crisis was passed. The decisive action taken by the central government increased its prestige by showing that the prime minister and parliament could move swiftly to meet threats to the stability of the state. Following the Action Group crisis, a new Mid-West Region was created on August 14, 1963, with much of its area drawn from the old Western Region. The houses of parliament of the Western Region were decreased in size after the creation of the new region. The Action Group charged that this constitutional revision was taken to weaken the Western Region and permit NCNC-NPC inroads into Yorubaland. The majority coalition argues that the region was created to give greater representation to various ethnic groups.

The Nigerian constitutional provisions for division of powers between the central and regional governments have a tendency to reinforce the status quo and restrict social and economic change, since significant areas of economic and social policy are excluded from federal control and direction. For example, land reform, agricultural development, health, and primary and secondary education are regional powers. Those who have held positions of economic or social power in the region may remain entrenched in the regional parties. Emphasis upon regional differences promotes the perpetuation of regional parties and restricts the growth of a unified national movement. The regionally based multi-party system has necessitated the reliance upon coalition cabinets and coalition politics, which limit the government's ability to act decisively and swiftly.

On the other hand, the federal approach allows for representation of differences in the regions and permits experimentation in regard to policy and programs. Local differences and desires may be taken into consideration in drafting and implementing regional legislation. Since uniformity of policy in every area of governmental power is not required, a greater degree of diversity may be permitted. Although this restricts unity, it may promote greater freedom. Considering the cultural, social, and political differences among regions, the federal system may represent the most workable compromise at present.

The federal government has certain powers that may play a significant role in the future expansion of federal influence and prestige. One example is the central government's exclusive control of export and import taxes. The revenues from these taxes form the principal source of federal funds. A percentage of these tax revenues is redistributed to the regional governments and represents one-half of the total revenue of the regions. It is possible that a grant-in-aid program similar to that of the United States may be developed to provide federal supervision over the use of funds and to establish federal standards for the programs. If the central government develops control over the type of programs that may be undertaken and the standards to be followed, greater uniformity may be encouraged. Grants-in-aid have been a significant means for expansion of federal powers in the United States. Although no trend toward such federal controls is clearly obvious at this point, federal control over the principal source of regional revenue may become significant in the future.

The growth of a united national party also would encourage deemphasis of regionalism, which presents the potential and constant danger of secessionist movements and the breakup of the state. Several forces exist that promote nationalism and that may become significant in the future. Since the African bureaucracy often served in regions other than its own during the colonial period, it developed a Nigeria-wide outlook. The college student group also has tended to be educated away from regionalism. This is particularly evident among those students who studied overseas. The growth of an urban population also has decreased regional and tribal loyalty. Since these groups have been active in nationalist movements, their influence may promote the eventual growth of a national party.

However, recent elections in Nigeria do not point to the early growth of a united national party. In the 1959 federal elections, the NPC won 134 seats, NCNC 89, and the Action Group 73. The votes in each region indicated strong regional or tribal voting. In the Eastern Region the NCNC won almost 65% of the vote. In the

West, the Action Group won close to 50% of the vote, and in the North the NPC won over 61% of the vote. In Lagos, the vote was split more evenly between the NCNC and the Action Group, but the NPC polled less than 1%. In the Western elections of 1960, the Action Group increased its support and won seats in parliament two to one over its nearest rival, the NCNC. In the Northern Regional elections of 1961, the NPC almost eliminated any opposition with the Action Group and the NEPU (ally of the NCNC in the North) gaining only 10 out of the 166 seats. A similar pattern was found in the Eastern Region, where the Action Group carried only 15 of the 121 seats while the NCNC won all the rest. These elections illustrate a continued one-party domination pattern in the regions and the regional or tribal base of the parties.

The Nigerian single-member district system based upon population creates problems for this regionally based multi-party system, since the Northern region's population represents a majority on the federal level. Fear of Northern domination of the federal parliament stimulated the NCNC and Action Group to greater activity in the North prior to the 1964 federal elections. The NCNC and Action Group, hoping to increase their percentage of the votes in the North, formed the United Progressive Grand Alliance composed of the NCNC, Action Group, and the Northern Peoples Front. The unions threw their support to the Alliance because of NCNC and Action Group support of their general strike in 1964. Southern concern over Northern domination and general agreement on socialist policies overcame Yoruba-Ibo tensions. Although this Southern union may be a hopeful sign of the decrease in East-West tensions, it does not point to a North-South union. In response to the formation of the UPGA, the North formed the Nigerian National Alliance composed of the NPC, the Nigerian National Democratic Party, the Middle Democratic Front, and the Niger Delta Congress. Outside of the NPC, these were dissident groups within the other regions. For example, the Niger Delta Congress is a party composed largely of Ijaws who have campaigned for division of the Eastern Region in order to separate the Ijaws from the Ibos.

Protests were voiced prior to the election over campaigning restrictions in the North and over the drawing of legislative con-

tution. After many unsuccessful attempts, a compromise was reached that centered around a regional system based on the federation of twenty-one tribally based regions or states. In the division of powers, the central government is given responsibility for foreign affairs, defense, customs, currency, foreign trade, immigration and communications. Other powers are reserved to the states. Included in regional powers are responsibility for economic development, law and order, administration and control of mineral rights. Differing from the Nigerian bicameral pattern, the federal level will have a unicameral parliament. Similar to the Nigerian constitution, the federal government is given emergency powers that may be used in cases of regional instability or crisis. The provisions for the federal executive may represent an attempt to compromise between the presidential and parliamentary pattern. Rather than being a ceremonial office, the presidency is to have significant powers, such as the declaration of a state of emergency, and the prime minister may become an administrative official rather than the *de facto* executive authority.

After achieving this compromise, President Kasavubu appointed Moise Tshombe as a "caretaker prime minister" to guide the state through ratification of the constitution and the election of a president. The outbreak of violence and the continued rebellion of the "revolutionary forces" caused postponements of the parliamentary election, but they finally opened on March 18, 1965, with 166 seats in the National Assembly at stake. In order to avoid a multiplicity of parties with the resultant coalition politics, Tshombe attempted to work out an alliance or coalition ticket. He was partially successful with the formation of the National Congolese Convention (Conaco). After releasing Gizenga from prison, Tshombe had attempted a reconciliation with the former Lumumba forces, but he failed to enlist their support for Conaco, and the National Congolese Movement (MNC) opposed Conaco. In addition, many smaller parties endorsed candidates. For example, in the seven house seats at stake in Leopoldville, 65 parties nominated 305 candidates to stand for election. Abako won 3 of the 7 with the other 4 split between Conaco, MNC, Balikilo, and Luka parties.

Despite the multiplicity of parties, Tshombe appeared to have won a victory in parliament, capturing 47 of the 73 seats decided in the lower chamber. A number of races were in doubt as a result of charges involving election irregularities or disputed contests, such as the MNC protests that it was not allowed to run candidates in Yele, Upper Congo, Maniema, Lamani, or Sankuru. Tshombe had invited African states to send delegates to observe the election procedures, and their reports concluded that the elections were run fairly despite such problems as the shortage of ballots in Leopoldville. They also expressed astonishment at the popular support that Tshombe commanded.

The presidential election was scheduled to be held six months after the completion of parliamentary elections. Although the parliamentary election ended on May 15th, the six-month schedule was to be extended in view of the large number of contested seats. Kasavubu announced his presidential candidacy, but Tshombe remained silent concerning his plans. Conflicting reports began to filter out of the Congo concerning Kasavubu's relationship with Tshombe. A number of politicians indicated that Kasavubu intended to remove Tshombe to eliminate a threat to his presidential aspirations. This action finally was taken in the fall of 1965. Although Kasavubu may have thought the way was open for his presidential election, General Mobutu moved with unexpected swiftness before the end of the year to remove Kasavubu and assume the presidency himself. Mobutu announced that his action was necessary as a result of political squabbling and the threat of renewed internal civil strife. Parliament formally elected Mobutu president for five years, and the new president assured the Congolese that the new constitution would be enforced. Kasavubu, Tshombe, and other political leaders were allowed to assume their seats in parliament. In view of the unexpected twists and turns that have characterized Congolese politics since independence, it would be premature to predict that the Mobutu coup has stabilized the situation for the next five years. In fact, some politicians are still proposing an abandonment of the new constitution in favor of some other approach.

In the original constitution adopted by Kenya prior to independence, a regional system also was adopted. Differing from Nigeria and the Congo, the Kenya African National Union had emerged as a majority party and Kenyatta as the national leader. However, issues of tribal loyalties and regionalism were raised in pre-independence campaigning, and the Kenya African Democratic Union was formed as an opposition party. KADU charged that the major tribes, particularly the Kikuyu, would dominate the state after independence. Fear was expressed that the Kikuyu might use their powers to deny the smaller tribes privileges, protections, and land rights. White settler concerns over post-independence policy also entered into KADU campaigning.

In the constitution negotiated prior to independence, Kenya was divided into seven regions plus the Nairobi area. Division of powers between central and regional governments was provided with the central government being granted residual powers. The central government had jurisdiction over all matters not exclusively reserved to the regions. One power reserved was land and land transactions. This provision met the KADU fear of possible land alienation by the Kikuyu. The central government was given emergency powers that permitted it to supercede regional reserved powers in periods of crisis. The central legislature, following the Nigerian pattern, was composed of two houses, a Senate and a House of Representatives. The Senate was to have powers similar to the British House of Lords and was composed of forty-one senators representing the districts of Kenya and Nairobi. The House of Representatives was composed of 117 members representing single member constituencies. Regional assemblies also were created. The central government executive was composed of a prime minister and a unitary cabinet system. A governor general was provided as the symbolic head of the state. The civil service of the federal and regional governments was administered separately with provisions for appointments, tenure, and promotions handled by each level of government.

KANU and Kenyatta expressed their disapproval of the regional system and their concern that dead-center government would result. They argued that Kenya was too small a state to warrant so many levels of government and duplication of personnel and effort. The ability of the federal or regional system to promote stability and progress was tested in the immediate post-independence period. Kenyatta implied that it would be thrown out if it did not work well. Upon his return from the Commonwealth Conference in the summer of 1964, Kenyatta announced that he would propose a presidental system for Kenya. KADU leadership countered by a threat that secession would follow such action. Despite KADU protests, Kenyatta moved to create a one-party state on November 10, 1964. Since KANU controlled approximately three-fourths of the House seats, KADU was not in a position to prevent this move. Ngala, the KADU leader, was persuaded to join KANU and to dissolve the opposition party. After this change was completed, a new constitution was proposed replacing the parliamentary system with the presidental. The president will be the leader of the majority party in parliament. His term of office coincides with the parliamentary term of office. The president appoints his cabinet, which will be responsible to the parliament. These provisions appear to be a compromise between the parliamentary system and the Gaullist presidential pattern, although they do attempt to strengthen the office of the executive. The regional system was not abandoned in the constitution, but it was altered significantly. Regional assemblies will be continued, but they will have no exclusive authority or legislative competence. Regional and local authorities will be employed as the agents of the central government rather than maintaining a separate civil service. These changes are intended to permit greater centralization of power and uniformity of policy. The emergence of a national one-party system facilitated the revision of the federal system. By these new provisions, Kenya has moved closer to the pattern found in the majority of African states toward greater centralization of power, uniformity of policy, and de-emphasis on the forces of division and disunity.

Attempts have been made to create federations of various states of Africa. One example is the Ghana, Guinea, and Mali union, which remains pretty much on paper without implementation of the common government, currency, and other provisions. A more successful federation attempt came between Tanganyika and Zanzibar. In 1964, the Afro-Shirozi Party let a successful coup against the government. The revolution was a protest by the African majority against the Arab minority and the constituency system, which was felt to prevent Africans from gaining control of the government. After the coup, the Afro-Shirozi Party was declared the one legal party in Zanzibar, and a Revolutionary Council of thirty ruled by decree. Concern was expressed over the stability of the state and the growing dependence upon Chinese Communist support and assistance. On April 23, 1964, Tanganyika and Zanzibar signed an act of union creating the single sovereign State of Tanzania. In implementing this union, the Tanganyika cabinet was enlarged to include five Zanzibar members. The act of union proposes a united government with a common cabinet, parliament, court system, and bureaucracy. These steps are to be taken gradually.

Various explanations have been given for the creation of the union. One was that Zanzibar was not economically viable and would have to rely on outside assistance. Another was that Tanganyika was concerned over the growing Chinese influence in Zanzibar and feared the use of the island as a training center for the eventual subversion of the mainland. It was also suggested that President Karume and his supporters in the Afro-Shirozi Party were apprehensive over growing Chinese influence in Zanzibar and doubted their ability to remain in control of the situation. They may have hoped that Tanganyika machinery for control might assist them. The official explanation for the Union was that it was a step forward in the creation of African unity and the goal of the federation of East Africa (PAFEMECSA).

Despite the apparent enthusiasm for East African unity, Tanganyika had notified Kenya and Uganda in April, 1964, that she would withdraw from the East African Common Market unless immediate steps toward federation were taken. Kenyan and Ugandan officials interpreted this action as a move to break up the Common Market and forestall any hope of federation. Tanganyikan steps to create a separate currency, freeze the volume of trade between the three states, and levy tariffs on the products of the other two was viewed as additional evidence of a movement away from federation with Kenya and Uganda. One major point of controversy surrounded the question of new industry and economic expansion in the three states. Kenya and Uganda had proposed a "fair share" formula, but Tanganyika had demanded that all expansion should occur in its territory in order to bring it closer to the Kenyan economic level. Although the creation of Tanzania was heralded as a first step in the creation of an East African federation, these problems raise doubts concerning further expansion to include other East African states.

CHAPTER 4

Policy

INTERNAL DEVELOPMENT POLICIES

AFRICAN GOVERNMENTS ARE UNDER PRESSURE TO ACCELERATE the economic growth rates of their states. Independence campaigns equated *Uhuru,* freedom, with economic and social development, improvement of living standards, and expanded educational facilities and employment opportunities. The people of the newly independent states expect their governments to achieve noticeable results in the immediate post-independence period. The failure to realize these expectations has contributed to instability and demonstrations against the government. Examples are the revolts in Tanganyika, Uganda, and Kenya by the servicemen demanding increased salaries. Labor also has been vocal in its demands for higher wage levels and expansion of employment opportunities. Many states have experienced widespread strikes and protest demonstrations. In June of 1964, Nigerian labor called a general strike to express grievance over the government's failure to meet its wage demands. The strike closed most industries, port facilities, railways and airlines. Water supplies were cut off in Lagos and the Health Department warned of possible epidemics. The week-long strike seriously crippled the Nigerian economy and showed the strength of the labor movement. The government finally agreed to a slight wage raise, although it could not meet labor's demands because the economy could not absorb the increase. In Kenya, 16,000 railroad workers called a general strike demanding higher wages and dismissal of all officials with a "colonial mentality." Sympathy strikes were threatened by postal and transport workers. The government protested the strain on the economy caused by wage demands. Ghana invoked emergency powers to prevent strikes for higher wages. Nyerere adopted strict controls to limit strike activity and urged labor leaders to support government policies in avoiding economic instability. Dahomey has asked for a strike ban until the standard of living has been raised throughout the state.

Labor unions are encouraged to adopt a "to each according to his needs" principle for the division of the wealth of society. Labor's function is viewed as production, and unions are reminded to concentrate upon the expansion of the productive capacity of the state rather than demanding an ever-rising living standard for union members. TANU has pressured the Tanganyika Federation of Labor to get its support for increased production quotas and to keep the demands of its members within proper limits. A "fair share" standard attempts to regulate the income of laborers so that it is in proportion to other areas of the economy. Wage increases are opposed, since they upset government planning and divert funds intended for development projects. It is feared union demands may encourage an urban-rural imbalance, since higher urban wages tend to stimulate an increasing exodus from rural areas. African governments wish to avoid rural depopulation, which would upset agricultural development and bring increased population into urban areas where unemployment is already a problem. Senghor points out that Senegalese government officials' average annual income is 360,000 CFA francs, union members 180,000, and farmers 10,000. Trade Union members' average monthly wage is 18 times higher than that of the peasant. Senghor criticizes union members for pressing for social security and welfare programs when they already have achieved "economic security." He has proposed a temporary freeze on all salaries and adoption of a system to assure proportional increases throughout the economy. Since the peasants form 90% of the population, Senghor argues their welfare must be protected against the union member or the government bureaucracy. Despite the claims of classlessness of African society, many governments express fear that the union member may develop into an economic elite. In order to prevent the growth of a labor class, African leaders reject the concept of union independence from the party. Nkrumah has stated that no one is an honest labor union leader unless he is a loyal member of the CPP. Union leaders who work only for the good of the union member are said to affect adversely the growth of the society and ultimately the union member. Nyerere terms the doctrine of independence of the union movement an "absurdity."

Many states also are experiencing the growth of an entrepreneurial class. For example, a Ghanaian middle class is beginning to grow up around cocoa farming. In Senegal, a similar class is emerging among the peanut exporters. Most governments have not taken action to prevent the growth of the entrepreneurial class, but the leadership has warned against "personal adventures" by party members and bureaucracy. Nkrumah has warned against the creation of a ruling class of self-seekers and careerists. Party discussions stress the evils of bureaucratism, careerism, and nepotism in the party or in the government. Contrary to Ghanaian and Senegalese policy, Mali and Guinea have adopted state trading as one method to prevent the growth of the middleman. Touré and Keita have campaigned against the creation of a selfish and privileged class and have admonished party members for counting their personal gains and desires ahead of the party. Despite these actions, the Mali Minister of Development has admitted that classes will evolve as modernization of the economy occurs.

Many states argue that the organization of all classes of society within the one-party system will prevent class warfare and struggle, since all members of society will be united in a common movement. African leaders view the rise of an educated African privileged class as another potential danger. They argue that European and Asian settlers who formed a privileged class are on the way out and will eventually disappear, but they fear that the African educated elite may replace the European and become a new "capitalistic group." The co-operative movement is another means adopted to control the growth of the middleman or the entrepreneurial class, and deter the development of an African bourgeoisie.

Governments favor a policy of greater equality of income among all members of society. Nyerere has indicated that when one group feels it should receive a larger proportion of the resources of the economy than another, it is exhibiting a "capitalistic attitude of mind." This attitude, according to Nyerere, involves the exploitation of fellow men. Nyerere refers to the traditional society in which everyone was a worker and contributed to society, and no one lived off the labor of another. He proposes to establish a communal system in which everyone is considered to produce something of intrinsic value to society. Although one person may have greater training than another, one may contribute a product of greater value, or another may have greater skill or ability, they all produce something of value. Nyerere concludes that any society has only enough productive capacity to supply the basic needs of its members. In the African Socialist System, each man will contribute according to his talents and be paid according to his needs. Senghor, in commenting on equality of income concludes that it could not serve the public interest to follow policies that would increase the disproportion between the living standards of the classes of workers now in the process of formation.

In attempting to achieve desired economic growth, African states face a number of similar problems. Government programs propose to shift the economy from subsistence agriculture to modern industry. It is estimated that eighty to ninety percent of the African population presently is engaged in agricultural production. A large percentage involves subsistence agriculture in the self-sufficient village system. Not all production is of this type since a cash-crop pattern was introduced during the colonial period. However, cash-crop production primarily concerns one crop, for example, in Senegal, the peanut; in Ghana, cocoa; in Tanzania, sisal; and in the Ivory Coast, coffee and cocoa. One crop production forms the bulk of the export of the African states and represents a principal source of export revenue. Reliance upon one crop for overseas credits has proven unreliable as a steady source of income. In the past few years, revenues have fallen as a result of lower world prices for many agricultural products. The resulting decrease in overseas credits has forced the postponement or readjustment of development programs. In some cases, the decline in revenue has necessitated some degree of economic retrenchment further aggravating the demands for wage increases. For example, Ghanaian economic plans were revised downward as a result of a five-year decline in cocoa prices, and investment projects have been restricted. In 1963, visible imports were up 11%, while export earning declined from £G 46m in 1962 to £G 28m. This decline was accompanied by inflation of prices on locally grown products. The serious economic effects of the decline in agricultural prices also may be indicated by export volumes. Although Ghanaian co-coa export rose 5% in volume from 1960 to 1961, revenue was down 15.4%. Cameroon revenue was down almost ten million dollars because of cocoa price decline. In the Ivory Coast, revenue was up about ten percent, but export volume rose over forty per-cent. Senegalese revenue totals increased only slightly despite a twenty-five percent production increase in ground nuts. In Guinea, coffee exports fell from 11,500 tons in 1958 to 7,000 tons in 1963 and bananas from 80,500 in 1958 to 50,000 tons in 1963. Part of the explanation was increased local consumption and lowered pro-duction. Some observers of the African economy conclude that a sustained demand for the primary products of African agriculture is of greater significance to economic growth than foreign aid pro-grams. Falling raw material prices have had a serious effect upon revenue totals that foreign aid has not been adequate to offset.

Mineral exporters have not experienced the same revenue de-cline and resulting economic entrenchment. Their income pattern has improved as a result of rising mineral prices on the world market. Iron ore and bauxite exports from Guinea were primarily responsible for higher revenue levels. Not all of the African states have significant mineral deposits for export, and in some cases these deposits are not developed. Therefore, a mixed mineral and agri-culture export pattern is not necessarily the answer to the prob-lem of falling revenues.

In attempting to stabilize agricultural prices, some states have created government trading corporations or boards. These agencies control the export of products for market and attempt to regulate world market prices by monopoly trading. In the World War II period, the British established trading export monopolies to regulate inflationary pressure in her colonies. Farmers were paid less than world market prices, and the surplus was invested in sterling secu-rities. In the 1950's, economic development projects were financed by use of these reserves. After independence, the newly emergent governments also called on these reserves to spur economic growth. Falling world prices on some agricultural products made it im-possible to rebuild the reserves or stabilize the prices that farmers received for their products. Although Ghanaian cocoa farmers were promised price stabilization when they accepted lower prices during World War II, such subsidy payments were impossible because the reserves were depleted. Sierra Leone has adopted stringency measures because of the pressure on its reserves.

States are attempting to promote diversification of agriculture, which is intended to eliminate reliance upon one-crop production and maintain revenue figures at more stable levels. If prices on one crop are down on the world market, prices on another may be high enough to offset the loss. Diversification of agriculture and the increase of production levels require the agricultural community to adopt new techniques. Improved methods of planting, seed research, and crop rotation are being studied and government projects for education have been undertaken. In Senegal, over seven thousand "rural promoters" were selected for a three-week course of study on improved agricultural methods. These promoters or county agents are responsible for the teaching and adoption of new methods in their rural districts. Increase in production levels may require re-allocation of land ownership patterns, since holdings are sometimes too small to permit effective cultivation, and since the traditional land holding pattern in some states is communal. Governments have moved slowly on the question of the adjustment of individual ownership but have encouraged co-operative development utilizing the communal land system as a base. In Tanzania, the Kilimanijaro National Planters Association was formed to coordinate the activity of African coffee producers. Its primary function was the co-operative marketing of coffee, but the Association gradually moved into the management of coffee factories. Its membership grew to over three hundred thousand. The Association also opened a college to provide greater educational opportunities for its members. This type of co-operative development is strongly encouraged by the government. The Tanzanian five-year plan proposes to double income by 1980 by emphasis on the co-operative sector. The government subsidizes co-operative development by utilizing co-operative organizations in administering and implementing government programs supervised by the Tanzania Agricultural Corporation. A serious problem impeding the development of co-operatives is the lack of membership personnel with needed clerical or administrative experience. Several states promote village co-operatives to encourage adoption of new agricultural methods and communal use of tools and skills. The Cameroon has divided the rural areas into departments. *Com-*

munautés villageoises with populations of 20,000 to 30,000 are to
be developed in each department. The Guinean government has
created state farms and livestock herds and moved toward collectivization of all land. In response to rural opposition to the PDG
plans for rural communities, the government has pledged full economic mobilization and intensified education programs to overcome
rural unwillingness to participate. Peasant opposition may be a
factor in decreased agricultural production levels in Guinea. Most
states reject collectivization of agriculture, but model farms have
been established to serve as examples for the farmers in the region
and as research and experimental stations. Ghana has developed a
number of state farms that also are producers of foodstuff requirements helping to decrease Ghanaian foodstuff imports.

Development plans emphasize that agriculture should supply
the raw material needs of the state. It is hoped that a diversified
and modern agricultural system will provide the food requirements
of the population and the raw material uses of industry. The shift
from one-crop production to a more nearly self-sufficient agricultural economy will decrease the reliance upon overseas imports
of foodstuffs, which would free funds for purchase of needed heavy
capital goods. Although a shift from cash-crop production would
decrease agricultural exports, it is expected that the loss of export
revenue would be offset by industrialization.

African governments have established a priority system for al-
locating resources in attempting to stimulate industrial growth.
Given top priority is the development of power plants to run an
industrial complex. The Nigerian project envisions an output
equal to the 1954 output of Austria. In Uganda, the Owen Falls
project already supplies power for Nairobi, and there are proposals
for expansion. Ghana places great emphasis upon the Volta River
project, and the Inga project under study on the Congo River
projects a plant ten times the size of the Grand Coulee Dam. These
power developments also are intended to supply the water and ir-
rigation needs of urban and rural areas.

Communication expansion is considered essential to industrial
and agricultural growth and generally receives secondary priority
status in development plans. Internal market development is dependent upon good roads, water transport, or air communication.
The inability to transport goods from producer to market seriously

hinders internal development, and many states devote as much as thirty percent of their budgets to communications projects. Expansion of agricultural production is pointless unless the product can be transported to market. In some areas, dry-weather roads and portage by foot are the only means available at present. In the rainy seasons, flooding and the closing of dry-weather roads make transport to market virtually impossible.

In the colonial period, capital and business ownership in the newly independent states tended to concentrate in the hands of foreign investors and firms. Since foreign investment is an important source of development funds, African states hope to expand it if possible. The encouragement of foreign investment presents a dilemma, since the states have adopted goals of Africanization of the economy and the ending of "neo-colonial" control. Since governments find it difficult to justify the continuance of a foreign business community that is not reconciled with a poorer African population, they assert their right to regulate activities of foreign corporations. Stringent government controls over the foreign business community have stimulated an undesired flight of capital, and restrictive policies have precipitated the withdrawal of investments and the exodus of the foreign community. Although this results in "Africanization" of the economy, it does not promote needed foreign investment. For example, Tunisia lost one-half its foreign population after independence partially as a result of stringent policies. This exodus contributed to an annual three percent decline in gross national product. The Tunisian example is well known in other African capitals, and governments are attempting to avoid a similar flight of capital. Nigeria and Senegal hope to attract foreign business by giving guarantees of no nationalization of foreign investment. In addition, the Senegalese Government insists upon a share of the ownership in foreign enterprises, to assure some government direction over policy. Despite moderate policies, the Senegalese level of foreign investment has been lower than anticipated. As a result, the four-year plan was revised downward cutting industrial estimates from 80 to 60 percent, and health and education projects were retrenched. Guinea nationalized some foreign investments and shut down foreign banks and trading houses in the immediate post-independence period. These actions had the effect of decreasing the rate of investment. After 1961, foreign investment was again encouraged, but it proved awkward since Africanization of the economy had been a pre-independence slo-gan of the PDG. In 1964 the PDG returned to the monopoly of the State Trading Corporation and ended licenses for private trading. Foreign business has been reluctant to invest large sums in Africa because of doubt over future government policies toward private enterprise, concern about government instability, and the inability of the states to supply needed technicians and skilled labor or ade-quate distribution and transportation facilities. The shifting back and forth on policy that has occurred in states such as Guinea accentuates these concerns.

To promote rapid industrial expansion, states have established varying degrees of government controls over the economy. The Guinean State Trading Corporation is given power to regulate all import and export operations and fix prices. Generally, govern-ment controls over the economy are not this broad. Attempts at tight regulations meet with qualified success, since government machinery is weak and the people object or refuse to co-operate. Most states follow a policy of mixed state, co-operative, and pri-vate enterprise. Kenyatta has indicated nationalization is not nec-essary for the Kenyan economy, but some consolidation will be undertaken by establishing state-owned companies acting as focal points for reorganization and export trading. Senghor maintains that private capital should be encouraged, since private enter-prise will train African personnel, reinvest part of its profits in the state, and contribute to state revenues by taxation. Senghor pro-poses three sectors for the Senegalese economy: a social sector for agriculture, a mixed sector for public utilities, and a free sector for banking and commercial industries, which will be regulated by excess profits taxes. Senghor concludes that underdeveloped soci-eties that adopt nationalization policies kill the goose that lays the golden eggs.

Development of industry involves the expansion of the skilled labor and professional force. African governments place high pri-ority upon the expansion of educational opportunities in order to build this trained labor force as well as an educated citizenry. Many states devote thirty to forty percent of their budgets to educational expansion. Since literacy rates fall below 50 percent in most states, elementary education is of primary concern. However, plans also emphasize the need to expand higher education. For example, Tanzania hoped to increase high school certificates from 104 in 1960 to 620 in 1964. Expanded college enrollment at home and overseas is encouraged by government scholarships or assistance, and new college and university facilities are being built in many states. Development plans hold the creation of a national education system and state control over curriculum and teaching personnel as a goal. Mission schools are to be discontinued at the earliest date possible. However, few states have established a national education system with government regulation exercised at all levels. Although mission schools have been closed in Guinea and the government regulates all curricula, mission schools still play a role in many education systems and receive subsidies in a few states. Mission schools help to meet the shortage of trained teachers as well as inadequate facilities. The Tanzanian five-year plan admits the necessity of relying on 1200 expatriate teachers over the entire five-year period. These shortages make the closing of mission schools more difficult.

Expansion of educational facilities has not kept pace with the demands for training in many states. For example, the Kenyan Government estimates that 120,000 students will take the KPE exams in 1965, but only 10,000 will be able to continue study at the secondary level. The government study concludes that a minimum of 95,000 of this student group will not find educational opportunity and that employment possibilities for them are dim. Where significant numbers of the younger population are blocked both from advanced education and employment, governments face a potential force for unrest, discontent, or even violence. Employment opportunities must be expanded to meet the demands of the elementary graduate and absorb the growing numbers of secondary school graduates. Although Africanization of the economy requires increased numbers of professional and technical workers, the elementary graduate is not necessarily trained to fill these positions and the secondary graduate may not have the necessary skills either. If employment opportunities for the elementary graduate do not keep pace with education expansion, serious problems may result. Despite emphasis upon the training of African cadres, many states must continue to rely on outside assistance. Senegal has asked for French technicians, nurses, teachers, and engineers to fill personnel shortage. The Peace Corps also helps to fill the gap in many states.

A more detailed description of the development programs of the African states may be of interest to the reader. Although planning varies from state to state, analysis of over thirty programs would exceed space limitations. A member of what is termed the "militant socialists" and one of the "moderate socialists" may serve to illustrate some of the differences in approach, of which Ghana and Nigeria serve as examples.

Kwame Nkrumah has termed the CPP philosophy *consciencism*. He argues that the three segments of African society—traditional, Western, and Islamic—coexist but are in conflict with each other. Consciencism will permit traditional African society to be reconstituted with the Western and Islamic segments representing only "experiences" of the traditional society. The goals of consciencism are the "egalitarianism of human society" and the "logistic mobilization" of resources to achieve this end. In discussing the egalitarian nature of man, Nkrumah stresses that man is one and that all arise from the same evolution. Conditions for the development of one should become the conditions for the development of all. Each man should be treated as an end and not merely a means. Planned development is considered essential if the egalitarian society is to be protected. Government plans are designed to prevent emergence or solidifying of classes. The CPP opposes the breakdown of society into classes of "exploited" and "exploiters." All groups within the society are encouraged to ally closely with the party and work through it in promoting their interests.

The first step in the restitution of African society is the liquidation of colonialism wherever it is found on the African continent. After independence, the orientation away from the "destruction of colonialism" will be the period of "severest danger." The state must seek to contain the spread of interests created by the "capitalistic habits of colonialism." The negative force of neo-colonialism will be countered by socialist positive action backed by the mass party. The multiple party parliamentary system will be abandoned since it may be used by capitalist interests to perpetuate the *have* and *have not* struggle.

CPP planning proposes to divide the economy of Ghana into five sectors. The first is the state sector in which state enterprise and ownership will be exercised. The second is the state-private sector in which state and private enterprise will co-operate jointly in development programs. The state will either control part of the stock of the private companies or supervise their operation. The third sector is the co-operative, which is emphasized as a means to eliminate the growth of the middleman in rural areas and an entrepreneurial class in industrial areas. Individual land holding is not outlawed, but co-operative marketing and farming are encouraged. The fourth sector is the private-enterprise sector. The CPP recognizes that "private capitalist investment" has a place in Ghanaian economic plans, and the socialist program does not envision an economy in which all private capital and ownership has disappeared. The CPP platform admits that its brand of socialism is compatible with a vigorous private sector. However, state control over the basic resources of society is considered essential to economic growth. The Trade Ministry is authorized to issue licenses for import or export. Its powers have been used to shift resources from the private sector to the joint sector. For example, the Ministry has refused to renew the licenses of certain private industries that have been reluctant to participate in state programs. The significance of this power may be indicated by the three thousand unemployed created in the private sector by a recent Trade Ministry refusal to renew certain licenses. Finally, the fifth sector of the economy is the workers-enterprise section. In discussing the organization of society into these five sectors, the CPP does not prescribe what percentage of the total resources or wealth should be devoted to each sector, although emphasis is placed on the state and co-operative sectors. Several modifications in resource allocation have taken place in response to export revenue decline and popular pressure.

The plan envisions more complete state planning and controls in the future with the government determining the percentage of resources to be spent on the various sectors of the economy and the percentage of income to be taxed. Maximum income levels will be established and controls over individual wealth are to be instituted gradually. Eventually, the types of agricultural and industrial production will be government controlled with quantity and quality regulated. Planning includes the educational system and the curriculum to be taught at each level. The numbers of engineers, doctors, agricultural workers, and machinists are to be designated and the government will use various inducements, such as scholarships, to assure that the desired number enter each field. The University of Ghana underwent re-organization as a part of educational planning. Instruction in agriculture and applied science was added to the curriculum, and the state assumed control over course content and instruction in order to assure that graduates would have the type of training needed in economic planning. It has been charged that these controls have been used to prevent opposition to the government as well as to promote economic growth. The requirement that all college students be instructed in "ideology" receives the greatest criticism.

In promoting the egalitarian society, the CPP supports a series of welfare services and programs. A Housing Corporation was created to supervise the construction of public housing programs in the cities and improved facilities in the villages. Self-help is a part of this type of program. The government provides equipment and technical advice, but those receiving aid are expected to supply labor and contribute a part of the cost of the project. The Welfare Department normally waits until it receives a request for aid before acting. Some requests are for projects that the department does not consider essential to development. For example, many villages requested a post office in the early post-independence period. The Welfare Department attempted to encourage the construction of sanitation facilities, but it met resistance or apathy in several cases. Welfare administrators discovered that it was easier to interest village members in sanitation after they had a post office. One step in modernization apparently encouraged others. Therefore, requests for nonpriority projects are allowed when budgets will permit it to overcome apathy toward those of higher priority.

The Department of Social Welfare has established a National Health Service. The Service includes vaccination centers and research laboratories for diseases such as yellow fever, sleeping sickness, and malaria. Scholarships for medical training are available for qualified applicants, and the government has subsidized a medical college and nursing training centers. Public health centers have been opened in several areas, and public health education programs are carried on periodically. A rehabilitation program is administered under the Ministries of Social Welfare, Health, and Labor. The Minister of Social Welfare is responsible for collecting information on disabilities, and the Minister of Labor is charged with notifying the Ministry of Health of any disabilities that occur in the labor field or that are discerned in registration for employment. Three thousand pounds are devoted annually to subsidize rehabilitation training. The Minister of Education is responsible for providing special classrooms and facilities, and one school for the blind has been opened. In addition to education programs, disabled workmen are also paid lump sum awards.

The Social Welfare Department provides a number of urban welfare services. Child-care centers and day nurseries have been opened for children of working parents. Boys and girls clubs and centers provide recreation and amusement facilities. Youth organizations such as the Boy Scouts have been superseded by the Young Pioneers Movement. Some centers have been opened to care for the aged and the senile. Such a center exists at Bekwai and accommodates about seventy older persons. Family Welfare Centers are provided to assist with marital difficulties and reconciliation. The Kwame Nkrumah Trust Fund, which is financed by private contribution, is distributed to community organizations such as the Red Cross.

In addition to the funds devoted to the elementary and secondary school systems, adult education programs are planned. An adult literacy program has been instituted to encourage extension classes in reading and writing both for urban and rural areas. Industrial schools have been opened to provide vocational or applied scientific training, and government assistance in the form of scholarships or living allowances is available to those with ability.

As the final step in achieving consciencism and the restitution of African society, Nkrumah emphasizes the creation of a political union of all independent African states. This union is necessary to achieve the egalitarian society, overcome the forces of colonialism and neo-colonialism, and avoid Balkanization, which he considers to have deterred the growth of Latin America.

The economic report for the first six months of 1965 indicated serious problems in Ghana. The cost of living jumped 30% since January, 1965 and the national debt soared to $185 million despite higher taxes. In 1964, Nkrumah attempted to raise cocoa prices by withholding the 1964 crop from the world market until a price of $533 a ton was reached. Since Ghana was responsible for 38% of the world production, it was hoped this action would succeed. However, other cocoa producers increased their shipments by 25% and the trading board was forced finally to dump the 1964 crop on the market at a price of $336 a ton. As a result, Ghana faces a critical foreign exchange crisis and has been forced to seek overseas economic aid.

In contrast to militant Ghanaian socialist philosophy, Nigerian plans are moderate. The Nigerian five-year plan and policy statements of the former majority party coalition generally endorse the socialist system or pattern. Socialism is defined as the means to lay the foundations of a welfare society in which equal opportunity for all will be maintained and in which there will be a steady rise in the standard of living. The welfare society will be based upon the "pure values" of freedom and respect for the individual. British Fabian Socialism or Scandinavian Socialism are models of the system Nigeria wishes to create. The maintenance of democracy is stated as a primary goal of the Nigerian approach. However, democracy is equated with equal opportunity rather than majority rule, minority rights, or recurrent elections.

The Nigerian development plan for 1962 to 1968 has as its goals to maintain and eventually surpass the four percent growth rate of the country, to reinvest fifteen percent of the gross national product each year, and government control over imports and exports to regulate revenue gains and losses. Inflationary spirals are feared, and the government is authorized to try to prevent rising prices on consumer goods.

The Nigerian plan is similar to the Ghanaian in emphasizing agricultural development as the first step in economic growth. Four-fifths of the Nigerian population is involved in agricultural production and is dependent upon such production for its livelihood. Agricultural exports represent over fifty percent of the total national product. Nigerian revenue figures have not been as adversely affected as the Ghanaian by decline of world market prices since Nigeria is less dependent upon one-crop production. The greater diversification of agriculture assists in maintaining a more stable income. The proposed modernization of agriculture envisions im-

proved farming techniques, research and development of soil fertil-
ization programs, and improved seed production. Agricultural research stations and training programs are proposed. Land-tenure
problems need to be tackled, but adjustment of fragmented and
inefficient size holdings moves slowly because of conflict with the
traditional system. Rural production is affected adversely by inadequate methods of distribution and marketing and by poor communications systems, which make transportation to market difficult and unreliable. Lack of proper storage facilities aggravate the
problem of inefficient distribution and marketing. Government
planning proposes state subsidies to the private land holders as
the means to correct these problems. Co-operatives, state farms,
and model farms play little part in Nigerian planning.

Nigeria has an advantage over some states, since significant
deposits of mineral wealth exist that may be exported for revenue
or utilized in industrial development. Petroleum, tin, and iron ore
are found in quantities sufficient for exploitation. The government
gives top priority to the development of hydro-electric power on
the Niger River to run the proposed industries. The five-year plan
envisions an iron and steel complex and the establishment of an
oil refinery, and government funds have been made available to
subsidize these projects. Present planning does not include a state
enterprise sector of the economy or nationalization of industry or
basic resources. Rather, Government revenues will be used to
stimulate growth of the private sector and private enterprise. Government controls have been established to prevent monopoly
growth and regulate mineral exploitation, but direct government
ownership of industry is not proposed.

To spur economic growth, a Nigerian Investment Company was
formed in 1959 with a capital of five million pounds. It serves as
a development bank for the country and attempts to stimulate
rapid rates of investment both by domestic industry and foreign
business and investors. The Investment Company is authorized
to subsidize projects that will promote long-term development and
assist in the rise of the growth rate. High priority sectors of investment are designated by the government and private capital is re-
strained from other areas of the economy as much as possible.
This high priority status is given to water power and the Niger

Dam, communications, the iron and steel complex, and the petroleum refinery. It is assumed that each of these will stimulate growth in other areas of the economy and overseas revenues.

Education is included in the area of maximum investment for government funds. Nigeria allocates from thirty to forty percent of its budget for educational programs. The Federal Government is directly responsible for education in the Lagos area. The 1962-68 Lagos plan proposes an elementary education system to include one hundred fifty thousand children; an expansion of secondary education to allow fifteen percent of the primary school graduates to go on to advanced work (from 960 in 1961 to 1650 in 1968); a sixth term for twenty percent of the secondary graduates; and a teacher education program to handle five thousand students per year. In addition to the Lagos program, the federal government subsidizes regional education through a grant-in-aid program. Grant-in-aid regulations include provisions for a national high school in each region under the direction of the Federal Government. Under the Nigerian constitution, regional governments have primary responsibility for education. From 1954 to 1960, the free primary education student population rose from 456,600 to 1,124,788. Secondary education students increased from 59 in 1954 to 167 in 1960. Approximately thirty percent of the regional budgets are devoted to educational expansion.

The Federal Government also proposes a comprehensive welfare program. The Federal Health Ministry maintains health centers throughout the country, and Lagos University receives grants to provide medical and teacher training. University College Hospital at Ibadan also receives funds for expansion of medical training. The government supports a children's hospital and research and vaccination laboratories. The health program is similar in scope to Ghana.

A National Providential Fund is created and supervised by the government. Employers are required to contribute five percent of the wages they pay to this fund with employee payroll deductions of the same percent. The credits that are built up in this fund are available for use by the employee in cases of prolonged unemployment, permanent incapacity, or retirement. This program is somewhat similar to the Social Security Program of the United States.

The two plans contain similarities and contrasts. The Nigerian five-year plan proposes more encouragement of the private sector and private enterprises and emphasis upon individual initiative than the Ghanaian. Ghanaian consciencism places greater emphasis upon state control, state enterprise, and the co-operative sector. Both plans envision a welfare state espousing economic equality, but Ghana has instituted more controls over income, revenue, and import-export trading. Both states argue that they have adopted African Socialism; the Nigerian approach, however, appears to be closer to regulated capitalism than state socialism. Although the Ghanaian approach involves more state enterprise and government intervention in the economy, it does not propose a completely state-run economy. The contrasts in government planning reveal differences in attitude toward the role of government in the economy. Although the development plans of other states contain additional variations in policy, states such as Guinea or Mali would be closer to the Ghanaian position and states such as Senegal or Kenya closer to the Nigerian.

FOREIGN POLICY

The Foreign Policy positions of individual African states are conditioned by their geographic positions, economic needs, strategic considerations, political alignments, and statesmanship decisions and ability. Interests are not identical, and policy positions reflect these differences. Despite variations, foreign policies of the states have several common characteristics. Most governments describe their foreign policy as "positive neutralism" or "positive nonalignment." States emphasize nonparticipation in the East-West power struggle, since the cold war is not considered of primary significance to African development. It is feared that alliance with one side or the other might pull Africa into political struggles in which she has no direct interest, and divert African resources from internal economic development. African leaders express their determination to develop their states according to African interests and needs. Participation in cold war politics may threaten independence of action if the states are persuaded to follow outside direction rather than pursuing their own separate course. When Tanzania accepted a Chinese military mission, Nyerere commented that Tanzanian foreign policy remained what it had always been, that is nonalignment. He emphasized that in the present world, "try as we will," Africa will not be left alone. Admitting that many states would not approve the decision to accept the Chinese mission, Nyerere concluded that he did not like Tanzania to be "subjected to the need to balance one set of facts against another" in order to obtain the necessary aid for development of the state. African leaders also stress the uniqueness of the African personality and assert the right of Africans to express their own individuality, develop their own way of life, and protect their customs, traditions, and culture.

A second characteristic of African positive neutralism is opposition to colonialism anywhere it is found. African leaders are quick to condemn colonialism in Africa or the denial of political rights to Africans. Angola and the Republic of South Africa receive the severest criticism. A series of resolutions have been introduced at the United Nations protesting discrimination against Africans by South Africa. Boycott of strategic goods and other economic measures have been adopted by African governments, and a few leaders have discussed the possibility of military action for the liberation of the two areas.

Neo-colonialism is considered a danger to the independence of Africa since colonialism may continue in this form with the perpetuation of the economic and social dominance of the former colonial power. Policy has vacillated on the question of trade and aid ties with the former colonial power. In the immediate post-independence period many states protested association with the European Economic Community as the continuation of neo-colonialism. However, by the summer of 1964, fourteen former French territories had ratified agreements to become associate members despite such protests. The Belgian Congo remained in *de facto* relationship with EEC for a period after independence, but eventually took action to associate formally. Former British areas such as Nigeria, Tanzania, Uganda, and Sierra Leone have expressed interest in finding a formula for association with EEC. Even Ben Bella of Algeria was interested in association. Guinea and Ghana remain firm in their opposition to what they consider entanglement with European politics. African states view EEC association as a way to receive more favorable tariff advantage on agricultural products and a share of EEC development funds. The fifteen associated states have received significant economic advantages. For example, in 1962 the EEC undertook an economic survey of the Congo and recommended a 250-million-dollar development program. Another example of a shift in policy in regard to colonial aid and trade may be the African attitude toward French assistance. Heated debate developed in France over the Cartier Plan for aid by France to her former African territories. Several French politicians recommended ending all programs. Ironically, African leaders, such as President Yameogo of the Upper Volta, entered the debate to refute the critics of continuing French aid to Africa and to endorse the Cartier Plan.

The positive side of African neutralism is based on the belief that it is Africa's mission to express law and morality in the international community. Africans feel their independence from major power politics and interests places them in a position to exert pressure for maintaining peace, ending the armament race, and promoting international justice and harmony. They argue that nonaligned states can judge impartially the actions of either power bloc and hold the major powers to a standard of international morality. Nkrumah concludes that Africa may save the world from disaster, since it is the mission of African civilization to restore ethical principles to world politics. Nkrumah feels that the African personality has a special contribution to make to world peace and morality.

> The African by virtue of his detachment, his direct vision, and his innate kindness, is qualified to bring humanitarianism to the materialistic concepts of the western world.[1]

Another common characteristic of African foreign policies is the fear of Balkanization and the expressed desire for eventual political unity. African leaders feel that Balkanization of Africa is encouraged by former colonial powers to keep the continent divided and weak. Balkanization is viewed as a deterrent to economic development, since it fosters overlapping of activity and competition among states. Latin America is mentioned frequently as an example of a Balkanized area that has remained disunited and failed to develop. The Congress of Vienna is accused of de-

---

[1] Kwame Nkrumah, as quoted by Armattoe, Raphael Earnest Grail, *Golden Age of West African Civilization* (London, 1946), p. 18.

liberately adopting a Balkanization policy when it created a number of small, independent states in Eastern Europe. African leaders argue that these small states provided the soil in which national jealousies and dissensions could grow, resulting in World Wars I and II. Divide-and-rule is to be avoided in Africa by forming a united continent. Although African leaders differ on the timing of the eventual political federation of Africa, they all pay at least lip service to it.

It would be impossible to discuss African foreign policy without including the Pan-African movement. Through it Africans express their determination to resist commonly colonial and neo-colonial pressures. Pan-Africanism involves a number of concepts. For some, it implies the search for the African personality; for others, it represents United Negritude and advancement of African civilization. Some describe it as a nonviolent, modernist, and socialist movement. To others it signifies the nonaligned position in the cold-war struggle. It is associated closely with African nationalism and the movement to independence, freedom, and economic and social progress. Its ultimate goal is held to be the creation of a Commonwealth of Free African States or a United States of Africa. This goal is discussed everywhere on the continent. Despite widespread enthusiasm, the creation of a federated Africa has encountered difficulty. Many conferences have been held to discuss unification, and many groups or organizations have been formed to encourage its creation. Among these were the Brazzaville, Casablanca, and Monrovia Organizations. The policy statements of a few of these meetings may illustrate some of the problems that have arisen in regard to federation.

The Brazzaville Powers, twelve members of former French Africa, met in December, 1960. Conference resolutions expressed their determination to remain friends of France; to solve the questions of Algerian independence and Congo stability; and to discourage the Communist presence in Africa. The Brazzaville States urged peaceful settlement of the Algerian war and opposed East-West intervention in the Congo. They rejected immediate political unification of Africa, but urged joint economic co-operation and co-ordination of planning as the first step toward eventual federation.

The Casablanca meeting, held in January 1961, was called in

part as a reaction against the Brazzaville Conference. Its members were Algeria, Ghana, Guinea, Mali, Morocco, and the United Arab Republic. The Brazzaville Powers were criticized for adopting a pro-Western or pro-French position on the Algerian question. The Casablanca Powers viewed Brazzaville as a threat to the cohesion of the Afro-Asian bloc and the maintenance of a strict nonalignment policy. At the 1961 meeting, Presidents Nkrumah, Touré, and Keita issued a communiqué condemning "all regrouping of African states based on the language of colonial states" and appealing to the Brazzaville Powers to return to the "healthier and higher conception of African Unity." The Casablanca group has been described as "militant, neutralist, and revolutionary." In their conference resolutions they reaffirmed their vigilance against colonialism and neo-colonialism and their determination to discourage the maintenance of foreign troops and bases in Africa. The French referendum in Algeria was condemned, and the Casablanca Powers expressed their support "by all means" for the Provisional Government of Algeria.

In May 1961, the Monrovia Conference was called in part to attempt a *rapprochement* of the Casablanca and Brazzaville Powers. President Senghor initiated the idea for the conference to work out a common policy for the Congo. Leaders of three states who were not members of either Casablanca or Brazzaville sponsored the meeting: Olympio of Togo, Tubman of Liberia, and Abubakar of Nigeria. Two Casablanca members, Guinea and Mali, and two Brazzaville members, Ivory Coast and the Cameroons, agreed to co-sponsor the conference. It was hoped that this joint sponsorship would bring representatives of all the independent African states to Monrovia, thus reconciling the Brazzaville-Casablanca differences.

Difficulty arose almost immediately over the question of Algerian participation in the conference. The Casablanca Powers insisted that the Provisional Algerian Government be invited, since Ben Bella was a signatory to the Casablanca Treaty. The Brazzaville Powers objected on the ground that Algeria was not yet an independent state. Casablanca charged that the Brazzaville Powers were being directed by France in this position. The uncommitted states attempted to find a compromise but were unsuccessful. As a result, Guinea and Mali withdrew as co-sponsors, and no Casablanca power attended the Monrovia Conference. The Monrovia Powers decided to go ahead in the hope of bringing about eventual unification. It was left open for the Casablanca Powers to participate at any time they might choose to do so. Among the twenty states attending the Monrovia Conference were the twelve Brazzaville states plus Nigeria, Sierra Leone, Togo, Ethiopia, Liberia, Tunisia, Libya, and Somalia. The U.A.R. accused Bourguiba of Tunisia of betraying Arab nationalism by attending a "pro-French" conference.

Monrovia followed the lead of Brazzaville on the Algerian question. It urged the French and the Algerian Provisional Government to establish a cease-fire leading to eventual independence for Algeria. The Casablanca powers viewed these resolutions as pro-French and charged that the Brazzaville powers had influenced the adoption of weak resolutions in order to avoid angering the French. Behind the scenes conversation hinted that France was using economic pressure to keep the Brazzaville states in line. Nahdatu Ifrigya expressed the contempt of the U.A.R. for the Monrovia position.

. . . So imperialism compels certain countries which are under its influence to get together and take decisions meant to weaken the struggle for national liberation in Africa. This is why the Monrovia Conference was called with its members impelled to carry out western orders.[2]

When Algerian independence was granted, this issue dividing Casablanca, Monrovia, and Brazzaville was partially resolved.

A second area of division centered around stability in the Congo (Leopoldville). The Congo question, like the Algerian question, served to emphasize policy differences between the three groups. The 1960 Brazzaville resolutions urged other African states to avoid political interference in the Congo and condemned efforts by any great power to "recolonize" the country. The Casablanca powers were critical of United Nations policy in the Congo. They protested the treatment accorded Patrice Lumumba and the return of Belgian technicians to Katanga. Mali, Guinea, and the United Arab Republic pressed for the recognition of the Stanleyville government, charging that the West was using the chaos to

[2] As cited by Jacques Baulin, *Arab Role in Africa* (New York, Penguin, 1962), p. 76.

assure that a pro-Western government would emerge. They reserved the right to take "appropriate action" if the United Nations did not re-establish the constitutional government with Patrice Lumumba as prime minister. By the end of 1960, they threatened to withdraw their troops from the United Nations Congo Force. President Nasser proposed a joint African military action to restore Lumumba to power. After the Security Council vetoed their proposals, all Casablanca powers, except Ghana, announced the withdrawal of their troops. President Nkrumah urged that the United Nations be given a last chance to settle the problem. After the death of Lumumba, all recognized the Gizenga Stanleyville government.

In contrast to the Casablanca position, Monrovia and Brazzaville supported the United Nations' action in the Congo and recognized the Kasavubu government as legitimate. Resolutions were adopted re-affirming the faith of the members in the United Nations, "which in spite of past weaknesses and mistakes in its work, is best adapted to achieve a real solution of the Congo problem." They appealed to African states to desist from hasty recognition of break-away regimes and siding with rival groups. Prime Minister Adoula of the Congo was invited to attend the Second Monrovia Conference to show support for the United Nations policies in the Congo and encourage Congolese leaders to adopt a moderate approach to foreign policy. When the Adoula Government brought some measure of stability to the Congo with United Nations' support, the tensions over Congo policy lessened. Problems arose again with the appointment of Tshombe as the "caretaker prime minister." Tshombe attempted to attend an Independent African States Conference in Cairo. When he arrived at Cairo airport, he was placed under house arrest by Nasser and was returned to Athens without attending any of the meetings. Tshombe has received general criticism from other African leaders because of his close association with Belgian officials in Katanga. The Casablanca powers have led the military support for the revolutionary forces in the hope of overthrowing Tshombe and placing the Gizenga forces in power. Despite the Casablanca view, Tshombe received a polite hearing before the Organization of African Unity. Many African states are hesitant to establish a precedent of aid to revolutionary forces, since such a policy might be used against them in the future. Former Monrovia states emphasize non-interference in the internal affairs of another state.

The Algerian and Congo problems revealed policy divisions among the African states and served as temporary stumbling blocks to the unification of Africa in the immediate post-independence period. Since political unification is held as a major goal of Pan-Africanism, the resolutions and views of the three groups on the question of a United States of Africa may indicate whether there are any basic or permanent points of division that may work against its creation.

The resolutions of the Monrovia Conferences[3] on the question of unification expressed support for the principles of absolute equality of African states; noninterference in each other's internal affairs and respect for state sovereignty, and emphasis was placed upon the inalienable right of each state to develop its own personality. The Monrovians hoped to achieve "unity of aspirations and action," but "political integration of sovereign African states" was not considered practical in the early independence period. In his opening address to the Monrovia Conference, President Senghor urged that the African states concentrate on technical and economic co-operation in attempting to achieve unity. He concluded that some African states wished to "run too fast" toward political union without the "necessary study and co-operation to bring it about."

At the Second Monrovia Conference, which met in Lagos from January 25 to 30, 1962, a similar attitude toward political unification was expressed. Dr. Azikiwe opened the conference by declaring that a "basic difference of an ideological nature" existed between the Monrovian and Casablanca Powers. He pointed to the "conspicuous absence" of a declaration by the Casablanca Powers that they recognized the rights of African states to legal equality, self-determination and to safety from interference or subversion in their internal affairs. Emphasizing that economic co-operation should precede any attempt at political unification, the conferences passed resolutions aiming at the gradual development of a common market; establishment of a system for regulating cur-

[3] Since the Brazzaville powers were members of Monrovia, their views on these questions did not differ significantly from the Monrovia resolutions.

rency exchanges; stabilization of prices on basic products; harmonization of development plans; and creation of an African Bank and a private investment guarantee fund. Resolutions also supported co-operation in expansion of facilities for control of disease, welfare of workers, transportation and communication, and education. A permanent organization was created to carry out these objectives. It included an Assembly of Heads of State, which met once a year to discuss general policies and actions, a Permanent Secretariat, an Association of Economic Co-operation and Development, and a Permanent Conciliation Commission to settle disputes among members by peaceful means. It was agreed that nothing in the Monrovia Charter should impair the commitments of the members under the Charter of the United Nations.

The Casablanca Conferences placed more emphasis upon political unification and the creation of a United States of Africa as an immediate or short-run goal. The Ghanaian view may be represented by a statement of President Nkrumah:

> So dear is this African unity to our hearts, that in our proposed republican constitution, a definite provision has been incorporated by a concrete proposal that Ghana's sovereignty should be surrendered in whole or in part as a contribution towards the attainment of the great objective. The greatness of this objective so transcends all other purposes and its sublimity is so profound that it behooves each and everyone in the leadership of this struggle to endeavor to subdue his own little interests, his individual pride and ego and other petty considerations. . . .[4]

A Ghana-Guinea union was formed in 1959 as the nucleus for a federated Africa. It was open to all independent African states. The union was empowered to create a common economic and monetary policy and hold periodic meetings among the heads of states. Each state would continue to determine its own defense policy and retain its own individuality and governmental structures. Mali joined the union in December of 1960.

At the Casablanca Conference, Presidents Nkrumah and Touré urged the adoption of the union approach. However, the question of immediate political unification was bypassed and a functional approach adopted. The UAR *Scribe* described the Casablanca

[4] Kwame Nkrumah, *Africa Speaks,* James Duffy and Robert Manners (eds.), (Van Nostrand, Princeton, New Jersey, 1961), p. 57.

approach to Pan-Africanism as the desire to promote co-operative development of Africa economically and socially.

> The desired African unity will not entail the disappearance of the peculiar characteristics of each country or, more exactly, of every region on the continent. It is not founded, as Arab unity, on ethical, linguistic, historical and religious community, but it is notably justi-fied and sought by reason of the necessity to co-ordinate all efforts in order to attain identical objectives, based on a similar situation. That is why there is no contradiction whatsoever between nationalism and the extolled unity.[5]

The Casablanca Powers agreed to create a Political Committee that would meet periodically, an Economic Committee to foster joint planning and co-operation, an African Cultural Committee to expand educational facilities and study of African culture, and a Joint African High Command to develop a common defense for Africa. The Economic Commission met at Conakry in July, 1961 and proposed the removal of customs and tariffs and the estab-lishment of a Bank for African Development.

The Monrovia Technical Commission, meeting in Dakar, adopted similar resolutions for economic, financial, and social welfare co-operation. An African customs union was proposed to encourage freer trade and agreement on a common external tariff. States were to harmonize their development programs to create a connecting network of railways. The Casablanca and Monrovia resolutions for the creation of an African Common Market and for co-opera-tion in the economic and social fields were nearly identical. How-ever, no provision for a joint African High Command was made by the Monrovian group. Rather than the Casablanca approach of a "NATO" for Africa, the Monrovians preferred consultation among the Council of Ministers.

Although Casablanca and Monrovia members referred fre-quently to their differences over the question of a united Africa, their resolutions indicated a greater degree of similarity than dif-ference. Both seemed to follow a functional position. Even the provisions of the Ghana-Guinea Union emphasized economic and social co-operation and political consultation rather than political federation.

Tension developed between the Casablanca and Monrovia

[5] *The Scribe*, Ministry of Information (Cairo, Egypt, July 23, 1962).

groups over the question of leadership for a united Africa. President Tubman of Liberia in opening the first Monrovia Conference revealed some of his doubts.

> There are those who feel that Liberia should assume leadership based on the fact that she is the oldest African Republic and is riper in political experience to assume leadership of Africa. . . . There are others who hold that Ghana should assume that role because she is physically more developed and embraces larger territories. It will require more than development and larger territory to assume leadership of Africa. And there are yet those who opine that Egypt with its rich traditions dating back to the remotest antiquity, should do so. It will require more than rich traditions of antiquity. It will require, in my opinion, the aggregate of all three of these and more besides. It will require the best of all three or the best that is in all compounded in such a manner as to represent the divisibility of Africa indivisible.

> Let me conclude by reiterating that while the idea of a universal political order is debatable at this stage of our political experience, the necessity for better cooperation among us is obvious. But any form of unity must be a voluntary process. Political union is attained by virtue of agreement. In the absence of a free agreement, any form of political union is but imperial domination.[6]

Tubman's remarks were a thinly veiled slap at Casablanca, revealing a fear that Nasser and Nkrumah wished to dominate the continent and assume control over the newly independent states.

Concern over the ambitions of the Casablanca leaders was indicated also by the late Sylvanus Olympio. He observed that political unification was desired only by those leaders who believed they would "come out on top in such unions." He expressed concern that ambitious men might lead Africa to conflicts in their attempts to force political union.

Chief Awolowo speaking of Nasser's role in Casablanca, observed:

> . . . with his undisguised totalitarianism, his territorial ambitions in Africa and the Moslem world, effective cooperation with Nasser, in any field at all, would be possible only if the black races of Africa were prepared to remain as satellites in Egypt's orbit. . . .[7]

[6] *African Summit in Monrovia*, Federal Ministry of Information, p. 9.

[7] Abafemi Awolowo, *Awo: The Autobiography of Chief Abafemi Awolowo* (London, Cambridge University Press, 1960), p. 312.

An editorial in the Nigerian *Sunday Post* expressed concern over the personal ambitions of Nkrumah. The editorial concluded that Nkrumah's continual detention of people in Ghana made nonsense of his plea for unity. The editorial observed that no one would wish to associate with a man who thinks he is always right and everyone else is always wrong.

> . . . If only President Nkrumah will realize that his doctrinaire democratic centralism, designed for export to independent African states, is no less neo-colonialist than American or British capitalism or the European Common Market philosophy. . . . Much of what plagues this self-styled African Man of Destiny will clear the air for genuine understanding among the new nations of Africa when, and only WHEN, he learns to think of other African leaders as people with some sense and a love and hope for the future of Africa.[8]

Concern over the possibility that one man would gain control of the African community is clearly expressed in these statements. The leadership is reluctant to surrender its newly gained status and power to a central body. Although each one might be willing to become the head of a United States of Africa, they are not anxious to see another African assume this position.

If a major stumbling block exists to the unification of the African states, it may center around the question of leadership and direction of a united Africa. The Casablanca Powers opposed the Monrovian approach on the grounds that it would lead Africa to a moderate, pro-Western, and neo-colonial status. The Monrovians feared that the Casablanca Powers in their desire for political unity would trample under state sovereignty, national identity, and internal governmental structures. These doubts might indicate a developing power struggle for influence and dominance in Africa among the newly independent states. They also illustrate a trend that has been observed in European attempts at political integration—that is the reluctance of sovereign states to surrender power, prestige, and status to a unified central organization. Since independence and sovereignty are highly prized by the African states, the reluctance to surrender what has been won so recently may be understandable.

[8] "Unity in Africa, Some Will Need to Think Again," *Sunday Post* (July 8, 1962), 10:6.

Despite these problems, African leaders did succeed in calling a conference of all newly independent states in the hope of avoiding permanent splits and rivalries. The Conference of Independent African States, which met in Addis Ababa in 1963, brought together the representatives of Brazzaville, Casablanca, and Monrovia. Committees were created to study and make recommendations on the development of economic cooperation and an African Common Market, the expansion of facilities for study of African civilization, and the steps desirable for the achievement of political federation. Implementation of these areas is still under study and consideration.

The Addis Conference emphasized the desire of African leaders to achieve common programs for economic and social advancement. Hope was expressed that joint and united effort would speed growth rates and avoid wasteful duplication and overlapping. Addis meetings devoted considerable effort to healing the rift between the Monrovian and Casablanca Organizations. Before the conference ended it was agreed to disband the Casablanca and Monrovia Organizations and form a united group. Discussions stressed the danger of rivalries, which could lead to conflicts and deter joint economic and social co-operation.

The Addis approach also favored functionalism rather than immediate political federation. Economic co-operation was viewed as the first step toward eventual political integration. Some positive steps toward co-operation have been taken. On May 25, 1963, the Addis Ababa Conference signed a charter creating the Organization of African Unity in which the African states pledged themselves to promotion of African unity and solidarity; co-ordination of economic advancement; defense of their independence; eradication of all forms of colonialism; and encouragement of international peace and co-operation. These principles were adapted from the basic goals of Pan-Africanism. The Monrovian view of state sovereignty may have influenced the signatories of the Organization of African Unity, since the charter supports the principles of sovereign equality of all member states and noninterference in each others internal affairs.

The OAU created an Assembly of Heads of State, which meets annually, and a Council of Foreign Ministers convenes at least twice a year. Member states have one vote in these bodies and a two-thirds majority is required to pass resolutions. A permanent secretariat is provided, and specialized commissions may be created as deemed necessary. Such special committees study policies in relation to education, health, economic and social development, or defense. One special committee is the Coordinating Committee composed of Ethiopia, Algeria, Uganda, the UAR, Tanzania, Congo-Leopoldville, Guinea, Senegal, and Nigeria. Its responsibility is to reach agreement on the assistance that African states should provide to national liberation movements. The Committee manages a special fund created to support such movements, but the status of the fund has been a closely guarded secret. The committee recommended that the first major effort be concentrated on the consolidation of the "disparate nationalist forces" in Angola and Portuguese Guinea.

After Tanganyika, Uganda, and Kenya called back British troops to suppress uprisings of servicemen, a new committee composed of twelve nations was formed at the February, 1964 OAU Conference. It studied the creation of an African police force that could be called into service in similar cases. This African force would maintain government stability. An African force would eliminate the necessity to call upon British or other outside troops. President Nyerere referred to the calling back of British troops in the military uprisings as a "national disgrace." It was suggested that such a force could have been used to settle the Congo crisis without the need for United Nations troops. Tshombe has appealed to this Committee for assistance in quelling the revolutionary forces. The police force also could be used to contain conflicts such as the Ethiopia-Somali border difficulties. The OAU did work out a truce agreement and truce committee to supervise the Somali-Ethiopian border problems. It also provided good offices in the Morocco-Algeria border fighting. These actions taken by the OAU may be the forerunner for closer cooperation and eventual unity. Although many of the OAU recommendations are still primarily only on paper, the future growth of a Common Market, an African Police Force, and joint consultation on African problems may pave the way for eventual political federation. However, many stumbling blocs remain before this goal is reached.

AFRICA IN THE UNITED NATIONS

The African role in the UN has assumed greater significance in the last few years. One reason is the rapid growth of the number of African states in the General Assembly. In 1958 the African Continent had nine representatives. By 1964 their membership had jumped to 34 and additional states will shortly be admitted. Presently, African states represent 30% of the total UN membership. They also form a significant percentage of the total membership of various blocs. For example, they represent over 60% of the Afro-Asian bloc.

At the 1958 Conference of Independent African States, a formal agreement was signed by the nine members of the UN that affirmed the desire of the states "to safeguard their independence, sovereignty and the territorial integrity of Africa." It was felt that united action in the UN would assist in the promotion of these goals. The states wished to create some formal procedure for coordinating their efforts and reconciling differences in approach to UN issues. Leaders feared that other blocs might attempt to split African votes and water African strength in the United Nations. The creation of the formal organization also was stimulated by the desire to bring African "positive nonalignment" influence into the UN. The belief that it is the African role to moderate East-West tensions and conflicts has been discussed. The Conference of Independent African States urged that united policies be maintained so that the role of harmonizer could be performed effectively. The formal agreement expressed support for the principles of the UN Charter, the Universal Declaration of Human Rights, and the Bandung Conference of Non-Aligned States. The only independent African state that is not a member of the bloc is the Republic of South Africa.

The African states created an Informal Permanent Machinery to co-ordinate the activities of the African bloc. The Co-ordinating Body, composed of representatives of all member states, meets once a month and can be called into special session by the request of any member state. Chairmanship of the Co-ordinating Body is passed each month following an alphabetical order of states arrangement. At the meetings of this body, the states attempt to resolve policy questions and arrive at common positions on UN agenda items. The monthly meetings permit African representatives to discuss their viewpoints and positions on international questions. Although reconciliation of positions is not always achieved, the meetings afford representatives a source of information on how other states will vote and what resolutions they will introduce. There is less possibility of being caught off guard and unprepared for the maneuvers of other African states. Representatives are not bound to follow the Co-ordinating Body's decisions. Contact through the Co-ordinating Body also allows a regular procedure for planning African conferences and preparing agenda items for these meetings. Other blocs in the UN often request permission to address the meetings of the African bloc in order to gain African support for their resolutions.

The Permanent Machinery also created a Permanent Secretariat, which is composed of representatives of four states. The members are elected for a two year term by the Co-ordinating Body. The Secretariat staff attempts to keep members informed of the actions of the various state representatives and the items appearing on the UN agenda. This is a complex responsibility, since it involves information and co-ordination of the activities of the various UN bodies and of all UN committees and special commissions. The Secretariat performs a valuable service for many African states with small delegations and poorly staffed missions.

African states participate in several blocs in addition to the African bloc. As was indicated, they form over 60% of the membership of the Afro-Asian bloc. Several states also caucus with the Arab bloc and former British territories take an active role in Commonwealth bloc discussions. Until recently, the African bloc was divided into sub-blocs representing the Casablanca, Monrovia, and Brazzaville Organizations. These states caucused together as well as participating in the Permanent Machinery. The formation of OAU brought an end to these formal sub-bloc operations.

Many studies of the UN voting behavior of the African states have been undertaken. These surveys reveal that the African bloc has been able to maintain a united voting front on 45 to 50% of all UN votes. In the period from 1958 through 1964, cohesiveness of voting has centered on certain issues. When agenda items involve the Republic of South Africa or apartheid questions, the bloc has maintained a consistently united pattern of voting. The issue of South West Africa and the UN role over the former League Mandate area also reveals a consistently uniform vote. Condemnation of Portuguese colonial policies in Angola follows this same pattern. On these questions voting cohesion is close to 100%. On the 1958 resolutions concerning racial conflict in South Africa only Morocco and Sudan voted in opposition. In 1959, all states supported the resolution proposing UN condemnation of South African policy. In 1960, a South African resolution recommended that the UN should have no responsibility for South West Africa. All African states voted against this position and supported a series of resolutions affirming UN responsibility for the mandated territory. The 1961 and 1962 votes on racial problems in South Africa again revealed a 100% position by the African bloc. Resolutions concerning racial problems in Southern Rhodesia in more recent Assembly sessions also show a similar pattern.

A second issue that receives a consistently high degree of voting cohesion is disarmament and nuclear testing. The African bloc was united in its protests against French nuclear testing in the Sahara. Recent proposals to declare Africa a denuclearized zone received 100% support. Resolutions calling for control of nuclear testing, East-West disarmament, and banning of nuclear weapons also receive a very high percentage of support. One explanation for the cohesion on these two issues may be that they represent African objection to colonialism or denial of freedom to Africans and the African desire to harmonize international politics under a system of international law rather than armaments races.

Cohesion of voting on other issues does not reach this high level. For example, the voting on the Congo question and on Algerian independence revealed the split between the Brazzaville and Casablanca Powers. Congo policy problems developed when President Kasavubu discovered a Soviet promise to supply aid to Lumumba in quelling secessionist movements in Kasai Province. Kasavubu acted to remove Lumumba and replace him with Ileo since he viewed the Lumumba-Soviet agreement as a Communist plot to overthrow him and the government. Tunisia and the Brazzaville states were concerned that no external forces enter the Congo.

They supported UN intervention and a resolution against East-West military involvement. The UN entered the Congo as a "neutral" in the internal political struggle. In attempting to maintain stability, its forces took control of communications and transportation. This action prevented Lumumba from using these facilities in regaining power.

The Casablanca Powers protested the UN action as support of the Kasavubu forces. Lumumba had participated in Casablanca meetings and had indicated his support for the militant, socialist, and nonaligned position. The decision to seat Kasavubu in the UN as the legitimate representative of the Congo caused additional outcries from Casablanca. The death of Lumumba raised tensions to the boiling point. The Casablanca powers decided to pull troops out of the UN Congo Force in an attempt to restore the Gizenga regime to power. Nkrumah broke over this decision and Ghanaian troops remained in the Congo, but he went along with Casablanca in recognizing the Gizenga regime as the legitimate government. The Kasavubu government called a conference for a new constitution, which was held in Tananarive and decided to adopt a loose confederation approach. Nkrumah and Touré condemned this decision as encouraging instability and division since the confederation approach is contrary to the Ghana-Guinea support for the unified one-party state system. A subsequent conference at Coquiehatville endorsed a stronger federal system, but Tshombe refused to accept this compromise. Nkrumah and Touré charged that Tshombe was using his opposition to foster Belgian reentry into the Congo. The Brazzaville Powers supported Tshombe, since they hoped that a confederal approach in the Congo might promote an eventual unification of the Congo and French Equatorial Africa. The States of French Equatorial Africa also expressed fear of dominance by Ghana and Guinea and hoped federation with the Congo would deter expansion by the Casablanca Powers. The Monrovia Powers, led by Nigeria, maintained support for the UN intervention in the Congo. They were concerned that East-West power struggles be kept out of Africa and that stability return to the Congo. They approved the use of UN troops in the Congo and the federal approach as the best solution to the problems of secession.

Additional divisions were revealed when the Algerian question came before the UN. Brazzaville Powers supported resolutions recommending the ending of hostilities and Franco-Algerian consultation in bringing about a peaceful solution to the war. They refused to support resolutions condemning French colonial policy, the referendum proposal, or Algerian autonomy within the French Union. Casablanca viewed the Brazzaville votes as a defeat for Pan-Africanism and independence. Since the provisional Government of Ben Bella was a member of the Casablanca Organization, they took a strong stand for immediate independence, possible UN intervention to assist Ben Bella's forces, and condemnation of French colonialism in Africa. The Monrovia Powers, in attempting to find a middle ground between the two, avoided proposals for intervention but supported peaceful settlement and independence.

The question of Mauritanian membership in the UN also revealed a Monrovia, Brazzaville, and Casablanca split. Morocco called the Casablanca Conference in part over her objections to the French creation of Mauritania. Morocco argued that this involved loss of her territory and invaded her sovereignty. The Casablanca Conference condemned France for this action. When Mauritania sought membership in the UN, the Soviet Union lined up with the Casablanca Powers and vetoed the Security Council recommendation for admission. The Brazzaville States supported France in pushing for the seating of Mauritania in the UN. The Monrovia Conference supported the latter position and its members voted in favor of Mauritania in its second attempt to join the UN. On the second resolution the Soviet Union refrained from using the veto and membership was granted.

The voting patterns on questions involving the Congo, Algeria, and Mauritania follow the differences in policy that were discussed above in Casablanca, Brazzaville, and Monrovia Conference resolutions. Since the "African Session" of the UN, most of these points of division have been resolved and the African bloc has shown a greater degree of cohesion in voting in the more recent sessions. The OAU may assist in healing splits, because it has created permanent machinery for consultation. Despite the Brazzaville-Casablanca split, the African bloc percentage of unity on voting since 1958 is about 50%. Casablanca cohesiveness was much higher than this. This sub bloc broke only on one or two questions and voted together nearly 80% of the time. Brazzaville and Monrovia cohesiveness was much lower. Brazzaville unity was affected by a high percentage of abstentions and absences.

What is the significance of these voting patterns for the African bloc and the UN? Since the African bloc forms a significant portion of UN membership, unity on African questions may permit greater influence in UN decision making. The explosion of African numbers in the General Assembly has produced a shift in voting strength of the various blocs in the UN. East and West find it necessary to gain African support for their resolutions and positions in order to assure passage of tightly contested questions. Cohesiveness in voting and co-ordination of policy permits the African bloc to play a more significant role in UN power politics. However, UN voting behavior refutes to some extent the claim of the African leadership that all of Africa is united on international goals and policy. Splits have occurred when the interests of the individual states came into conflict. Although the Algerian and Mauritanian issues have been resolved at least temporarily, future crises may arise to produce further rifts. The question of Congo policy continues to plague the bloc, and states were split over their position in regard to Tshombe and the revolutionary forces. Although joint machinery for consultation exists, it is difficult to predict whether future problems will push the states toward closer co-operation or wider rifts. Consultation and conference by the bloc in the UN may pave the way for agreement on eventual closer co-operation and even federation. Despite the verbal support for the eventual creation of a United States of Africa, the realization of this dream remains in doubt.

Conclusion

AMONG THE GENERAL CHARACTERISTICS OF STABLE POLITICAL societies are the development of a sense of commitment to the state, agreement on the procedures by which the state should be governed, trust in the impartiality of government officials, and consensus on the goals and policies of the state. The survey of African governments has revealed problems in each of these areas. Tribalism and regionalism represent a threat to the development of a sense of nationalism or state loyalty. Secession is a constant danger to the unity of the state. Popular understanding or support for the governing processes and procedures is not well developed. High illiteracy rates and lack of experience with the political procedures aggravates the development of popular acquiescence to the government. Popular concern has been expressed in regard to the new African ruling elite and their impartiality in administration. Confronted by these factors, African leaders constantly reiterate the theme of the overriding need to provide leadership, direction, and unity.

In attempting to achieve stability, a clear pattern of structural centralization of powers has emerged, with power tending to concentrate in the hands of the executive or president. There has been a movement away from the collective responsibility of the parliamentary system. A separation-of-powers system is provided constitutionally, but the three branches of government are not assumed to be equal in power; and there is a tendency to view the legislative and judicial branches as arms of the executive. The role of the bureaucracy is stated to be an aid to the executive, and the concept of the neutrality of the bureaucracy is rejected or de-emphasized. On the question of internal division of power, the unitary form is preferred to a regional or federal system, since localism and regionalism are viewed as threats to unity. Non-governmental parties are de-emphasized or outlawed, and opposition movements often are equated with disloyalty or subversion. Opposition is feared as a stimulus to localism, regionalism, or secessionism. The chaos in the Belgian Congo has had a deep impact on Africa, and African leaders express their concern that if certain forces in their states are not controlled, a series of "Congos" could occur all over Africa.

Economic planning reveals a similar tendency toward centralization of power and government direction, although the degree of control varies considerably from state to state. State direction and regulation is considered an absolute necessity if rapid growth is to be achieved and "neo-colonial" pressures curtailed. Given the limited African private capital in the states, government intervention in the economy may be the only alternative if short-run expansion of growth rates is to be achieved. The Pan-African movement also stresses centralization of effort. An African common market, joint military forces, or co-operative power, communications, transportation, and educational projects are proposed to overcome limited state facilities and resources. The dangers of Balkanization are discussed everywhere. The final step in centralization is to be the creation of a United States of Africa that will mobilize the resources of the continent in the struggle for economic development and international status.

African leaders argue that centralization of power in the hands of the executive, whether in individual states or in a United States of Africa, follows traditional African political process and procedure. A glance at the constitutions might produce the conclusion that the African states have adopted Western systems and institutions, since the British parliamentary system or the French Gaullist system appear to have served as models. The turning to these Western forms may have represented a necessary compromise, since few common tribal institutions or procedures existed to which states could turn in writing the new constitutions. The adoption of Western patterns has been criticized by some observers of the African political scene who conclude that Western political procedures are not understood and cannot work effectively.

A more careful analysis of the operation of African constitutions reveals the attempt to blend Western and African political traditions and institutions. Although few common tribal institutions and procedures may have existed, there seems to have been general understanding and support for the role of the chief in society. This common tradition centered around the acceptance of power or authority as the "person" of the chief; support for the chief as the expresser of the consensus of the community; acquiescence to the power of the chief as enforcer of this consensus; and agreement that no opposition would be allowed once consensus had been achieved.

The presidential system lends itself to a blending of these traditional concepts with the Western Gaullist model. If power or authority is conceived as a "person," the presidential system is able to accommodate to this concept. The cult of personality found in some African states may be a carry-over from this tradition. The president can be viewed as an arbitrator of interests and a senser of consensus following the traditional role of the chief. Since the tribal system permitted no opposition after consensus was reached, the concept of one-party democracy blends the traditional government by discussion system with modern Leninist or democratic centralist models. Historical experience with government by consensus serves as a precedent for contemporary de-emphasis upon opposition parties and movements.

The tendency toward centralization of power in the hands of the executive has been criticized as a movement toward dictatorship or totalitarianism. African leaders respond to such charges by denying that the Western concepts of an opposition party, diffusion of responsibility, and division of powers have any meaning in African political tradition. These concepts are viewed as artificial and unnecessary to a democratic system. It is argued that the traditional concept of consensus follows the true Greek definition of democracy as "government by discussion."

In their emphasis on maintaining unity, African political structures raise doubts concerning the protections given the areas of diversity. Mass conformity can result from overemphasis upon uniformity of viewpoint. Equating opposition to disloyalty toward the state, preventive detention acts, state security courts, and procedural rights limitation enter into the attempts to assure commitment to the party, the government and the state. The fear that the operation of organized opposition or the representation of individual or local issues will result in the outbreak of secessionism suggests the gravity of the problems of disunity and instability.

African leaders admit that these structural arrangements are open to the danger of a man on a white horse. Concentration of power in the hands of the independence leader requires that he exercise a high degree of self-discipline if dictatorship is to be avoided. Lord Acton's warning concerning absolute power corrupting absolutely comes to mind in surveying structural concentration of power in one hand. However, the role of the independence party in checking abuse of power should not be overlooked.

African leaders conclude that emergent societies must give primary consideration to achieving stability. The balance between unity and diversity must receive secondary attention until power is consolidated. Present concentration of power in the executive is promoted by mass support and loyalty to the independence leader. As these leaders pass from the political scene and governmental policies incur opposition, the provisions for structural unity may be revised. Areas of opposition are already observable in the one-party structures. When the transition period is passed, these elements of diversity may become more significant.

The theme of the overriding need to provide leadership, unity, and direction in the period of transition may not be peculiar to African governments. For example, emergent states in Southeast Asia have turned to guided democracy, benevolent dictatorship, and one-party structures in order to provide stability and respond more quickly to the pressures for change. Although Western observers express concern over the African centralization of power patterns, these systems may not lead inevitably to dictatorship. After the transition period is passed, power structures may be liberalized. The series of military coups coming at the end of 1965 may point to a continuing concentration of powers and restrictions upon the independence party in performing its check on executive abuse of powers. Future developments will reveal whether African states have achieved the equilibrium between unity and diversity which they seek.

Bibliography

Chapter 1—POLITICAL CULTURE

Books

Africa, A Foreign Affairs Reader, edited by Philip W. Quigg (New York, Praeger, 1964).

Africa in the Modern World, edited by Calvin W. Stillman (Chicago, University of Chicago Press, 1955).

African Political Systems, edited by M. Fortes and E. E. Evans-Pritchard, published for the International Institute of African Languages and Culture (London, Oxford University Press, 1950).

Alderfer, Harold F., *Local Government in Developing Countries* (New York, McGraw-Hill Company, 1964).

Church, Harrison, *Environment and Policies in West Africa* (Princeton, N.J., D. Van Nostrand Company Inc., 1963).

Essays on African Population, edited by K. M. Barbour and R. M. Prothers (New York, Frederick A. Praeger, 1961).

Fage, J. D., *An Introduction to the History of West Africa* (Cambridge, Cambridge University, 1962).

Hailey, William Malcolm, *An African Survey: A Study of Problems in Africa South of the Sahara* (London, Oxford University Press, 1957).

Hodgson, Robert D. and Stoneman, A., *The Changing Man of Africa* (Princeton, N.J., D. Van Nostrand Company Inc., 1963).

Herskovits, Melville J., *The Human Factor in Changing Africa* (New York, Alfred A. Knopf, 1962).

Kent, Raymond K., *From Madagascar to the Malagasy Republic* (New York, Frederick A. Praeger, 1962).

Kimble, George H. T., *Tropical Africa,* Vol. I, *Land and Livelihood* and Vol. II, *Society and Policy* (New York, The Twentieth Century Fund, 1960).

Kup, A. P., *A History of Sierra Leone 1400-1787* (Cambridge, Cambridge University Press, 1961).

Panikkar, K. Madhu, *Revolution in Africa* (New York, Asia Publishing House, 1961).

Seligman, C. B., *Races of Africa* (London, Oxford University Press, 1959).

Skeffington, Arthur, *Tanganyika in Transition* (London, Fabian Commonwealth Bureau, 1960).

Wingfield, R. J., *The Story of Old Ghana, Melle and Songhai* (Cambridge, Cambridge University Press, 1961).

Worldmark Encyclopedia of the Nations: Africa (New York, Harper and Row, 1963).

Young, Roland and Fosbrooke, Henry, *Land and Politics Among the Luguru of Tanganyika* (London, Routledge and Kegan Paul, 1960).

Government publications

French Africa, A Decade of Progress, 1948-1958, Investment Fund for Economic and Social Development in French West and Equatorial Africa (Ambassade de France—Service de Presse et d'Information, New York, 1956).

Handbook of Tanganyika, second edition, edited by J. P. Moffett, printed and bound by the Government Printer, Dar es Salaam, 1958.

Information Brochure on Kenya, as revised, May 1962.

Information transmitted to the Secretary General of the United Nations by Her Majesty's Government in the United Nations, In Accordance with the Provision of Article 73 (e) of the United Nations Charter concerning the Territory of Kenya for the Year 1961 (H.M.S.O., London, 1962).

Nigeria: The Making of a Nation (British Information Services, New York, An Agency of the British Government, Reference Division, June 1960).

Notes et Etudes Documentaires, La République de Côte d'Ivoire (Paris, 7 November, 1959), No. 2, 588.

Notes et Etudes Documentaires, La République du Congo (Paris, 17 December, 1960), No. 2, 733.

Nyasaland 1960 (London, H.M.S.O., 1961).

Statistical Information for the United Nations Organization Under Article 73 (e) of the Charter of the United Nations in Respect of 1961.

Tanganyika: The Making of a Nation (British Information Services, New York, August, 1961).

Uganda (British Information Services, New York, January, 1962).

Chapter 2—POLITICAL PROCESSES

Books

Almond, Gabriel A. and Coleman, James S. (editors), *The Politics of the Developing Areas* (Princeton, N.J., Princeton University Press, 1960).

Apter, David E., *Political Kingdom in Uganda* (Princeton, Princeton University Press, 1961).

Awolowo, Abafemi, *Awo: The Autobiography of Chief Abafemi Awolowo* (Cambridge, Cambridge University Press, 1962).

African Independence, edited by Peter Judd (Dell Publishing Company, 1962).

Baulin, Jacques, *The Arab Role in Africa* (Baltimore, Maryland, Penguin, 1962).

Bennett, George and Rosburg, Carl G., *The Kenyatta Election: Kenya 1960-1961* (Oxford, Oxford University Press, 1961).

Carter, Gwendolen M., *African One-party States* (Ithaca, N.Y., Cornell University Press, 1962).

Coleman, James S., *Nigeria, Background to Nationalism* (Berkeley, California, University of California Press, 1958).

Creighton, T. R. M., *Southern Rhodesia and the Central African Federation: The Anatomy of Partnership* (New York, Frederick A. Praeger, 1960).

Duffy, James and Manners, Robert A. (editors), *Africa Speaks* (Princeton, N.J., D. Van Nostrand Inc., 1961).

Hughes, John, *The New Face of Africa South of the Sahara* (New York, Longmans, Green, and Co., 1961).

Kenyatta, Jomo, *Facing Mount Kenya* (London, Secker and Warbury, 1938).

Kruger, D. W., *South African Parties and Policies 1910-1960* (Capetown, Human and Rousseau, 1960).

Legum, Colin, *Pan-Africanism, A Short Political Guide* (New York, Frederick A. Praeger, 1962).

Lumumba, Patrice, *Congo, My Country* (New York, Frederick A. Praeger, 1962).

MacLure, Millar and Anglin, Douglas G. (editors), *Africa: the Political Pattern* (Toronto, University of Toronto Press, 1961).

Mboya, Thomas, *Freedom and After* (Boston, Little, Brown, 1963).

Merriam, Alan P., *Congo: Background of Conflict* (Evanston, Illinois, Northwestern University Press, 1961).

Nkrumah, Kwame, *Ghana, the Autobiography of Kwame Nkrumah* (New York, Thomas Nelson and Sons, 1957).

Nkrumah, Kwame, *I Speak of Freedom* (New York, Frederick A. Praeger, 1961).

Nkrumah, Kwame, *Consciencism* (London, Heinemann, 1964).

Okumu, Washington, *Lumumba's Congo: Roots of Conflict* (New York, I. Obolensky, 1963).

Rothchild, Donald S., *Toward Unity in Africa: A Study of Federalism in British Africa* (Washington, D.C., Public Affairs Press, 1960).

Segal, Ronald, *Political Africa—A Who's Who of Personalities* (New York, Frederick A. Praeger, 1961).

Senghor, Leopold Sedar, *On African Socialism,* translated by Mercer Cook (New York, Frederick A. Praeger, 1961).

Shepherd, George W., *The Politics of African Nationalism: Challenge to American Policy* (New York, Frederick A. Praeger, 1962).

Sklar, Richard L., *Nigerian Political Parties, Power in an Emergent Nation* (Princeton, N.J., Princeton University Press, 1963).

Spiro, Herbert J., *Politics in Africa: Prospects South of the Sahara* (Englewood Cliffs, N.J., Prentice-Hall, 1962).

Taylor, J. Clagett, *The Political Development of Tanganyika* (Stanford, California, Stanford University Press, 1963).

Tilman, Robert O. and Cole, Taylor (editors), *The Nigerian Political Scene* (Durham, North Carolina, Duke University Press, 1962).

Wallerstein, Immanuel, *Africa: the Politics of Independence* (New York, Random House, 1961).

Zolberg, Aristide R., *One-party Government in the Ivory Coast* (Princeton, Princeton University Press, 1964).

Articles

Bourguiba, Habib, *Neo-Destourian Socialism,* Publications of the Secretariat of State for Information and Tourism, June 24, 1961.

Diamond, Stanley, "Weight of the North," *Africa Today,* Vol. X, No. 1, January, 1963, p. 4.

Emmerson, Donald K., "African Student Organizations," *Africa Report,* Vol. X, No. 5, May, 1965, p. 6.

Harris, Richard, "Nigeria: Crisis and Compromise," *Africa Report,* Vol. X, No. 3, March, 1965, p. 25.

Moore, Henry Clement, *The Mass Party Regime,* a paper presented to the African Studies Association, San Francisco, 1963.

"New Tribalism in Kenya Today," *Africa Today,* Vol. IX, No. 8, October 1962, p. 23.

"Nkrumah Declares War on Patronage, Nepotism," *Africa Report,* Vol. VI, No. 5, May, 1961, p. 11.

Pelissier, René, "Political Movements in Spanish Guinea," *Africa Report,* Vol. IX, No. 5, May, 1964, pp. 3-7.

Sanger, Clyde, "Kenya—New Man at the Stern," *Africa Report,* Vol. VII, No. 11, December, 1962, p. 11.

Sanger, Clyde, "The Outlook in Kenya," *Africa Report,* Vol. VII, No. 6, June, 1962, p. 3.

"Single Party Discussed," Congo (Brazzaville), *Africa South of the Sahara,* Agence-France Presse, Paris, No. 990, August 5, 1963, p. 19.

"Subversion Factors," Federation of Nigeria, *Africa South of the Sahara,* Agence-France Presse, Paris, No. 991, August 12, 1963, p. 13.

Young, Crawford M., "Congo Political Parties Revisited," *Africa Report,* Vol. VIII, No. 1, January, 1963, p. 14.

Van den Berghe, "The Role of the Army in Contemporary Africa," *Africa Report,* Vol. X, No. 3, March, 1965, p. 12.

Zolberg, Aristide R., "Government for the People," *Africa Today,* Vol. IX, No. 4, May 1962, pp. 4-7.

Party platforms and constitutions are available at party headquarters and in a few cases through government printing offices.

Chapter 3—GOVERNMENTAL PROCESSES

Books

Ashford, Douglas, *Political Change in Morocco* (Princeton, N.J., Princeton University Press, 1961).

Baade, Hans W., Editor, and Robinson, O. Everett, Associate Editor, *African Law, New Law of New Nations* (Dobbs Ferry, N.Y., Oceana Publications, Inc., 1963).

Bretton, Henry L., *Power and Stability in Nigeria: The Politics of Decolonization* (New York, Frederick A. Praeger, 1962).

Hatch, John, *Africa Today—and Tomorrow: Outline of Basic Facts and Major Problems* (New York, Frederick A. Praeger, 1960).

Hennessey, Maurice, *The Congo* (New York, Frederick A. Praeger, 1961).

Hughes, John, *The New Face of Africa South of the Sahara* (New York, Longmans, Green and Co., 1961).

Jesman, Czeslaw, *The Ethiopian Paradox* (London, Oxford University Press, published for the Institute of Race Relations, 1963).

Landau, Rom, *Mohammed V King of Morocco* (Rabat, "Morocco" Publishers, 1957).

Lemarchand, René, *Political Awakening in the Belgian Congo* (Berkeley, California, University of California Press, 1964).

Leys, Colin and Pratt, Cranford (Editors), *A New Deal in Central Africa* (New York, Frederick A. Praeger, 1960).

Liska, George, *The Greater Maghreb* (Washington, Washington Center of Foreign Policy Research, 1963).

Macmichael, Sir Harold, *The Sudan* (London, Ernest Benn Ltd., 1954).

Mair, L. P., *Native Policies in Africa* (London, George Routledge and Sons Ltd., 1936).

Maesel, Albert Q., *Africa: Facts and Forecasts* (New York, Duell, Sloan and Pearce, 1943).

Perham, Margery, *The Government of Ethiopia* (New York, Oxford University Press, 1948).

Ullendorff, Edward, *The Ethiopians* (London, Oxford University Press, 1960).

Zartman, I. William, *Government and Politics in Northern Africa* (New York, Frederick A. Praeger, 1964).

Articles

"An Ivory Coast Militia," Ivory Coast, *Africa South of the Sahara*, Agence France-Presse, Paris, No. 997, August 29, 1963, p. 11.

Azikiwe, Nnamdi, "Essentials for Nigerian Survival," *Foreign Affairs*, Vol. 43, No. 3, April 1965, p. 447.

Castagno, Alphonse A., "Ethiopia: Reshaping an Autocracy," *Africa Report,* Vol. VIII, No. 9, October 1963, p. 3.

"Chief Enahoro," Nigeria, *Africa Digest,* Vol. X, No. 6, June 1963, p. 201.

"Emergency and Security Measures," Ghana, *Africa Digest,* Vol. X, No. 3, December 1962, p. 106.

"Emergency in Ghana," *Africa Report,* Vol. VII, No. 9, October 1962, p. 19.

"Ghana's Nkrumah Faces Internal Crisis," *Africa Report,* Vol. VI, No. 9, October 1961, p. 9.

Hatch, John, "Nkrumah's Ghana," *Africa Report,* Vol. VII, No. 8, August 1962, p. 9.

Milcent, Ernest and Meisler, Stanley, "Two Views of Senegal," *Africa Report,* Vol. VII, No. 8, August 1962, p. 13.

"Minister of State Dismissed," Gabon, *Africa South of the Sahara,* Agence France-Presse, Paris, No. 1007, October 3, 1963, p. 23.

"Mr. Adjei's Trial," Ghana, *Africa South of the Sahara,* Agence France-Presse, Paris, No. 991, August 12, 1963, p. 13.

Nyerere, Julius, "How Much Power for a Leader," *Africa Report,* Vol. VII, No. 7, July 1962, p. 5.

Rawick, Allen Jay, "Some Political Paradoxes of Nationhood," *Africa Today,* Vol. VIII, No. 3, March 1961, p. 7.

"Tanganyika," *Africa Digest,* Vol. X, No. 5, April 1963, p. 161.

"Terrorist Chief Sentenced to Death," Cameroon Federation, *Africa South of the Sahara,* Agence France-Presse, Paris, No. 1001, September 12, 1963, p. 18.

"Treason Trial," Liberia, *Africa Digest,* Vol. X, No. 6, June 1963, p. 201.

"Treason Trial," Nigeria, *Africa Digest,* Vol. X, No. 3, December 1962, p. 107.

"Treason Trial in Accra," Ghana, *Africa Digest,* Vol. X, No. 6, June 1963, p. 200.

"Trial by Jury to be Abolished," Kenya, *Africa South of the Sahara,* Agence France-Presse, Paris, No. 989, August 1, 1963, p. 16.

"Uganda," *Africa Digest,* Vol. X, No. 4, February 1963, p. 133.

"Upper Volta Minister Arrested for Theft," *Africa Report,* Vol. VII, No. 8, August 1962, p. 21.

"Violence May be Necessary: Mr. Nyerere," Tanganyika, *Africa South of the Sahara,* Agence France-Presse, Paris, No. 989, August 1, 1963, p. 17.

"What Happened in Dakar," *Africa Report,* Vol. VIII, No. 1, January 1963, pp. 6, 30.

Government publications

Kenya: *Africans in Senior Posts in the Kenya Civil Service.*

An Economc Survey, Barclays Bank D. C. O., 54 Lombard Street, London, July 1960.

Economic Conditions—Part II, A. International Trade.
Economic Conditions—Part II, B. Agriculture and Livestock.
Economic Conditions—Part II, C. Forestry.
Economic Conditions—Part II, E. Mining and Mineral Oils.
Economic Conditions—Part III, D. Labour and Employment Conditions.
Economic Conditions—Part IV, Educational Conditions, 1961.
Process of Legislation in Kenya in 1961.
Training Schemes, Institutional, 1961.
Literacy Campaign, Department of Social Welfare and Community Development, Gold Coast, 1952, West African Graphic Co., Accra.
Monthly Bulletin of Statistics, United Nations, Vol. XVII, No. 12, December, 1963.

Constitutions of the African states are available through the government printing offices. Legislative debates and information on constitutional negotiations are available through government printing offices, for example:

Legislative Council Debates, Nigeria.
Proposals of Tanganyika Government for a Republic, December, 1961.
Uganda 1960, London, H.M.S.O., 1961.

Chapter 4—POLICY

Books

Hovet, Thomas, *Africa in the United Nations* (Evanston, Illinois, Northwestern University Press, 1963).
Padmore, George, *Pan-Africanism or Communism? The Coming Struggle for Africa* (New York, Roy Publishers, 1956).
Rivkin, Arnold, *Africa and the European Common Market* (Denver, University of Denver Press, 1964).
Rivkin, Arnold, *Africa and the West* (New York, Frederick A. Praeger, 1962).
Roper, J. I., *Labour Problems in West Africa* (London, Penguin, 1958).
Shepard, George W., "The Ideological Factor in Ghanaian Foreign Policy," paper presented to the African Studies Association Annual Meeting, San Francisco, October, 1963 (unpublished).
Stillman, Calvin W. (Editor), *Africa in the Modern World* (Chicago, University of Chicago Press, 1955).
The United States and Africa, The American Assembly, Columbia University, June, 1958, Background papers prepared for the use of participants and the final report of the Thirteenth American Assembly, Arden House, Harriman Campus of Columbia University, Harriman, New York, May 1-4, 1958.

Periodicals

"African Eleven," *The Economist,* Vol. 197, No. 6123, December 31, 1960, pp. 1388, 1390.

"African Leaders Convene at Rival Summits," *Africa Report,* Vol. VI, No. 1, January 1961, p. 11.

"Britain and the E.C.M.," *Arab Observer,* June 18, 1962, p. 28.

"Casablanca Economists Discuss Custom Union," *Africa Report,* Vol. VI, No. 8, August 1961, p. 11.

Diamond, Stanley, "Still a Key But Not a Showplace," *Africa Today,* Vol. IX, No. 6, July 1962, p. 7.

Emerson, Rupert, "Pan-Africanism," *International Organization,* Vol. XVI, No. 2, Spring, 1962, pp. 275-90.

Friedland, William H., "Paradoxes of African Trade Unions," *Africa Report,* Vol. X, No. 6, June 1965, p. 6.

Gareau, Frederick H., "Bloc Politics in West Africa," *Orbis,* Vol. V, No. 4, Winter, 1962, pp. 470-89.

"Ghana-Guinea-Mali Union, Union of African States," *International Organization,* Vol. XVI, No. 2, Spring, 1962, pp. 443-44.

Houser, George M., "At Cairo—The Third All-African People's Conference," *Africa Today,* Vol. VIII, No. 4, April 1961, pp. 11-13.

Howe, Russell, "The Monrovia Conference," *Africa Today,* Vol. VIII, No. 5, May 1961, p. 4.

Irvine, Keith, "African Nationalism and the United Nations," *Current History,* Vol. 38, No. 226, June 1960, pp. 352-57.

Jack, Homer A., "The 'African Assembly,'" *Africa Today,* Vol. VII, No. 9, November 1960, p. 2.

Kamarck, Andrew, "Some Unanswered Questions about Africa's Economic Potential," *Africa Report,* Vol. X, No. 1, January 1965, p. 5.

"Kenya, Prelude to Independence, a Summary of the New Constitution," *Africa Today,* Vol. X, No. 4, April 1963, p. 10.

Klomon, Erasmus H., "African Unification Movements," *International Organization,* Vol. XVI, No. 2, Spring, 1962, pp. 373-77.

Landis, Elizabeth S., "1960 Agenda-Africa U.N. Report," *Africa Today,* Vol. VII, No. 6, October 1960, pp. 11-12.

Legum, Colin, "Deceptive Calm in Nigeria," *Africa Report,* Vol. VII, No. 10, November 1962, p. 23.

Legum, Colin, "Peking's Strategic Priorities," *Africa Report,* Vol. X, No. 1, January 1965, p. 19.

Lichtblau, George, "The Dilemma of the ICFTU," *Africa Report,* Vol. X, No. 6, June 1965, p. 18.

Maslow, Will, "The Afro-Asian Bloc in the United Nations," *Middle Eastern Affairs,* Vol. VIII, No. 11, November, 1957, pp. 373-77.

"Monrovia Group Finds Agreement in Dakar," *Africa Report,* Vol. VI, No. 8, August 1961, p. 11.

"Monrovians Muddle Through," *The Economist,* Vol. 202, No. 6180, February 8, 1962, pp. 431-32.

Morgenthau, Ruth Schachter, "African Socialism: Declaration of Ideological Independence," *Africa Report,* Vol. VIII, No. 5, May 1962, p. 3.

"Nkrumah's Goals for Ghana," *Africa Report,* Vol. VII, No. 1, January 1962, p. 13.

"Out of Africa: Reports from our Correspondents; Transcending Differences, Casablanca," *Africa Today,* Vol. VIII, No. 2, February 1961, pp. 8-9.

"Pan-African First Steps," *The Economist,* Vol. 199, No. 6140, April 29, 1961, pp. 454-56.

Pick, Hella, "The Brazzaville Twelve and How They Came to Be," *Africa Report,* Vol. VI, No. 5, May 1961, pp. 2, 8, 12, 15.

Rake, Alan, "Ghana's Economic Crisis," *Africa Report,* Vol. X, No. 3, March 1965, p. 47.

"Resolutions and Amendments—Notes and Chart," compiled by Elizabeth S. Landis, *Africa Today,* Vol. VIII, No. 1, January 1961, pp. 7-9.

"Road from Casablanca," *The Economist,* Vol. 198, No. 6125, January 14, 1961, pp. 121-22.

Roberts, Margaret, "Summitry at Casablanca," *Africa South of the Sahara,* Vol. 5, No. 3, 1961, pp. 68-75.

Rosberg, Carl G., Jr., and Segal, Aaron, "An East African Federation," *International Conciliation,* May, 1963, No. 543, Carnegie Endowment for International Peace, p. 72.

Sears, Mason, "The Congo, Africa and the U.N.," *Africa Today,* Vol. VII, No. 5, September 1960, pp. 14-15.

Shepperson, George, "Notes on Negro American Influence on the Emergence of African Nationalism," *Journal of African History,* Vol. 1, No. 2, 1960, pp. 299-312.

Spencer, John H., "Africa at the United Nations," *International Organization,* Vol. XVI, No. 2, Spring, 1962, pp. 375-86.

Sterne, Joseph, "The Lagos Conference," *Africa Report,* Vol. VII, No. 2, February 1962, pp. 3-6.

"The Brazzaville Twelve," *Africa South of the Sahara,* Vol. 5, No. 3, April and June, 1961, pp. 76-84.

"The Cooperators," *The Economist,* Vol. 199, No. 6143, May 20, 1961, p. 766.

"The Osagyefo and Others," *The Economist,* Vol. 197, No. 6123, December 31, 1960, pp. 1366-68.

"Unity in Africa, Some Will Need to Think Again," Nigerian *Sunday Post,* July 8, 1962.

Government publications

African Statistics, Annex to the Economic Bulletin for Africa, Vol. II, No. 1, January, 1962.

African Summit in Monrovia, published on behalf of the Federal Ministry of Information and printed by the Nigerian National Press Limited, Lagos, Nigeria, 1962.

"African Unity," a speech by Osagyefo, Dr. Kwame Nkrumah, President of the Republic of Ghana on opening of the African Unity House in London, March 18, 1961, Republic of Ghana.

Annual Report of the Department of Social Welfare and Community Development For the Year 1960, Government Printer, Accra, 1960.

Current Documents, Resolutions of the All-African People's Conference, December 5-13, 1958, Accra, Ghana.

Digest of Statistics, Vol. II, Federation of Nigeria, No. 2, April 1962, Lagos: Federal Office of Statistics.

East African Posts and Telecommunications Administration, Kenya, 1961.

East African Railways and Harbours, Kenya Colony, Report to the United Nations Organization, 1961.

Economic Bulletin for Africa, published by the Secretariat of the Economic Commission for Africa, Vol. II, No. 1, January, 1962.

Economic Survey of Nigeria, 1959, published by direction of the National Economic Council, printed by the Federal Government Printer, Lagos.

Explanatory Notes on Road Traffic Statistics, Kenya Colony and Protectorate, 1962.

Government Servants and Teachers Selected For Government Service Sent on Courses in the United Kingdom and Elsewhere in 1961, Kenya.

Kenya, An Economic Survey, Barclays Bank D. C. O., 54 Lombard Street, London, July 1960.

Pan-African Freedom Movement for East, Central, and Southern Africa, Addis Ababa Conference, February 2-10, 1962, published by the African Department of the Foreign Office, Addis Ababa.

Programme of the Convention People's Party for Work and Happiness, published by the Ministry of Information and Broadcasting and printed by the Government Printing Department, Accra, Ghana, 1961-62.

Proposed Charter of the Inter-African and Malagasy Organization, formulated by the African and Malagasy Heads of States and Governments assembled in Lagos, Nigeria, January, 1962.

Report of the Committee of the Education, Rehabilitation and Employment of Disabled People in Ghana, December, 1960, Government Printer, Accra, Ghana.

Resolutions—Lagos Conference of Heads of African and Malagasy States and Governments, January 25-30, 1962.

Setting Up a Joint High Command, Government Printing Office, Accra, Ghana, 1962.

The Kariba Hydro-Electric Scheme, British Information Service, An agency of the British Government, November, 1959.

Western Nigeria Development Plan 1962-1968, Government of Western Nigeria, Government Printer, Ibadan, Nigeria, 1962.